THE HISTORY OF THE
FUTURE IN COLONIAL MEXICO

THE
HISTORY
OF THE FUTURE
IN COLONIAL
MEXICO

MATTHEW D. O'HARA

Yale

UNIVERSITY PRESS

New Haven and London

Published with assistance from the foundation established in memory of Calvin Chapin of the Class of 1788, Yale College.

Yale University Press books may be purchased in quantity for educational, business, or promotional use. For information, please e-mail sales.press@yale.edu (U.S. office) or sales@yaleup.co.uk (U.K. office).

Set in Janson type by IDS Infotech Ltd.
Printed in the United States of America.

ISBN 978-0-300-23393-3 (hardcover: alk. paper)
Library of Congress Control Number: 2018935323
A catalogue record for this book is available from the British Library.

This paper meets the requirements of ANSI/NISO Z39.48-1992 (Permanence of Paper).

10 9 8 7 6 5 4 3 2 1

For my parents, Jackie and Wally,
now a part of my past
but always a part of my futuremaking

Contents

Preface

Are innovation and tradition compatible?

In contemporary usage, the answer seems straightforward: No.

To describe something or someone as innovative almost always implies a great rupture with the past. "Disruption," the word of the moment in Silicon Valley—considered by many to be the epicenter of economic innovation—emphasizes intense alteration. In this world, "to disrupt" means to enact radical change. Indeed, innovation seems to be measured by the degree to which it breaks from tradition.

We don't have to look far for examples. A well-known technology conference, TechCrunch Disrupt, sells itself as a springboard for "revolutionary startups" and "game-changing technologies." Disruption, in the future-oriented world of Silicon Valley and its startups, means leaving the past in the past. It is understood to be an unalloyed good.

Yet it turns out that innovation and tradition have often been quite compatible. Indeed, many historical examples suggest that innovation not only complements tradition but also, in fact, requires it.

Even in Silicon Valley, if one strips away the posturing of technologists and the marketing of their firms, it is clear that past, present, and future interact in more subtle and complex ways than "disruption" might imply. Steve Jobs, the cofounder of Apple Computer, while usually held up as the paradigmatic disruptor, was also famous for his obsession with product evolution, adaptation, and iterative change.

Moving beyond the rhetoric of contemporary innovation is important, for it raises a set of questions that are at the heart of this book and at the center of human experience, namely, what are the cultural and intellectual resources available for making futures? What were the tools available to historical actors as they interpreted the past, navigated the present, and created different ways of being in the world? Getting this history right is critical, since change, adaptation, innovation, and creativity have become yardsticks that we use to take measure of ourselves and historical subjects. Sometimes we do this explicitly and self-consciously, but more often we do so implicitly, as part of an undeclared folk sociology, a commonsense understanding of the world.

This book probes these questions through historical case studies in a place and time not known for innovation: colonial Mexico. In the following chapters I examine how individuals thought about, planned for, and manipulated futures full of uncertainty and risk.

Why look for innovation in a place where conventional wisdom tells it was absent? When we begin to look in unexpected places, surprising examples of futuremaking abound: a shift toward empiricism developed as much from the market for astrology as it did from the ideas of the scientific revolution; preachers stoked political imaginaries by reading the future through Old Testament exemplars; farmers and traders used a sophisticated understanding of theology to demand new types of financial instruments. Surprising, perhaps, but such findings should also make us wary of the assumptions we bring with us into the past, whether that of Mexico or elsewhere.

This historical perspective suggests that we need to rethink the relationship between innovation and tradition, between future and past, between our need for continuity and our desire for change. It is worth contemplating these other futures, not to celebrate the past, or even less to suggest a return to a time that was so deeply vexed by intolerance, inequalities, and hierarchies of many forms. Instead, it is a way to remind ourselves of different ways of relating to time that have shaped human experience and different ways of integrating past, present, and future.

This is an important task for historians, especially at a time when our present futures seem so diminished, offering us an imagined time-to-come that rejects the past completely or a retreat to a winsome moment in a past that never was.

Acknowledgments

MY DEBTS ARE MANY, quite a few profound, some perpetual.

First, my family. Thank you, Susie, Farrin, Bridgid, and Maeve. You make this life sparkle. Here's to many more adventures and laughs. Susie, I didn't need to comb the archives to know you complicate my sense of time, merging past, present, and future in wonderful ways.

To my brothers and sisters and extended family, lots has changed in the last few years, but I hope we manage to cling together in those to come.

To my Santa Cruz superextended family of friends, academics argue endlessly about the meaning of community. I'd hold you all up as a great example of what it can be.

I owe an enormous, long-term debt (for the terms of the deal, think colonial *censo*, with no collateral and zero interest) to the many scholars, archivists, and staff who helped me at various stages of this book. I'll begin with some of my fellow historians and academics who read or commented on various versions of the chapters or their previous lives as conference papers or articles. These included Andrew Fisher, Javier Villa-Flores, Eric Van Young, Eddie Wright-Ríos, Sonya Lipsett-Rivera, Jessica Delgado, Michelle Molina, Paul Ramírez, David Tavárez, Karen Melvin, Sylvia Sellers-García, Sean McEnroe, Martin Nesvig, Ben Vinson, Dustin O'Hara, Neil Safier, Pablo Gómez, Pamela Voekel, Margaret Chowning, Dorothy Tanck de Estrada, Brian Connaughton, and Bill Taylor. Some of my colleagues at UC Santa Cruz offered outstanding critique and advice, including Nathaniel Deutsch, Kate Jones, Cindy Polecritti, Alan Christy, Gail Hershatter, and María Elena Díaz. To the rest of my colleagues in the History Department, thanks for making it such a great place to be. The department staff deserves special mention: Stephanie Hinkle, Stephanie Sawyer, Kayla Ayers, Cindy Morris, and Rose Greenberg.

My deep thanks go to the many archivists and library staff who've helped me over the long haul of this project. In Mexico, the staff of the Archivo General de la Nación, especially at the home of colonialists, Galería 4; the Archivo Histórico del Arzobispado de México, above all, Berenise Bravo Rubio and Marco Pérez Iturbe; the staff of the parish of Santa Veracruz; in Spain, the Archivo General de Indias and the Archivo Histórico Nacional; in the United States, the librarians of the University of California, Santa Cruz, the Sutro Library, Bancroft Library, and the John Carter Brown Library.

A number of institutions and foundations provided crucial financial support for this book. The University of California not only kept me employed but also provided travel and other research support, including through UC-MEXUS. At UC Santa Cruz, I'd like to recognize the Humanities Division, the Committee on Research, and the Humanities Institute. An American Council of Learned Societies Fellowship funded an important period of my research and writing. Toward the end of the project I was lucky to receive an Early Career fellowship in the Enhancing Life Project, headed by William Schweiker at the University of Chicago and Günter Thomas at the Ruhr-Universität Bochum, supported by the John Templeton Foundation. In addition to Gunther and Bill, I want to recognize my fellow ELP scholars, who helped me think through the meaning of my work, especially for those readers outside the discipline of history. Thanks also to Markus Höfner and Sara Bigger, who made that complicated machine run so smoothly.

At Yale University Press, my gratitude goes out to Jaya Chatterjee, a superb editor and champion of this project, production editor Phillip King, indexer David Luljak, and my excellent copyeditor, Lawrence Kenney.

Earlier version of chapters 5 and 6 appeared, respectively, as "The Supple Whip: Innovation and Tradition in Mexican Catholicism,"

American Historical Review 117, no. 5 (2012): 1373–1401, and "Anxiety and the Future at Mexican Independence," in *Emotions and Daily Life in Colonial Mexico*, ed. Javier Villa-Flores and Sonya Lipsett-Rivera, 198–220 (Albuquerque: University of New Mexico Press, 2014).

THE HISTORY OF THE
FUTURE IN COLONIAL MEXICO

CHAPTER ONE

Introduction

MOST ACADEMIC BOOKS TAKE a long time to publish. While working on these projects, we authors end up having plenty of conversations about ideas that seem to be forever in the works. To give some form to these invisible labors, we come up with quick descriptions of our projects. These are "elevator-ride" accounts of a book—punchy and short enough to be delivered to a distracted colleague or conference goer. One hopes they will captivate in an instant, but at the very least they might explain what you've been up to when not teaching courses.

Such was the case when, in the middle of researching this book, I ran into a Peruvian friend, also a historian, at one of our yearly conferences. The standard conversation began: "What are you working on?" he asked. "The history of the future," I replied, a bit puckishly. "It's about how people made their futures in the colonial period." I was sure I could anticipate his response, since up to that point most people had replied with a pause, wondering what I really meant. They were to be forgiven for their confusion and I excused for my lack of clarity. I had intentionally framed my working title as something of a paradox.

So I was ready. Now I'd tell him what I was *really* writing about. I'd follow up with some descriptions of concrete topics and chapter titles.

Before I could do so, he countered with his own bit of mischief: "But Latin Americans don't think about the future." Delivered with a wry smile by someone from the region who had spent most of his adult life in the United States, the irony was thick and expertly applied. It drew a laugh from us both.

At the same time, what made the joke work was its anchoring in reality. That is to say, it referred to a long tradition of cultural commentary. The notion of Latin America and Latin Americans as a place and people locked in the past, consumed by the present, and unconcerned about the future is a classic stereotype of the region. Sometimes it has been voiced from within, from the perspective of a local or insider, as delivered ironically by my friend, but also a Latin American elite that sometimes questioned the capacity and aptitude of other people in the region. Often it came from without, most bitingly as a way of explaining and denigrating Latin America's difference when compared with the United States, including the region's supposed lack of political, economic, or even cultural development.

Although we might recognize the origins and errors of such accounts, they have a pernicious relationship to historical practice. They frame our perspective of the past, even before we've cracked a book or walked into an archive. As a result, these traditional narratives potentially blind us to the many ways in which historical subjects sought to shape their futures; how they aspired to improve their individual and collective lives; how they innovated from current conditions. In short, how they engaged in futuremaking.

This book recovers some of those lost futures through a series of historical case studies in colonial Mexico. Based largely on archival materials, the following chapters explore a range of practices and ideas, from topics we usually associate with religious studies (prayer, divination, preaching) to others that are typically the domain of economic or political historians (credit, futures markets, collective motivation). The combination of seemingly disparate subjects is intentional. In bringing together these diverse topics, which are rarely treated in one book, I mean to foreground the historical problem of time experience and futuremaking rather than the concerns of traditional subfields.

Placing time experience at the center of analysis forces us to rethink our interpretation of Mexico's past. Colonial Mexico developed a culture of innovation, human aspiration, and future-making that was subsequently forgotten in part because it did not fit with later definitions of modernity and innovation as secular phenomena and things untethered to the past or tradition.

This choice of historical method and topics is driven by a desire to step outside some of the dominant paradigms in the study of Latin America and colonialism in general. Historians of Latin America have spent a great deal of energy studying historical legacies. Whether one examines how the colonial past shaped the new republics of the nineteenth century or the role of historical memory in contemporary politics, the notion that the past weighs heavily on the present is a standard mode of historical analysis. While Latin American history offers one of the best examples of the imposing past narrative, it is an organizing concept for many historical subfields and even for history as a subject of investigation and study.

Often used to describe societies with an especially turbulent history or a strong sense of historical memory, the maxim is a favorite way to gesture to historical legacies of one sort or another. This is done whether the heritage is economic inequality, ethnic or racial divisions, religious conflict, slavery, or some other weighty historical conditions whose effects continue to be felt in the present. These histories are understood to be burdensome, creating heavy labor for those places and peoples bearing them in the present. Scholars of postcolonial societies have written extensively about the colonial legacy, including the ways in which the transition from colony to nation could be fraught with unresolved questions and conflicts.[1]

This vein of inquiry has a long and distinguished record in Latin American history. Classic studies have tackled economic, political, and cultural legacies and tried to pinpoint their origins in historical processes from the colonial era, a period that in most parts of Latin America ran from the sixteenth century through the early nineteenth century. Beyond works that directly engage the problem of colonial legacies, much scholarship on the colonial period is implicitly concerned with them, and quite understandably so since one of the traditional imperatives of history as an academic discipline is to examine the origins of later conditions. In the case of Mexico these objects of historical explanation are many and diverse: the political development of the Mexican nation-state after it broke free of the Spanish empire in 1821; persistent challenges of economic development and underdevelopment; and the origins of Mexican nationalism, among many other concerns. My own previous work joined this conversation by examining the history and legacies of the category Indian in colonial Mexico, one of the prime examples in world history of ethnogenesis, or the creation of new social identities.[2]

But in its most extreme form, such analysis frames the colonial period as a moment of original sin. This mode of explanation finds modern Latin America forever tainted by earlier societies that were weaned on racial hierarchy rather than pluralism, religious rigidity instead of tolerance, absolutist politics that offered little opportunity for grassroots associative culture or experience in proto-democratic practices, or cultures of status that valued honor, ostentatious displays of wealth, and rent seeking over thrift, capital accumulation, or entrepreneurship. This list goes on and on.[3]

For example, in terms of its political institutions and patterns Latin America has often been described via narratives that stress temporal lags and backwardness. In such accounts, supposed shortcomings of Latin America are emphasized when compared with the United States or some other marker of progress. Relative political turbulence is often highlighted in this analysis, but studies of shortcomings have run the gamut from questions of culture to economics and many things in between. The tradition of diagnosing Latin America as being deficient in some important quality or behind according to a significant waypoint has derived not only from voices in the United States or other outsiders, nor is it a recent construct. Historical actors from the region itself voiced similar concerns. Early Mexican liberals, to take one potent example, paid special attention to what seemed an obvious example of difference: the United States. By the early nineteenth century some offered their own explanations of the success of the young republic to the north alongside what seemed to be utter failure in Mexico. Fray Servando Teresa de Mier, a prominent intellectual and political figure at the time of Mexico's independence from Spain, collapsed many of the potential points of comparison. In his assessment of what he considered Mexico's sad current condition as of the early nineteenth century he wrote, "The prosperity of that neighbor re-public [the United States] has been, and currently is, the trigger of our America because the immense distance between them and us has not been pondered enough. [They were a new people,] homogenous, industrious, enlightened, and full of social virtues as educated by a free nation; we are an old people, heterogeneous, with no industry, enemies of work and lovers of public jobs as are the Spaniards, as ignorant as our fathers were, and degraded by the vices derived from three hundred years of subjugation."[4]

The study of Latin America as a place of faults and shortcomings is also found in contemporary scholarship, whether the object of study is some point in Latin America's past or the current moment. One prominent example from recent years is Francis Fukuyama's edited collection *Falling Behind: Explaining the Development Gap Between Latin America and the United States*, which, as its title suggests, seeks to interpret the region's economic failure to thrive over the previous three centuries when compared to the juggernaut to the north.[5] How is it, the editor asks, that Latin America and British North America enjoyed comparable levels of development at the turn of the eighteenth century only to diverge widely and permanently? Economic historians have asked much the same questions, as in an anthology from some years ago, *How Latin America Fell Behind: Essays on the Economic Histories of Brazil and Mexico, 1800–1914.*[6] As one might imagine, the answers to these riddles themselves diverge widely and include the failure of political systems, misguided economic policies, differing resource endowments, and weak institutions.

This book has no direct quarrel with such approaches or the conclusions these scholars might reach, but it offers an alternative frame of analysis and other vistas on the past. These perspectives might complement those that attempt to explain the supposed failures of Latin America, but they might also lead us to question some of those previous interpretations. In either case, we should rethink a historical practice that takes as a point of departure a teleology: the attempt to isolate and explain historical winners and losers. As E. P. Thompson has so eloquently argued, much is lost when one focuses exclusively on historical examples that are deemed to be harbingers of "subsequent preoccupations," whatever those later preoccupations might be, whether modernity, democracy, scientific rationality, or others. When history is done this way, Thompson writes, "Only the successful (in the sense of those whose aspirations anticipated subsequent evolution) are remembered." Select historical endpoints are celebrated at the expense of broader historical process. The widespread appeal of this paradigm explains the fondness historians show for precocious moderns: we delight in those who seem to have acted like us and thought like us before our time. Taken too far, this attitude toward the past becomes a form of historical narcissism, an obsession with finding the familiar in the far-off. If we follow this method exclusively, we do a great violence to the past, above all by silencing historical subjects who do not fit this mold. We also do a great disservice to ourselves in that the contingencies, possibilities, and meanings of the past are thus foreclosed, along with our ability to think creatively about our present and future.[7]

What if one were to replace an implicitly comparative vision, which emphasizes how a region shackled by tradition and burdened by the past fell behind, with one that considers how historical actors related to past, present, and future in their own historical moments? The benefit of this different perspective is that it allows us to take Latin America's and Mexico's past on their own terms rather than view them through a prism of relative underdevelopment or political pathologies.

What if we take as our starting point an examination of historical futures rather than historical legacies? We might find ourselves surprised by the intensely forward-looking sensibilities of those apparently past-oriented historical subjects. This book uncovers some of those unexpected histories, including some of Thompson's "lost causes" and "blind alleys." It foregrounds the many ways in which residents of New Spain, as colonial Mexico was then known, grappled with time. It discusses how they adapted to myriad challenges. It evaluates how they created new futures. It highlights futuremaking in the study of the past.

In fact, historians, ethnohistorians, and historical anthropologists of Mexico and Latin America have long investigated events and incidents we might call future oriented. Studies of utopian or millenarian religious, social, and political movements come immediately to mind. But even in these cases, rarely have the qualities of historical futures been scrutinized like those of historical pasts.

Indeed, some of the best work on millenarian movements privileges pastmaking—the crafting of historical memory and the relationship to the past—over futuremaking. The most celebrated book on historical time in New Spain positioned itself as a study "dedicated to recovering the diverse images of Mexico's past created by the successive generations that have reconstructed, mythicized, hidden, deformed, invented, ideologized, or explained the past."[8] Historical memory, in this and many other examples, has received the lion's share of scholarly attention. While this framing has yielded rich insights, it has put blinders on others, including the historical meaning of the future.[9]

Part of the challenge lies in the vocabulary and categories we use to study the future in the past. It is clear that some of the dominant frameworks for understanding the experience of time fail to explain the role that religious cultures play in imagining and bringing into being potential futures. Foremost among these is the category of modernity. Reinhart Koselleck, one of the leading theorists of time experience, defined modernity as the moment when the past is no longer a source of guidance for the future.[10] If this is the case, what are we to make of instances in which individuals and groups self-consciously looked to tradition as a vehicle for innovation? What happens if we try to interpret such examples through the modernity framework, whether Koselleck's version or the many competing models, most of which assume a similar temporal rupture?[11] One danger is analytic fuzziness, given the proliferating definitions of modernity.[12] An equally serious concern is that the term "modernity" tends to focus attention on temporal breaks, dramatic transitions, and inflection points and thus might distract us from longer-term transformations, subtle changes, and reproduction.[13] This is not to say that these accounts of a modernist relationship to the past are themselves inaccurate, but simply that they are not applicable to many other historical settings. Finally, while variations on the modernity frame have pointed out the multiple experiences of being modern, some of which tended to be overlooked in previous, Eurocentric narratives, they have been less successful at explaining how decidedly traditional and at times "unmodern" cultural practices could be vehicles of innovation.[14] In all of these ways modernity as a category of analysis throws a jealous and smothering embrace around the qualities sometimes associated with modernity, spurning other ways of explaining these characteristics.

At this juncture it makes more sense to set the modernity paradigm completely to the side and instead consider how and when traditional practices are redefined as current, future-oriented, or forward-looking and what historical factors are involved in that process. Doing so opens a new vista onto the traditional elements of innovation; no longer exotic tagalongs on a journey toward the modern, we are instead able to focus on their necessary role in the repetition and transformation of cultural practices.

Historians have also struggled to understand futuremaking in the past because we have tended to examine future-oriented events primarily through the study of ideas. This sort of approach naturally accentuates the imagined future, which is part of human futuremaking, but overlooks the concrete steps involved in attaining any future. In work on Latin American history, this analytic move can easily devolve into an implied conflict between the future-oriented ideas imported from outside, such as eighteenth-century Enlightenment thought or nineteenth-century liberalism, and the supposedly past-oriented ideas indigenous to the region. While paying careful attention to the development of ideas, this book also analyzes historical *practices* of futuremaking, the day-to-day activities in which individuals engaged the future, activities that at times were quite ordinary and could easily escape the historian's trawling through the archive.[15] Creative futuremaking, it turns out, usually took place not through the occasional, radical idea but through common, everyday practices.

Indeed, if we bring together these two methods—complementing the study of ideas and concepts with attention to practices and strategies—it is clear there was a widespread grammar of futuremaking in colonial New Spain, based in part on Catholic law and theology. The common aspects of colonial futures suggest that we should be careful about the labels we use to describe this history: Was the futuremaking of popular culture opposed to the high culture of the elite, church officials, or civil authorities? Were seventeenth-century diviners part of an unorthodox practice clearly opposed to the orthodox knowledge of Catholicism? Did small-scale lenders in the countryside have a different view of credit and economic horizons than the learned theologians of the church or the colonial bureaucracy?

The people studied in this book demonstrate that such categories can distort the shared forms of practice and the networks of knowledge found in New Spain, many of which crossed standard social markers of wealth, occupation, ethnicity, gender, and literacy, among others. At the same time, I am reluctant to jettison completely such distinctions because these labels do recognize forms of social power. In the chapters that follow I try to balance these two issues: paying attention to the reality of power and inequality when studying historical practices, yet keeping in mind how such practices could be widespread and how they could be unifying in ways that might even undermine some of those same hierarchies.

To survey some of the shared activities and mental frameworks that guided futuremaking in New Spain, this temporal commons, we'll need to follow an analytic path that varies somewhat from that of the existing historical literature. Scholarship on New Spain, my own previous work included, has quite naturally given a great deal of attention to the attempted evangelization of native peoples and Indigenous religious experiences in general. Given the centrality of these themes to the history of the Americas and the fact that New Spain is one of the prime examples of a missionary project during the period of European global expansion, it is, as might be expected, critical to consider the differences and divergences in spiritual and religious activity in the colonial world. Historians have done just that, for example, describing the initial waves of evangelization and the institutional spread of the Roman Catholic Church, the messy process of translating ideas and symbols across cultural and linguistic boundaries, and what David Tavárez describes as the "invisible war" over spirituality that was waged between church authorities and Indigenous spiritual leaders.[16] Some works have examined similar themes more generally in New Spain, investigating how officials struggled to maintain orthodoxy and control over New Spain's religious expression, whether on the part of Indigenous peoples or others.[17] There is also a substantial body of writing that examines the history of the church itself, its institutions, practices, and clergy, often in relation to broader social and cultural themes.[18] Perhaps the greatest strength of this literature is the way in which it maps major fault lines in the region's history: conflicts between native peoples and Europeans, between the clergy and the laity, between authorized and unauthorized practices and beliefs.

Yet, as a number of these works suggest, we also need to pay attention to the many historical moments when the boundaries of analysis are not so clear. This means being cautious about the qualities and historical roles we sometimes assign reflexively to groups of historical actors, whether Indians, Spaniards, priests, *castas* (persons deemed to be of "mixed" heritage), or other social categories from the time in question. We need to consider the styles of time-oriented thinking, acting, and doing that many individuals employed, that were often more consistent than divergent, and that informed futuremaking throughout the colonial era. In other words, the diversity of religious experiences across time and space in New Spain makes it easy to overlook the common elements of colonial Catholicism and the relationship of these things to time. Consider, at a most basic level, how the yearly ritual calendars in places as unlike as the great urban areas of Mexico City, Puebla, or Guadalajara and rural villages in, say, Chiapas or the Huasteca were often oriented around the same central events: most obviously in the key events of the liturgical calendar, the Lenten season and the celebration of Easter and Holy Week, the feast of Corpus Christi, the commemoration of the birth of Christ, and so on; as well as how the rhythm of the Christian week could be found in every corner of the viceroyalty in the rite of the Mass. Again, this is not to discount divergences in the celebrations of specific festivals and patron saints and the way such ritual and events could take on locally specific meanings, or even how relationships to Christianity could range from rejection to embrace to many points in between.[19] Instead, it is asking that we pay some attention to commonality alongside diversity. While many of the studies referenced above touch on these issues, I want to put some of these shared qualities of futuremaking at the center of analysis. This means at times exploring the orthodoxy of the supposedly wayward and the heterodoxy of those usually recognized as conformist.

One way to achieve this goal is through what historians might think of as historiographical cross-fertilization. Setting to the side our professional jargon, I mean simply drawing on the tools and techniques historians have used to study one topic in early Latin America and applying them in another area.[20] On one hand, I want to bring to bear some of the insights and interpretive approaches of the sophisticated literature on New Spain's ethnohistory and popular religion, which have focused on unique local inflections and the negotiated character of much religious expression. Broadly speaking, this scholarship has pointed out that religious activity and thought were the result not of a monologue of the Catholic hierarchy but of interaction and dialogue between the laity and church leaders. We can take these findings and turn them back on the institutional church, its authorities, and others in positions of power. While colonial officials are usually interpreted as first movers in historical explanations, we need also to observe how they adapted and responded to popular practice, local conditions, and other sources of transformation and innovation. On the other hand, I also want to draw from some of the strengths of more traditional religious or church histories, using their perspectives and methods in the study of popular practices and ideas. This involves remaining open to the possibility that people with little or no formal education could engage with sophisticated theological and legal concepts; it means recalling the ways in which those same people interpreted their world and futures through ideas that were orthodox as well as heterodox; it requires that we entertain the notion that nonelites are also part of a history of ideas, though their thoughts and attitudes might be embedded in diverse kinds of historical activity and records.

Early Mexico, it turns out, is an ideal place and time to study these problems. A locus of encounter and invasion during the cataclysmic sixteenth century, it became one of the centers of colonial administration, economic activity, and intellectual life. Its records reflect these realities. They are copious and record debates and conversations about all of these problems and possibilities of historical interpretation. Many records were generated by the church, whose position as a gatekeeper on a range of issues relating to the future, including salvation, offers us a way to survey the raw materials of futuremaking.

Some of these building blocks of the future are familiar and close to our own sensibilities, while others might strike us as strange and distant. Many were "religious" in nature, a term I've momentarily placed in quotes to point out how it can be deeply problematic for historical analysis. In New Spain, religious and nonreligious activities, ideas, and practices overlapped a great deal. As a result, religion does not always designate a separate domain of thought or practice the way it might in later historical times or in our own time as we look back on the past. Nonetheless, it remains useful and probably indispensable—both as a category of analysis (which we impose retroactively on the past) and as a category of practice (that formed part of the mental world of our historical subjects)—so long as we keep this important qualifier in mind.[21]

Is it possible this focus on things religious is a result of some selection bias—that is, we encounter them by leaning heavily on an archive generated by religious institutions? To some extent, no doubt. Historians must work with what they have. But in many cases the perspective of the future furnished by colonial documents, including those generated by the Catholic Church, is in fact a kind of peripheral vision. Frequently these documents offer information that is tangential and secondary to the original reasons for their creation, and thus I read them through sidewise glances. This fact gives me confidence that such sources can be used to piece together a history of futuremaking in New Spain broadly speaking, not just a history of those who generated the historical record.

Take the case of sin and salvation, two concepts that formed part of the intellectual commons of colonial futuremaking. Both ideas arrived in New Spain as part of a centuries-long conversion effort that introduced and reinforced key concepts and ritual practices among native peoples. And though such concepts are especially prominent in the records left by the missionary projects, they were also part of a centuries-long effort that cultivated ideas in the minds not only of native peoples but of all colonial subjects. In turn, much of the futuremaking I discuss leaned on this widely distributed knowledge about sin, salvation, and related ideas. To understand the historical futures that fill the following chapters, these shared foundations require attention at the outset because they created mechanisms for thinking and communicating about what is to come and then opened pathways for creating the future.

For example, both learned individuals and many people with little or no formal education grappled with the concept of free will and its paradoxical partner, the notion of divine intervention, or Providence. As subjects in New Spain considered such issues—occasionally in an abstract sense but more often in specific, sometimes very common-place situations, including many that were not overtly religious—they were forced to reckon with individual choice within a metaphysical framework and material reality in which one's actions could be sub-stantially constrained. In broad terms, these were tensions similar to what social scientists would much later call the problem of structure and agency, or the relationship between big, external forces and smaller units in shaping human life and experiences. The historical subjects found in this book grappled with comparable questions: To what degree do we control our actions? Do we command our own fate (in the world and beyond) or is it mostly determined by outside influences, whether material or spiritual?

The shared forms of futuremaking in colonial Mexico were deeply shaped, even driven, by a relationship to the past and the re-sources it offered. As noted above, many of these inherited re-sources were related to Catholicism: its institutions, its ideas, and a host of local practices. This might seem odd for a book that is con-sciously pushing back against the notion that the past weighs heav-ily on the present. I recognize this almost ironic twist: futuremaking in Spanish America and colonial Mexico often occurred when indi-viduals reached into the tools of tradition.

It is a paradox of sorts. But the creative adaptations described in the following case studies—the historical actors responding to individual circumstances and aspiring to improved futures, the in-dividuals and communities refashioning their lives—cannot be eas-ily accounted for in a narrative that assumes that Latin American and Mexican history, traditions, and legacies were simply burdens or engines of inertia.[22] As Jeremy Adelman has pointed out, persis-tence is not eternity.[23] Historical change and transformation can take place within the context of reproduction and persistence. Part of the interpretive problem lies in our tendency as historians to use sharp dichotomies to make comparisons across time and space, most notably the pair tradition / modernity, as if the times and places the terms describe were always discrete and separated by a crisp historical breakpoint or the qualities associated with modernity were antithetical to those of tradition.[24] Yet many historical examples, including those examined in this book, demonstrate that innovation and futuremaking often occurred as a result of individuals tapping into and modifying received concepts and techniques.

This is not to say that the past and tradition were always beneficial or even benign. Hardly. Nor does it mean we should champion these forms of futuremaking for our own times. Every chapter will reveal ways in which inherited knowledge and practices served as great constraints on human agency and reproduced unsettling historical patterns, including extreme economic inequality, social hierarchies, and religious intolerance. Like our own, these futures came with limits. They came with horizons, beyond which it could be difficult to see.

Even so, to reduce Mexican history to these things is to distort that history. As we will see, colonial Mexicans used these resources of culture and tradition in surprising and often unexpected ways. To do justice to these individuals and their lives, we need to think about a complementary historical narrative of resilience, ingenuity, and futuremaking.

In this model of history and human action, the past plays a critical, recurring role. We'll encounter it repeatedly. It is alive and active in ways that will at times appear unfamiliar and illogical to us. But in some ways the past can also be understood as a secondary player in that anticipation and prospection, creating expectations and evaluating future possibilities, were the energy that prompted individuals to reach into the resources of tradition.[25] In other words, there might be a partial resolution to the paradox just introduced. The future, at least when conceived of as an active human process of imagining, aspiring, and prospecting, was part of the engine that drove the present and past. Time, in a sense, sometimes flowed in the opposite direction from what we normally expect.

This is not a history easily captured in a single moment or subject. As a result, the book moves chronologically across New Spain's entire colonial period, from the European invasions and missionary projects of the early sixteenth century through the wars of independence in the early nineteenth century. The chapters are also organized thematically, as focused case studies, examining varied forms of colonial life but collectively piecing together a grammar of futuremaking.

Chapter 2, "Confessions," surveys the conceptual and practical tools of Catholicism that many colonial subjects used to shape their futures. While recognizing a great diversity in colonial spirituality, this chapter examines a common vocabulary that allowed for wide-ranging conversations about the limits and possibilities of the future. Christianity came with a host of ideas and practices that influenced one's relationship to the future, even the future of eternity in the form of salvation or damnation. Introduced via European missionaries in the sixteenth century, such concepts as free will and sin demanded new ways not only of thinking about religion and spirituality but also of living and relating to time. This chapter draws on a rich body of scholarship related to these themes but also delves into a unique set of primary sources, especially the intriguing genre of confession manuals. When examined over the arc of the colonial period, these sources reveal an evolving sense of individual futuremaking through the tools of Catholicism.

Chapter 3, "Stars," examines these concepts in practice, focusing on colonial modes of prediction, especially astrology and popular forms of divination. While most people in New Spain believed that heavenly objects could influence conditions on earth, there was great disagreement on the relative strength and importance of such forces and whether or not humans could (or should) discern them. The essence of these complicated, sometimes technical disputes was surprisingly well understood in the broader population, even by many who lacked a formal education. Colonial consumers of prediction understood the twin notions of free will / divine intervention and used a vernacular theology to evaluate diviners and their accuracy. As a result, by the eighteenth century many subjects in New Spain had adopted a more critical attitude toward the information produced by astrology and divination. As colonial subjects employed these tools of tradition, often in conversation with the Inquisition and its investigations, they helped to create a new culture of knowledge that championed a more precise and empirically grounded telling of the future.

Ideas about money and economic relationships had also transformed by the end of the colonial era, leading to a far more flexible system of credit and trade. By 1800 a more liberal market for credit and a new attitude toward risk and just pricing could be found throughout New Spain, from major cities and mining zones to villages and hamlets. Innovative financial instruments created opportunities for sophisticated financial hedging and risk management. Above all, fresh ideas had emerged about what constituted fair economic practices and an individual's or group's economic rights. Yet custom and values strongly influenced these innovations. They grew out of a tradition in Christian theology in which the church carved out a role for itself as a protector of the poor and where in theory, if not always in practice, its regulatory authority over economic transactions ensured some basic amount of market justice. Chapter 4, "Money," examines this shift in credit practices and its implications for how colonial subjects experienced the future.

Chapter 5, "Prayers," pieces together the logic of traditional innovation—how it worked, the resources it required—by investigating a form of sanctioned Catholic practice. In the eighteenth century a new movement flourished in many of the most important cities and towns of New Spain. Calling themselves Holy Schools of Christ, these groups combined collective piety sometimes associated with baroque Catholicism, such as the lashing of flesh, with an intense demand for self-regulation of an individual's thoughts and actions. As a result, the Holy Schools brought together practices of collective ritual and attitudes toward self-improvement that might seem temporally out of step. Like some of the other future-oriented individuals examined in this book, the participants in the Holy Schools might appear to us as surprisingly modern in their attitude toward controlling the future and their attempts to achieve individual or collective improvement. Yet to characterize this movement as a moment of hybrid modernity in which elements of the past persisted despite a turn toward the modern would be deeply misleading. For the members and supporters of the Holy Schools, as for the practitioners and consumers of astrology and divination, innovation required tradition. Individuals of this period, in other words, were often future-oriented without being modern.

Chapter 6, "Promises," moves to the realm of politics and collective motivation at the violent end of the colonial era. Sparked by a crisis in the Spanish monarchy in 1808 and the rebellion led by

Miguel Hidalgo y Costilla in 1810, more than a decade of uncertainty and violent conflict would lead to Mexico's independence from Spain in 1821. Through a reading of political rhetoric during this era, this chapter explores the use of biblical references and interpretation as a way of navigating the uncertainty of the present. For royalist preachers, this often meant emotional appeals to their flocks and a call for them to defend traditional forms of authority and hierarchy. Yet these tools of tradition, especially biblical typology, were also used most forcefully by supporters of new visions of political community, including the most radical leaders of the insurgency. Even during the collapse of the colonial order, futuremaking included a strong element of tradition.

I draw these case studies together to review the logic of futuremaking in colonial Mexico. This book offers a historical counternarrative to most writing on Mexico's history. Some of the qualities we associate generically with futuremaking, whether individualism or innovation, in fact had their origins in tradition. Examining this relationship between past, present, and future offers a way to reconsider Mexico's colonial era, its subsequent historical development, and how we have understood that history.

CHAPTER TWO

Confessions

THE PAST HAD FUTURES.

Of course, you say, that is what this book is about. Yet those historical futures also had pasts, and the relationship between the two requires a bit of explanation.

When we think of futures being created, what usually comes to mind is imagination, a mental process whereby an individual constructs a notion of what is to come. But an empty mind will find it hard to imagine. To imagine and construct a future, the mind requires a past. It requires materials.

In New Spain these materials included a common vocabulary of concepts and ideas. They also included shared practices, rituals, and institutional experiences. Together, these assumptions and activities influenced the possible futures in the colonial world. To use another metaphor, we could say that colonial subjects built their relationship to time with these resources, these raw materials of ideas and actions, as I suspect is the case for most historical contexts.

This is not to suggest that all subjects in New Spain conceived of the future using the same mental imagery or engaged it through the same rituals, practices, or techniques. That would be absurd, given the great range of human thoughts and experiences in any time or place. It would be especially misguided in a locale as diverse as colonial Mexico. New Spain brought together individuals from many parts the world—Europe, Africa, Asia, and many Indigenous peoples—all with unique cultural and linguistic traditions and living in varied socioeconomic contexts. As a result, even a casual reading of the region's history would uncover many ways of relating to time that might be quite different from those I describe in this book.

Yet common forms of futuremaking developed over the colonial period. These were not shared by everyone in New Spain or at all times, but they appear consistently in the documentary record, across multiple domains of practice, and among people with varied backgrounds.

I want to consider some of the ways in which these key concepts became established in the early colonial period, how they began to shape colonial futuremaking, and some ways they evolved over the long run. Two reminders are in order. First, this history of time is also about temporality, or the way historical subjects experienced time. As a result, when probing the history of the future we need also to look at the evolution of the individual as a historical subject: the individual's changing sense of self, the relation of individual to collective life, historical understanding of individual autonomy, responsibility, and so on. These themes will remain in our peripheral vision throughout much of the book, occasionally moving directly into the field of view. Second, in terms of the historian's methods it is sometimes difficult to separate these concepts from the practices that activated them. As a result, the following chapters are not about ideas in the abstract but about their relationship to material practices. They are about people doing things in the world and thinking about the implications. How did specific rituals and activities shape ideas about the future? Or, the reverse, how did ideas influence practices of futuremaking? How was thought embedded in practice and vice versa?[1]

Foremost among these practices was a new ritual that arrived in Mesoamerica with Europeans: the Catholic sacrament of penance, commonly referred to as confession.[2] Confession is a good example of how some of these core concepts of futuremaking spread widely in New Spain. Over the arc of the colonial period the sacrament of penance introduced or reconfigured ideas about how the individual related to time and the future. Through it and

other forms of communication (whether rituals, formal indoctrina-
tion, or casual conversations) colonial subjects, both Indigenous
and non-Indigenous, learned about sin, free will, the individual as
an agent of change, the future as a domain of (limited) individual
agency, and the soul, not only as an entity that transcended worldly
time but also as something that drove the human experience of
time. Returning to the concept of thought embedded in practice,
we could say that the ritual of confession was both a way to communicate ideas and a new way of relating to the future.

Confession was itself embedded in Christian and Catholic assumptions about an individual's relationship to the long-term future
of salvation or damnation. Confession rests upon the idea that humans are fallible and inclined to sin. Augustine emphasized both in
his influential assessment of human nature from the first centuries of
Christianity. Human beings, he argued, faced a constant danger of
corruption and of misusing the gift of free will. Augustine captured
this gloomy take on the human condition when he recalled an event
from his own life. It was a simple act, and one, on the face of it, not
especially horrendous or vile: he stole pears from an orchard while
out walking with friends. As he reflected on the event many years
later, he found the utter senselessness of it most disturbing. He
wrote, "We carried off an immense load of pears, not to eat—for we
barely tasted them before throwing them to the hogs. Our only
pleasure in doing it was that it was forbidden."[3] He stole the pears
because he could and because doing wrong felt good. He and his fellow humans, it seemed, were inclined to err, to pervert their essen-
tially good nature (being modeled, after all, on God), by directing
their desires away from the appropriate object (the divine) toward
base longings (sin). Though not all later Christian writers shared his
pessimism about the human predicament, this Augustinian outlook
regarding the dangers of sin and human weakness figured prominently in the Catholicism of New Spain.[4]

Augustine's account of sin and fallibility is probably familiar to
most of us in some general sense, if not in its historical specifics or
theological details. In broader political or social contexts, sin and
fallibility are often associated with an impulse toward order, tradition, and even forms of violence: projects of social control, the
maintenance of orthodoxy by authorities, and the imposition of

cultural norms in the form of missionary projects. They evoke power and, eventually, a kind of stasis or oppressive conservatism, as authorities place limits on religious expression and individual behavior. These assessments are often accurate, including for the history of New Spain. To take the most obvious example, which we will encounter later in this chapter, the eradication of sin and the quest for the salvation of souls became the key justifications for European settlers' and missionaries' demanding massive changes in the behavior and belief systems of native communities in the wake of conquest. In more cynical moments, they simply became cover for plunder and power.

What is less apparent are the ways in which these same ideas acted as engines of change, in the first instance shaping human experience of the passing of time but also animating human activity and serving as catalysts for human choices. This too was an essential component of Christian theology, as much as the dangers of sin and human fallibility. The God of the Old Testament gave humans free will, or the ability to make choices independent of divine control, whether for good or ill. From the Catholic perspective, few things could be more essential to the human condition than free will, since, as the great medieval theologian Thomas Aquinas (1225–74) later noted, individual choice and action opened a pathway to salvation.[5]

The problem of free will and the intellectual foundations of the future attracted a great deal of attention from intellectuals in early modern Spain and Spanish America, especially in the context of the challenges raised by Martin Luther, John Calvin, and other theologians of the Protestant Reformation. Is God's grace sufficient for human salvation or do individuals need to perform good works to earn that reward? Do individuals control their fate in this world and beyond or is all predestined by God? It was a particularly fertile moment for thinking about the subject. In the late sixteenth century the Spanish Jesuit Luís de Molina (1535–1600), for example, rejected the notion that human beings lived in a cage of limited choice created by God and therefore that the future was predetermined. God might be all-knowing, argued Molina, but not all-controlling. Indeed, God's knowledge is so profound, according to Molina, that it includes foresight not just of what will happen but of everything that *could* happen, sometimes referred to as the notion of *scientia media*, or middle knowledge. Within this vast range of possibilities humans are free to choose, potentially working in cooperation with God but perhaps at odds. In this intellectual move, Molina, Francisco Suárez (1548–1617), and other Jesuits, including many in New Spain, pushed the idea of free will even further than Aquinas and also tried to resolve the paradox of God's knowledge of all things alongside the uncertainty of human behavior.[6] Although other theologians in the Catholic world contested these ideas at the edges, part of a long-term debate about the ability to know the future and the degree of God's influence on the world, the core concept of human freedom remained strong. Free will and the danger of misusing it through sin and moral failings thus served as cornerstones in the theory of human behavior and agency that prevailed in New Spain.

What else did sin mean during this period? In the theology that made its way to New Spain in the early sixteenth century, sin referred to a specific type of moral transgression. It occurred when human beings failed to use their faculties of reason and committed an intentional, voluntary violation of divine law. Theologians explained that sin had the potential to cause damage, both in terms of its external, or material, consequences and certainly through its internal effects on the person who committed the sin.[7] Most significantly, the dogmas of Catholicism related sin to the status of the soul, the immortal essence of human beings. Sin, Catholics held, could extend one's time in purgatory, a medieval development in Christian thought that referred to a liminal space between heaven and hell. While souls in purgatory were understood to be ultimately marked for salvation and a place in heaven, the timing of that transition was uncertain and thus created an enormous sense of anxiety among some believers.[8] When left unatoned, more serious transgressions—mortal sins in the theological system of Aquinas—could lead to damnation. It was essential, therefore, to make amends for one's sins and seek a reconciliation with the church and God through the sacrament of penance, since confessors had the authority to grant forgiveness for many sins.

Early modern Catholics also believed that sin influenced events on earth in the form of divine retribution for human failings. The most well-known example in the Judeo-Christian tradition is the story of the flood in Genesis, where an angry God strikes back against a sinful humanity. Yet in the sixteenth century and beyond it was common to attribute other great calamities and natural disasters, such as earthquakes and crop failures, to divine retribution for human sin, usually sin committed on a collective scale.[9]

Indeed, intellectuals in New Spain in the late seventeenth century debated these very points. Should calamities be attributed to divine wrath or to natural causes? Did nature offer harbingers of such punishment in celestial events, such as the appearance of a comet? Did sin, or human action in a more general sense, trigger events in the future? Throughout the colonial era, whatever the specific answers to these questions, sin was generally understood to have potentially severe material consequences in addition to its more obvious spiritual repercussions. As a result, it offered a language and concept for talking about human action in relation to what is to come, both the short-term future of the material world and the longer-term future of the afterlife. The future in New Spain thus folded intricately on itself, an overlap between an ultimate reality in the beyond and a penultimate reality in the world. The relationship between these two futures was intimate and real.

When European missionaries arrived in the sixteenth century, they attempted to communicate these ideas to the native peoples they evangelized. A complicated process of cross-cultural translation ensued. Many Indigenous peoples of the region possessed concepts that shared some features with the Christian notion of sin. The Nahuatl-speaking communities of central Mesoamerica are a good example. Nahuas demographically predominated in much of the region that composed the center of the Aztec empire, which, after its conquest, became central New Spain, and they have been the subject of substantial ethnohistorical study. Nahuas, it turns out, also ordered their world according to a binary, in their case order and chaos rather than good and evil. To the Nahuas and many Mesoamerican peoples, order was an ideal state and something human actions should promote.[10] Chaos, entropy, or disorder were conditions to be avoided. The good-evil and order-chaos binaries both suggested desired states and acted as ethical principles, or guides to behavior. Yet they differed insofar as the Christian-European notions of good and evil referred to essential qualities and assumed the two categories were mutually exclusive. The Nahua-Mesoamerican concepts of order and chaos, on the other hand, described a mutable condition, not an essence, and thus covered a wider range or conditions, in fact suggesting a spectrum or continuum rather than a simple binary.

Such subtle but potentially profound differences in thought and symbolism could be seen in the translation of the term "sin" from the Spanish (*pecado*) or Latin (*peccatum*) into Nahuatl. Christian missionaries and Nahuas engaged in what Louise Burkhart describes as a "moral dialogue," a term she uses to emphasize that meaning and concepts flowed in both directions, not simply from the missionaries to native peoples or from Spanish to Nahuatl.[11] To translate "sin," for example, Spanish friars used the Nahuatl term *tlatlacolli*, which roughly translates as "damage" or "harm." "Any sort of moral error or misdeed could be labeled a *tlatlacolli*," Burkhart notes, "from conscious moral transgressions to judicially defined crimes to accidental or unintentional damage."[12] Some usages of *tlatlacolli* clearly overlapped with the idea of sin (theft, sexual transgressions), but others referred to damage that was of a different quality: "A weaver who tangled her weaving, a feather worker who ruined feathers, a warrior who erred in battle, a singer who failed to harmonize, a mouse gnawing garments, hail harming crops."[13] Above all, the difference between tlatlacolli and sin revolved around the relationship of transgression to time. The Nahua understood moral transgressions, such as those captured under the label of tlatlacolli, to influence primarily the present world. Christian thought left open the possibility of worldly consequences for sin but emphasized the strong, even determining influence of it on one's fate in the afterlife.[14]

We might draw upon many other examples of "moral dialogue" and cultural translation in the missionary projects in New Spain, let alone other parts of the New World. But, as I noted above, the goal in this chapter is not to revisit the missionary encounters but to explore how colonial subjects communicated with each other about the future.[15] Over generations the Christian notion of sin became one of the key terms colonial subjects used to talk about and argue over different forms of futuremaking. In some cases, as we will see, this meant a rather accurate understanding of the orthodox theology surrounding the concept. In other cases, individuals offered a much more fluid understanding of the term, sometimes accented with local interpretations and understandings, whether of Indigenous or other origins, such as the concept of tlatlacolli.

Sin was the primary category used by the church to create and enforce normative behaviors. In general, the church and its agents attempted to replace preexisting moral frameworks with those of Catholicism, although, as Burkhart and others have noted, sometimes this work entailed a great deal of cultural compromise. The Roman Catholic Church enforced these norms formally and informally, including through institutional means. Most notably, the church attempted to ensure orthodox thought and practice through the Inquisition and related institutions. Like many other areas in the early modern Catholic world, by the late sixteenth century New Spain had its own office of the Inquisition, and its records are a boon to those interested in the cultural and social history of the period.[16] At the local level, in the parishes and *doctrinas de indios* that formed the first layer of the church in New Spain, subjects of all backgrounds interacted with church authorities through doctrinal instruction, participation in the sacraments, religious celebrations, and so on.

As a result, the church and its records offer us a perspective not only on the enforcement of orthodoxy and social control but also on colonial futuremaking. These futures are perhaps most visible in the historical records describing lofty religious goals, such as the quest for salvation and the care of the souls of the departed, but, just as important, in all sorts of mundane events: when discussing economic transactions, community matters, and political events. So, on one hand, we can use the case files of the Inquisition, records of local piety, and other church documents as a way of reading some of the norms it attempted to impose. But we can also look to them as records of historical conversations about attitudes and practices related to the future that included the voices of many peoples, not just those of authorities.

Using confession as a lever to pry open these themes comes with some advantages. The ritual was relatively well documented in a general sense, given the numerous theoretical treatises on the theology surrounding the sacrament, so-called confession manuals (*confesionarios*) written as practical "field guides" to help priests in their work, grammars (*artes*) and dictionaries to aid in translation when confession took place across the boundary of languages, and many other related documents that touched on some aspect of the ritual. These texts have proven to be a treasure to historians for their specificity and the way they meditate deeply on subjects that are often quite scarce in other historical records, subjects like core assumptions about spiritual matters, the practice of religion on a small scale, even an individual's thoughts, memories, and emotions. They provide texture and detail, a human granularity. On the other hand, they are tricky texts to work with, for they raise difficult questions about method and epistemology—that is, the way in which we historians conduct our work, the sources we use to investigate the past, and the kind of information we can glean from these traces of the past that are available to us. Above all, they are highly mediated texts, deeply influenced by their genre. The confessional texts offer us an opportunity to listen to some historical conversations regarding futuremaking, yet almost always these are imagined conversations, and they are produced by only one side of the dialogue, the priest who wrote the manual. As a result, we should not assume they give us access to the individual penitents or priests in some unalloyed, pristine state. Finally, in New Spain the literature tends to be focused on the evangelization of Indigenous subjects, and historians have tended to use them in studies focused on questions of attempted conversion and evolving beliefs among native peoples. Yet they can be read for other purposes. They can tell us something about the self, time, and the future in colonial Catholicism. For this purpose, the historical records surrounding penance and confession are ideal.

Ritual atonement for sin had long been a part of Christianity and Catholicism. In the early centuries of Christianity rituals of forgiveness took many forms, often as an end-of-life or deathbed event meant to atone for years of sin, though some individuals performed it earlier in the life course in order to reconcile with their communities. Penance was frequently a public or semipublic affair and was not always carried out between an individual priest and penitent. In the late medieval period forgiveness rituals became formalized as the sacrament of penance, along with the other Catholic sacraments of baptism, confirmation, Eucharist, taking holy orders, extreme unction, and marriage.[17] In 1215 a church council, the Fourth Lateran, decreed that all the faithful confess at least once a year. Subsequent writings by theologians and church authorities affirmed the necessity of the ritual for the forgiveness of sins.

By the time early missionaries arrived in New Spain the form and meaning of the ritual had also evolved. One-on-one confession between a priest and penitent became the norm. The encounter was meant to be private—that is, shielded from the ears and eyes of one's community, though we know that in practice this rule was not always observed.[18] The ritual revolved around a narrative of sins in the context of a conversation, where the individual voluntarily confessed to the sins he or she had committed since the last confession. The description of sin was supposed to be complete, with attention given to the frequency and the specific instances when the acts occurred. Indeed, for a confession to be good or true in theological terms—that is, for it to confer upon the penitent the gift of divine grace—the accounting needed to be complete. Church authorities also affirmed that the priest-confessor had the power and authority to absolve sins, assuming that other qualities had been met by the penitent: most important, contrition, or a true sense of sorrow and desire to avoid future sins.[19] As a number of historians have observed, the purpose of the ritual had also changed. Whereas penance previously had focused on the expiation of sin and communal reconciliation—a largely public and exterior ritual—it was now a more private, interior act, imposing the norms of the church on the "inner forum" of the penitent's mind and conscience.[20]

This evolved sacrament loomed large in New Spain, partly out of historical circumstance. The initial evangelization of native peoples and the formation of the church in sixteenth-century New Spain occurred at the moment when the Roman Catholic Church faced the challenge of the Reformation, when Luther and other dissidents questioned the meaning and necessity of the sacraments. In response, the Catholic Church clarified its doctrine but ceded no ground. It reaffirmed the role of the sacraments as conduits for God's grace, most forcefully in the decrees issued at the intermittent meetings of church authorities known as the Council of Trent

(1545–63). This development led to a new emphasis on the sacrament of confession in Catholic ministry. It became a key part of the
pastoral work of the church in the New World, among native peoples and others, in the decades following the conquest of the Aztec
empire in the early 1520s.

The ritual figured prominently in the yearly liturgical calendar,
organized around the birth, death, and resurrection of Christ.
Although some church leaders and intellectuals advocated frequent
confession, most residents of New Spain confessed once a year, as
part of the *precepto anual*, a responsibility that all of the faithful
confess and take communion in the weeks leading up to Easter.
There is evidence that some individuals avoided the precepto, often as a result of a dispute with the local priest (or simply some
personal animosity), but it seems the vast majority of the laity completed the yearly obligation.[21] As a result, the Lenten season, the
forty days of spiritual preparation leading to Easter, was also a season of confession. In the weeks before Easter the rite occurred en
masse throughout the viceroyalty, from large, urban churches to
the most remote rural hamlets.

Given that the precepto anual was a moment when individuals
reaffirmed their connection to God and the church, the sacrament
offered an opportunity for priests to reinforce basic doctrine and
devotions. Many of the confesionarios (again, the manuals written
to aid priests in the performance of the ritual) included a primer of
doctrine and a collection of standard prayers, such as the Credo,
the Ave Maria, and the Pater Noster. They sometimes included a
more detailed discussion of the sacrament and the place of sin in
the Christian imaginary, such as moral conundrums the priest
might face in the confessional or advice for discussing particular
sins and their regional inflections.[22] The laity encountered these
prayers and basic tenets of doctrine in many contexts, including
sermons, but the yearly rhythm and intimate setting of confession
made it particularly well suited for priests to review them. It also
opened up space for penitents to raise their own questions about
the sacrament or other points of doctrine.

As noted, a verbal recounting of sins formed the core of the
sacrament. Not just any recollection would do. To complete a good
confession—a theological term of art that meant the rite was

successful and therefore conferred God's grace—the penitent had to approach the sacrament in a state of contrition and with a desire and intent to avoid sin in the future—one of our first hints of the dynamic relationship between the future and the past—and then give a full recounting of all major sins committed since the last good confession. Failing to confess one major sin ruined not only the current confession but also all future ones until the penitent confessed the missing sin. One confesionario author imagined such a scenario. After learning that a penitent had concealed a sin in four or five prior confessions, he warned, "Child, what is important to you now is to reexamine again all the sins you have committed in that time [while] you denied the sin. Because although you went to confession, by reason of failing to confess that sin you made your confessions null and void, even though you saw that they absolved you for your other sins. Now then go to your home, and examine and count how many sins you have committed since you hid that sin, so that when we are together you confess them again here where very willingly I remain awaiting you in order to help you, since for that purpose God put me here and commands me to do it."[23] It is hardly a surprise, then, that the moment of confession could be fraught with a great deal of spiritual uncertainty and that the approach and aftermath of confession might be as much part of the psychological experience of the ritual as the act itself.

Given this high threshold for success, much of the literature on the sacrament addressed how to achieve a complete accounting of an individual's sins. The confession manuals give us a good indication of how such dialogue could unfold. To begin with, the conversation between priest and penitent typically revolved around a series of questions from the priest to the confessant. Authors organized the manuals in such a way as to aid recall, for example, by listing potential questions under the seven mortal sins, the articles of faith, or some other rubric, most commonly the Ten Commandments, also known as the Decalogue. In a typical manual the initial set of questions concentrated on the first commandment, "You shall love the Lord your God with all your heart, and with all your soul, and with all your mind."[24] Related questions followed: "Have you doubted some teaching of the Holy Mother Church and the Faith?"[25] "Did you believe in [your] dreams? What did you believe or what did you

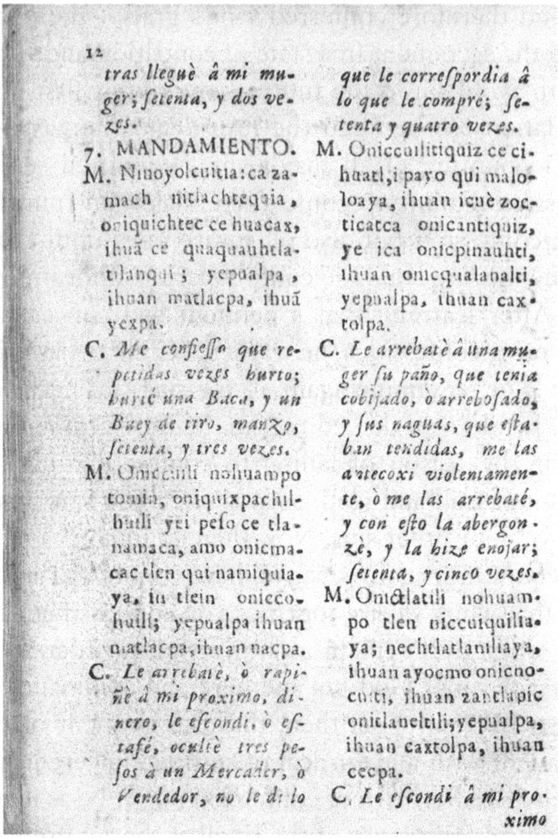

12

tras llegue à mi mu-
ger; setenta, y dos ve-
zes.

7. MANDAMIENTO.
M. Ninoyolcuitia: ca za-
mach nitlachteqaia,
oriquichtec ce huacax,
ihuā ce quaquauhtla-
tilanqui; yepoalpa,
ihuan matlacpa, ihuā
yexpa.

C. *Me confiessa que re-
petidas vezes hurto;
hurté una Baca, y un
Buey de tiro, manzo,
setenta, y tres vezes.*

M. Oniccuili nohuampo
tomin, oniquixpachil-
huili yei peso ce tla-
namaca, amo onicma-
cac tien qui namiquia-
ya, in tlein onicco-
huili; yepoalpa ihuan
matlacpa, ihuan nacpa.

C. *Le arrebaté, ò rapi-
ñé à mi proximo, di-
nero, le escondi, ò es-
tafé, oculté tres pe-
sos à un Mercader, ò
Vendedor, no le di lo*

que le correspordia à
lo que le compré; se-
tenta y quatro vezes.

M. Oniccuilitiquiz ce ci-
huatl, i payo qui malo-
loaya, ihuan icuè zoc-
ticatca onicantiquiz,
ye ica onicpinauhti,
ihuan omequalanalti,
yepoalpa, ihuan cax-
tolpa.

C. *Le arrebaté à una mu-
ger su paño, que tenia
cobijado, ò arrebosado,
y sus naguas, que esta-
ban tendidas, me las
aviecoxi violentamen-
te, ò me las arrebaté,
y con esto la abergon-
zé, y la hize enojar;
setenta, y cinco vezes.*

M. Onictlatili nohuam-
po tlen niccuiquilia-
ya; nechtlatlaniliaya,
ihuan ayocmo onicno-
cuiti, ihuan zantlapic
oniclaneltili; yepoalpa,
ihuan caxtolpa, ihuan
cecpa.

C. *Le escondi à mi pro-
ximo*

Figure 1. *Questions relating to the seventh commandment ("You shall not steal") in a Nahuatl–Spanish confession manual from eighteenth-century New Spain. (Carlos Celedonio Velázquez de Cárdenas,* Breve práctica y régimen del confessonario de indios, en mexicano y castellano . . ., *t PM4068.V3 x. Courtesy of the Bancroft Library, University of California, Berkeley.)*

dream?"[26] Depending on the length of the manual, additional questions might follow. The confesionario then proceeded through the rest of the commandments. This simple, rigid structure was meant to aid both the confessor's and confessant's recall, with the goal of achieving a complete recounting of sins. Armed with such rubrics of potential transgression, which themselves were understood to be comprehensive, confessional authors hoped priests and penitents would be less likely to pass over any sins, whether the omissions were inadvertent or intentional.

In this way, the confessional had a productive quality. In addition to a technique of recall, which uncovered memories of sin that the mind closeted or time entombed, confession created the thing that it sought. In a most straightforward way it produced sins, or at least their recollection, simply by demanding an accounting of behavior. Those demands could carry enormous emotional pressure. Many confession manuals suggested that the priest offer some form of exhortation to the penitent prior to confession. "If you don't tell me the serious sins you've committed," suggested one author, "God won't pardon you for your sins, and you won't clear your soul, and then you might die without confessing, and the Devil will take away your soul forever." Frequently, confessional authors advocated some combination of fear and tough love with consolation and appeals to trust. In the passage preceding this threat of damnation, for example, the priest noted, "I don't get angry when people confess with me, so don't be afraid, don't be ashamed."[27] This juxtaposition of tone is one striking example among countless in the literature of the sacrament that captures how confession was a ritual of emotions and the management of affect. The ritual elicited a particular perspective on behavior. It marked certain thoughts or actions as sinful and drew the penitent's attention to things that might otherwise have been passed over or digested in a very different manner. Emotions arose not only in relation to past action but also in the form of "affective residue," traces of feelings linking emotion to past actions that guided the evaluation of future action.[28] How would one feel in a certain scenario? In this way of thinking, confession did not necessarily document how an individual behaved in the world but created a new understanding of self in relation to the world.[29]

The practice of confession introduced and reinforced normative ideas. This is plain from the contents of the confesionarios and other descriptions of the sacrament in practice. Priests and penitents were required to catalogue and describe potential sins. This meant that the manner of questioning could be extremely detailed, even exhaustive in its depth and breadth. One of the most important native language confessionals from the colonial period, Alonso de Molina's *Confesionario mayor* (1565), included scores of questions about a vast range of activities, from marriages to market transactions to sexual practices. Although Molina's work is something of an outlier (most colonial confessionals were much shorter), the goal of the genre was clear: to elicit the penitient's detailed, comprehensive description of potential sins and to undertake a deep journey through the past. Indeed, priests understood that the printed questions were nothing more than starting points, the basic tools they would use, repurpose, and modify over the course of a lengthy confession. Authors of native-language confesionarios frequently combined them with grammars and dictionaries to foster improved communication and dialogue between the priest and penitent, all with the goal of ensuring a complete, good confession. Agustín de Quintana, who wrote a confesionario in Mixe, a native language spoken primarily in parts of Oaxaca in southern New Spain, addressed this relationship between language and knowledge. He told his readers that the manual included all the questions he thought might come up when discussing specific cases in the confessional. But he also pointed out that his primer didn't teach moral theology per se but something more powerful. He offered the language of Mixe itself, "so you can ask everything."[30]

Historians and poststructural theorists were not the first to recognize that confession could produce new ways of thinking. Colonial-era priests and confessional authors made a similar observation when they discussed the ritual. They described a most precarious balance in the potential of the sacrament to aid in salvation: a teetering between grace and sin. On one hand, the confessional dialogue needed to be sufficiently detailed to ensure that no sins were left uncovered. On the other, sin tended to beget sin. The language used to describe sin, that is, could put the penitent or even the confessor at risk by producing impure thoughts or tempting both parties toward some new transgression. This was most obvious in sections describing the sixth commandment, "You shall not commit adultery," which gathered questions related to all manner of sexual transgressions and usually made up the largest section of the confessionals.[31] The sample questions might go into great detail, but confessional authors frequently described the need for prudence and restraint in the examination. Be careful. Use good judgment. Discuss "only what is necessary," noted one, depending on the confessant's background, age, sex, and so on.[32] Another author

Figure 2. Alonso de Molina's Confesionario mayor *(1565), a detailed confession manual that runs hundreds of folios in parallel Spanish and Nahuatl text. (Alonso de Molina,* Confesionario mayor, en lengua castellana y mexicana. *Courtesy of the John Carter Brown Library at Brown University.)*

observed that the amount of questioning should always be left to the discretion of the minister, "which is part of being a knowledge-able confessor."[33]

Priests often described the danger of the confessional. They portrayed an economy of risk, in other words, where the enormous potential payoff of a future salvation required both parties to engage in a spiritual transaction that was marked by uncertainty and potentially disastrous outcomes. This precariousness is most clear in a remarkable late-colonial confessional written by a Discalced Carmelite who worked among diverse urban populations in the city of Valladolid (now Morelia) in western New Spain. The language of risk is peppered throughout the document and is used to describe a handful of related problems: the spiritual risk of sins left in silence; the sexual risk of temptation in the confessional; the mental risk that the language of the confession will pollute the thoughts of both the priest and penitent; and, as frequently as any of the others, the kind of external, material risks that accrue to sinners in addition to any spiritual dangers. The material harm the priest described included reprisals from aggrieved persons, financial loss, exposure to illness, and legal jeopardy, among others. By the late eighteenth century it seems colonial subjects might have begun to blend the language of risk with the language of sin, considering them complementary notions of self-discipline.[34]

Confession is thus implicated in the birth of the modern self—the notion of the individual as a tightly bounded, mostly autonomous being who is free to exercise choice. After all, the ritual revolved around a simple imperative: that the penitent look inward and reflect on her or his actions and thoughts. It also constituted a tool for authorities to discipline and control those individuals. The materials discussed so far certainly support both of these assertions. Much of the literature on the confessional in Europe and Latin America has taken on this problem, discussing in diverse ways how the ritual played a role in the historical emergence of the Western subject.[35] These are important topics for colonialists, given their attention to the ways in which individuals internalized norms and acted as agents of their own governance. Among other historical problems, they help us understand the relative success of the missionary project and the surprising stability of the colonial order, despite the limited administrative capacity and coercive powers of the church and crown.

What has received less attention was that the journey inward was also a journey outward in the experience of time. As we've seen, the rite of penance and the theological imperative of a good confession required a nimble relationship between one's past and future. The penitent needed to confess by looking toward the past and providing an accounting of activities, sometimes in phenomenal detail. He or she was supplied with techniques like mnemonics, rubrics, and other categories and organizing principles that helped the process of recall. "Go remembering and recalling through the passage of the days," urged one manual, "the nights, the weeks, the months and the years, counting up with kernels of corn, until reaching a year, two, etc."[36] Penitents were asked to develop an emotional state (contrition) that projected the individual self into the future in a most aggressive way, in a combined state of sorrow, hope, and confidence.[37] The mental accounting and subsequent narrative could function the same way, by delaying the emotional consolation and spiritual benefit of the ritual until a complete accounting and good confession had taken place. In some cases the priest might defer the confession or the granting of forgiveness (absolution) until the penitent had prepared a thorough review of past sins.[38] These techniques of self-reflection, though sometimes caricatured or overemphasized, formed a part of the mental landscape of many colonial subjects. In the confessional and the penitential culture that surrounded the ritual, individuals developed a relationship to time that integrated past and future, with the present as a potential locus of control and mastery over both.

Colonial subjects also connected memory, past, and future in ways that might seem unnatural to many of us in the present. Colonial confession engaged memory as a productive, creative technique much more than as a simple storehouse of information that was available for retrieval. This relationship to memory grew out of a medieval theory of mind, beautifully described by Mary Carruthers, that understood memory as a tool for thinking, like "a chisel or a pen," not a mechanism for summoning a fixed past or even producing specific outcomes.[39] Medieval *memoria* thus embraced our notions of both inventory and invention, words harvested from the same Latin root of *inventio*. "Having 'inventory,' " writes Carruthers, "is a requirement for 'invention.' " Memory was for doing and making as much as for summoning and recalling. Ideally, then, memory work brought the individual into a different mental state, as Michelle Molina notes in her study of Jesuit spirituality, engaging one's emotions and prompting action in the future.[40] This does not mean that the confessional prompted creativity in our contemporary understanding of the term—that is, as a kind of casual originality unburdened by the past or as a type

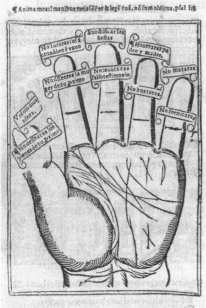

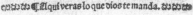

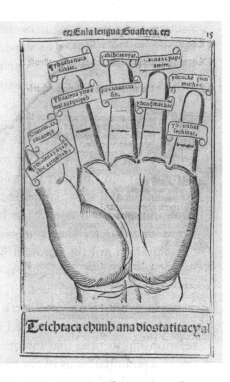

Figure 3. An example of the memory tools found in colonial confession manuals: the Ten Commandments arranged across the fingers of the hand. On the left are the commandments in Spanish, on the right are their equivalents in Huastec, a Mayan language spoken in eastern New Spain. (Juan de la Cruz, Doctrina christiana en la lengua Guasteca co[n] la lengua castellana *[1571]. Courtesy of the John Carter Brown Library at Brown University.)*

of pure novelty. Instead, it was an act of building and crafting with some strong fidelity to the materials at hand, in this case the memory of the penitent, which might be shaped and rearranged.[41]

We find this theory built into concrete practices of the confessional. Actions and events needed to be accounted for, of course, but a simple list of sins would render the penitent and the ritual inert. The list would be worthless. It wouldn't lead to a good confession. It was thus essential for the penitent to detail a comprehensive list (inventory) of past transgressions but also to craft (invent) a new future of thought and action. By tapping into these two qualities of *inventio*, the journey of confession placed penitents in an active role with the expectation that they would be transformed through taking part in the ritual. Could confession elicit guilt and shame? Of course. Could it also produce hope and consolation and act as a catalyst of future action? Certainly. Were these two states irreconcilable? Not at all. Memory work created new attitudes toward the past, but it was largely future oriented, even driven by the anticipation of future scenarios, and it was certainly meant to shape future emotion and behavior.[42]

These practices of memory and accounting, including the quick tacking back and forth between memory (or, in other cases, tradition, custom, "time immemorial") and the present, produced new perspectives on the past but always in service of the future. Indeed, as discussed earlier, it seems that the ritual of confession and the techniques associated with it should be thought of primarily as future-oriented activities. Guilt, moral accounting, and shame were never products of the past but means with which to contemplate the future—potentially the rewards or punishments that flowed from one's behavior in the world—and various ways of being in the world. Here we encounter one of the great paradoxes of the confessional and other forms of futuremaking examined in this book. Individuals dipped into the past not as a storehouse of ideas but as something alive that could be used to produce new perspectives on the present and future. As one did so, new futures came into being. They were imagined, mental constructs, scenarios, and situations from which one could then choose a particular orientation, a goal, and destination or even just an emotional hunch to follow or a fear to be avoided.[43]

As a result, when examining confession as a ritual of cultural domination and social control we need to be careful not to mischaracterize the relationship between priests and penitents. The very sources historians have used to argue the social control / discipline thesis—the confesionarios, *summae confesorum, advertencias*—also demonstrate that interactions in the confessional were turbulent, contingent, and uncertain. Church authorities, different religious orders, and even individual confessors, for example, often disagreed on how best to perform the sacrament. Should it be tailored to diverse groups of penitents (Indians and Spaniards, learned and uneducated, women and men, married and engaged, children and adults, and on and on)? Could it be modified in particular cases (for example, when communicating across language barriers)? How should it relate to previous Indigenous rituals of forgiveness or reconciliation (a concern especially in the early years of evangelization)?[44]

While we shouldn't discount the cultural violence and domination of which the confessional was at times a tool, in the messiness of lived experience the sacrament could include a remarkable amount of confrontation, negotiation, and, in a word, dialogue. In the mind of an urban confessor, his job was to win souls by imparting moral lessons, cutting through the noise and turbidity of the penitent's recollection, and achieving a good confession. If he succeeded, he would improve the confessant's chance of salvation and also his own.[45] This perspective of the sacrament is evident in many sources, and it tends to fit the standard interpretation of the confessional as a location where priests exercised power. Yet the ritual also placed the confessant in a position of power. After all, the interaction was a dialogue, not a monologue. Confessing depended on the speech and actions of both parties. Priests asked, penitents answered. But penitents could also parry, conceal, distort (intentionally or not), or ask their own questions. This was power working in the opposite direction, a scenario where the goals of the two parties diverged, where their intentions clashed. Many confessional authors anguished and complained about this reality.[46]

Initiative, moreover, could be more than oppositional resistance, a point the confessors sometimes noted. We need to recognize as well the agency of orthodoxy: the penitent's role in achieving a victory through a good confession by successfully integrating the confessional practice, the work of memory, and memory's temporal orientation. These were often conversations, in other words, in which both parties could demonstrate an ability to influence outcomes. So in addition to interpreting the confessional as a site of domination, control, and policing of norms, which it most certainly was, we need to acknowledge that it was a place where penitents honed a way to discuss normative behavior, ethics, sin, and the moral economy of risk. The journey into the confessional was part of a tradition of inventing the future through the manipulation of the past. Penitents not only were subject to this tradition but also subjected the tradition to their own ends.[47]

Figure 4. The title page of the Confessonario en lengua mixe, *an eighteenth-century confession manual with questions that probed the penitent's emotional state at the time of a sin. (Agustín de Quintana,* Confessonario en lengua mixe *[Puebla: Viuda de Miguel de Ortega, 1733]. Courtesy of the John Carter Brown Library at Brown University.)*

This inward journey and its temporal orientations were part of a long history of confessional practice and related forms of self-reflection. In New Spain it seems to have become more pronounced over the arc of the colonial centuries. A number of late-colonial manuals suggest there was a demand, in the eighteenth and early nineteenth centuries, to look deeper into the self. These confesionarios asked penitents to articulate their emotional states, desires, and intentions. What were you thinking at the time of a sin? Did simply thinking about sin bring pleasure?[48] While it is difficult to peg such intensification of confessional practice to any one cause, it is consistent with other shifts in eighteenth-century New Spain in which the individual was emphasized in different domains, most notably in piety and economic life.[49] The shift we see in the confessional language might be related to evolving opinions about sin and sexuality on the part of the clergy. Even so, the late-colonial confessionals, with their demands for penitents to scrutinize the self and the mind in a most rigorous fashion, seem to be responding to a broad ethos that affected other practices of futuremaking in New Spain. It was an outlook that emphasized individual responsibility but also efficiency and productivity in both the spiritual and material use of the term, qualities which eighteenth-century individuals often understood to overlap. Yet when subjects in New Spain pursued these seemingly modern objectives, they adapted, refined, or even repurposed traditional methods, at times, paradoxically, through the methods of collective Catholicism, rather than pursuing them through novel techniques. This was true for the clergy and the laity as well as for both authorities and those they governed.

As we will see in other case studies in this book, it would be a mistake to interpret these changes simply as products of external forces arriving from abroad in a sort of warped version of the Enlightenment. It would be a mistake to read them as products of a vaguely defined eighteenth-century spirit of rationality, for example, a ripple of modernity reaching the far shores of the Atlantic world. The foundations of these notions of the self, of individuality, and temporal orientation toward the future were laid deep in the colonial period and transformed slowly over generations. In the case of the confessional, these diverse origin points included the long Catholic tradition of a spiritual accounting of sins and techniques of self-reflection in Europe and elsewhere, but also the use of this tool on a massive scale in the long-term evangelization of native peoples in the Americas. Both were part of a transatlantic Catholic tradition, clearly, though sometimes the way they transformed in the global expansion of the Iberian-based empires has been overlooked. Indeed, Michel Foucault pegged the spread of the new confessional language—that is, when the church and confessors demanded that penitents offer a more comprehensive catalogue of sins—to seventeenth-century

Europe. Even then, he argues, it was limited in practice to an elevated stratum in society and was something that most of the laity would have been able to avoid.[50] Yet it is evident that the process began much earlier in the colonial space of New Spain—at the very least in the native-language confessionals produced by Alonso de Molina and others in the mid-sixteenth century—and in the actual practice of confession throughout the viceroyalty.[51]

A similar tempo of change shaped other forms of futuremaking in colonial New Spain, where core assumptions about these issues and techniques of manipulating time could be found early in the colonial period, but then evolved in surprising ways by the time of Mexico's independence in the early nineteenth century. One of these was the art and science of prediction, in which colonial subjects grappled directly with the problem of knowledge and its limits. To what extent could one know the future? Was doing so acceptable or was it a sin? If one could know the future, even if only in a partial sense, what did that mean for the ability of humans to influence it?

CHAPTER THREE

Stars

ON NOVEMBER 19, 1659, residents of Mexico City witnessed a grisly public spectacle, but not the one they expected. Don Guillén de Lombardo, an Irishman also known as William Lamport, was to be burned at the stake for crimes against the crown and the faith. By the time of his scheduled execution, Don Guillén had descended into madness, his condition undoubtedly inflamed by nearly seventeen years of imprisonment in the cells of the Inquisition. In the very center of the city, a pyre waited to take his life, slowly and painfully, after the Inquisition announced his offenses. Before the Inquisitors had their way, however, Lombardo quickly brought an end to the spectacle. He somehow managed to hang himself in front of those gathered to watch his punishment. In this desperate, tragic act he regained control of his fate.

Beyond this dramatic end, his life was extraordinary in other ways: the son of an anglicized member of the elite in the Irish town of Wexford, he was forced into exile at the age of ten, found refuge and schooling in Spain, served the Spanish crown in various capacities, made his way to New Spain in the entourage of a new viceroy. Once in the viceroyalty, he eventually hatched a plot to secure New Spain's independence from Spain, more than 150 years before the legendary *grito*, or cry, of Dolores given by Miguel Hidalgo that set off the Mexican war for independence. Lombardo's plot stewed in a rich stock of future knowledge, seasoned in part by his close connections to the viceregal court. It also relied on generous doses of peyote, a hallucinogenic plant associated with foresight in some Indigenous cultures of Mesoamerica, and on a sophisticated practice of astrology.[1]

Don Guillén was an outlier in many ways, yet this most exceptional of individuals was normal in other respects. Above all, he shows us how forms of colonial futuremaking, such as astrology, and the knowledge they purported to provide were highly sought after, deeply contested, and aggressively regulated in colonial Mexico. His case also demonstrates how many of the standard binaries used to analyze cultural activity in the past, such as high / low, elite / popular, or orthodox / unorthodox, need to be employed with a great deal of caution. For Don Guillén, it turns out, like many who sought access to the future, found information where it was available and often in networks of knowledge and practice that crossed these boundaries.

Over generations a new relationship to future knowledge emerged out of those sorts of networks in colonial Mexico. It was a knowledge culture that emphasized empiricism and precision, modern qualities that we often associate with the scientific revolution and the Enlightenment. Yet the origin points of this new form of futuremaking were very different. They were found in a long-term conversation about foresight between New Spain's Inquisitors, the practitioners of astrology and divination, and the many colonial subjects who demanded knowledge about the future.

Moving beyond the remarkable story of Don Guillén, a number of volumes containing documents from New Spain's Holy Office of the Inquisition cut to the heart of these issues. These collections hold scores of licenses that approved the publication of books of prognostication, sometimes called *libros pronósticos, calendarios, almanaques,* or *lunarios,* all of which claimed to open a window into the future. The texts in question were usually short manuscripts. Their authors hoped to publish them as pamphlets or booklets, objects you could hold easily in your hand or carry with you in a small pouch. They were written by some of the most learned individuals in New Spain, including the seventeenth-century polymath Carlos de Sigüenza y Góngora (1645–1700), a Creole, or Spaniard born in the Americas. They contained information about the coming year, such as important days in the liturgical calendar, like Lent, Easter, and Corpus Christi as well as days to celebrate the saints, and so on. But they also offered predictions, usually based on some astrological reasoning. They addressed a variety of topics: they forecast major celestial events, from conjunctions of the planets to eclipses; they predicted the weather, which was of interest to all and especially useful to farmers, merchants, and navigators; they even offered medical advice, including auspicious and inauspicious times to give medicine or conduct a bleeding.[2] While the content of these manuscripts occasionally ran afoul of the Inquisitors, the documentary trail left by the almanacs and libros pronósticos is generally a record of successful petitions for publication. The majority of these books of the future received not only the careful scrutiny but also the essential support of the Inquisition, the institution tasked with defending religious orthodoxy in New Spain. There was some censoring of individual works, but the genre was authorized by church and civil officials and consumed eagerly by colonial subjects. As a result, the licenses for publication of almanacs provide a record of one of New Spain's authorized forms of futuremaking.

Yet these same Inquisition volumes also contain denunciations, investigations, and trials (*procesos*) of accused astrologers, for example, Nicolás de Aste, a young man of twenty who was denounced to the Inquisition in 1617 and later admitted to practicing astrology. In the previous year or so, he told the Holy Office, he had used the stars to help interpret the lives and futures of at least fifty people in Mexico City. His astrology and divination, so he explained, conferred remarkable power. He successfully predicted a delay in the arrival of ships from Peru, one of the main trade routes in the Americas, and even knew where to find the lost treasures of Moctezuma, the fallen Aztec emperor.[3] As his detailed testimony revealed, Aste and his fellow astrologers, along with the people who consulted them, sought information about a much wider range of future events than was available in the almanacs and lunarios. The weather and medical guidance were areas of interest, but so too were specific financial troubles, the location of a rich vein of silver, the behavior of a difficult neighbor, the prospects of an unrequited love, even one's fate in the afterlife.

Those who sought out the services of astrologers also coveted the future. They wanted more types of information than that given in the published works. They also wanted more details. Like us, they might be intrigued by ambiguous generalizations and hazy allusions, but they craved specific information and sought out individuals who could provide it to them, even if the results sometimes failed to live up to their expectations. Those who supplied astrological prediction in New Spain, including the closely related techniques of chiromancy, or palm reading, tailored their information to meet local demands: in Mexico City a Mercedarian friar denounced some of his brothers for using astrology to predict the outcome of conflicts between their vicar general and the leader of their province; in the mining town of Zacatecas a prolific palm reader named Leonardo Bernabé claimed to know the location of silver lodes; in Acapulco a diviner named Cecilia correctly predicted the arrival of ships from China and Peru; in the capital a Spanish healer, or *curandero*, used a mix of astrology and chiromancy to predict the future and offered readings in a convent, foretelling which sister would become prioress.[4] Despite their broad, even cosmopolitan intellectual foundations, astrology and prognostication were by definition local affairs. Practitioners had to speak to local concerns and work within communities of knowledge production. They had to translate the universal language of the stars into the vernacular of the street.[5]

But if clients demanded detailed information, so too did the Inquisitors. They meticulously reviewed the writings and libraries of astrologers and attempted to reconstruct their practice by taking testimonies of the accused and any others who might have knowledge of their work. In the case of popular astrologers, palm readers, or other diviners, who could be individuals with little formal training and who left few written records, the Inquisitors relied more heavily on oral testimony, growing their witness lists like the branches of a tree.[6]

The investigations led to very different verdicts. While the Inquisitors generally approved of the knowledge found in almanacs, they strongly rejected the information offered by Aste and other stargazers. Rather than the imprimatur given to most calendarios and almanacs, astrologers received condemnation and punishments, from simple warnings to give up the practice to harsh sentences that might include years of forced labor. Aste himself was paraded through the center of Mexico City in a spectacular *auto de fe*, a ritualized event for Inquisitorial punishment, then given two hundred lashes and five years in the galleys. The investigations and trials could be a punishment in themselves. While alleged astrologers waited for the conclusion of their cases, they could spend months, even years, breathing the dank air of the Inquisition's secret jails, as did Don Guillén.[7] Whatever one's status in society, practicing unauthorized forms of astrology was a most dangerous activity in colonial New Spain.

Despite the brutal experiences of some who found themselves under Inquisitorial scrutiny, we should not take the Inquisitor's heuristics and typologies as our own. Their categories, which shape the records of colonial astrology that we have, do not necessarily mirror those of the accused or reflect even the norms and attitudes of New Spanish society as a whole. While the Holy Office tried to make a distinction between authorized and unauthorized prediction, in both theory and in practice the boundary was not at all clear. The Inquisition's own records reveal these ambiguities. As in many of the activities and ideas they investigated, the Inquisition sought to differentiate the wholesome from the unhealthy and to separate the heretical from the orthodox. But in the course of their investigations they gathered all sorts of information that suggested a more complex mix of practices and ideas, even if we view this material from the perspective of the Inquisitors. In many cases, their documents unwittingly reveal the common foundations of orthodox and unorthodox practices, including the shared epistemologies, or theories of knowledge, that we now consider unrelated: the science of astronomy and the superstition of astrology.

This blurry boundary was certainly the case in the seventeenth-century investigations of astrology. Whether the guidance received came from an authorized almanac or an unauthorized horoscope, all of these stargazers engaged in a remarkably similar activity: they used a reading of the stars to bring order to events that were beyond their temporal horizons. In some ways their attempts to understand the future were idiosyncratic and shaped by particular experiences, backgrounds, levels of education, social status, and desires, whether the search for silver in Zacatecas or ships in Acapulco. But in other respects they took part in a common project of futuremaking. They approached their shared problem of insufficient knowledge in common ways.

What should we make of this strange juxtaposition of high and low, or authorized and unauthorized futuremaking, via the stars? This theoretical question can be best answered by examining the practice of astrology in both its sanctioned and forbidden forms. Previous studies of New Spain have focused either on the publication and regulation of almanacs and other forms of authorized astrology or, less commonly, on unsanctioned astrological forecasting that drew the attention of the Inquisition and other colonial authorities. In the latter case, scholars have concentrated on a number of high-profile cases, such as the remarkable history of Don Guillén, or those linked to well-known intellectuals.[8] Historians have paid less attention to the many obscure records of popular astrology and divination. Moreover, these unauthorized forms of futuremaking have usually been studied as something qualitatively distinct from the knowledge found in almanacs. Such an approach assumes a strong boundary between orthodox and unorthodox forms of divination. Yet if this was the case, how can we account for common epistemologies, these shared ways of knowing? We of course need to recognize the diverse forms of prediction in New Spain and the many ways in which a particular context, including the power relations surrounding the astrologer and his clients, could influence the act of astrological forecasting. Nonetheless, there was broad conversation taking place throughout New Spain about the future and an evolving consensus on what could be known. We know of these conversations because the Inquisitors wanted to know. But what might explain some of the intriguing similarities between authorized and unauthorized forms of prediction?

If we turn to the voluminous writing about astrology in early modern Europe, part of this problem is easily solved. Astrology was one of the great bodies of knowledge, or sciences, of the late medieval and early modern periods. Individuals from all social strata and levels of education accepted it as a way of knowing. Monarchs, dukes, and diplomats purchased a glimpse of the future from the most learned practitioners, as did common people who bought readings from astrologers with more humble backgrounds. Astrology was everywhere in early modern Europe, from royal courts to alleyways, in the city and the countryside, in erudite Latin and rustic vernaculars.[9] As Anthony Grafton has noted, given astrology's ubiquity, it makes little sense "to draw firm distinctions between high and low, [or] elite and popular culture." "The preserved horoscopes and textbooks of astrology," Grafton continues, "mirror the hopes and expectations, anxieties and terrors of a whole society."[10]

Much the same could be said of astrology in seventeenth-century New Spain. Individuals from diverse backgrounds embraced its art and practice, including both its sanctioned and unsanctioned forms. In early New Mexico a Spanish soldier from Sevilla received a manuscript of astrological technique and "secrets of nature" from a Nahua blacksmith, a work the Spaniard used to predict the fertility of some local women and to sketch out the futures of their children; in Puebla an old man employed astrology and indigenous plants to find lost goods and grappled with marriage conflicts for Spanish women; in the neighborhoods of Mexico City a Creole and a mulatto astrologer plied their trades among the well-to-do and the working class.[11] Given the Inquisition's interest in regulating these sorts of astrological and divinatory practices, its records offer a rich sampling of a very widespread practice of colonial futuremaking.

But if astrology mirrored the emotional relationships to the future of so many people in the early modern period, capturing their "hopes and expectations, anxieties and terrors," then what exactly was it? In the seventeenth century, astrology was a more roomy label than our contemporary word. Astrology could refer to a general science of the stars, closer to what we would now call (and what some at the time called) cosmology and astronomy, including their mathematical foundations.[12] This form of astrology tried to understand the positioning and movement of the stars, planets, and other celestial bodies. But a second meaning referred to the interpretation of astral influence on earth. At the time, almost everyone believed that the heavens influenced the earth and its inhabitants. While the principle of celestial forces was generally accepted, along the lines of what Thomas Kuhn would later call "normal science," astrologers did not always concur on the degree or direction of that influence.[13] Thus a second meaning of astrology concerned the attempt to discern the details of celestial influence and its implications for humans. In a general sense this form of astrology, which might rely heavily on astronomical observations and calculation, included "any practice or belief that centered on interpreting the human or terrestrial meaning of the stars."[14] Understanding the position and movement of the heavens was a starting point. Then one could begin the real interpretive work. How did the stars and other celestial bodies influence the world? How might they shape the future?

While I will generally use "astrology" to refer to this second meaning—that is, the interpretive science of the stars and its popular practice—the nuances of the historical term are a source of ambiguity. The term's density of meaning at once captures the shared history of interpretive astrology and astronomy, their close relationship in the minds of some of their practitioners, and the sketchy boundary between diverse forms of astrological practice. One of the analytic pitfalls that may ensnare those who wish to understand practices that later became marginalized, especially scientific knowledge that was later found to contain flaws, is to apply our verdicts of what is irrational to an earlier period.[15] When we unmask erroneous knowledge in this way it misrepresents the role these ideas played at the time. In the case of astrology, it distorts the history of its practice, including how its eventual dethroning as reputable knowledge was a slow, piecemeal, and subtle process and how the practice of astrology was diverse and contested. In a general sense it blinds us to a critical mode of experiencing time, as astrology was an act and epistemology of futuremaking that shared a great deal with practices that would maintain their intellectual credibility. We can go even further. Astrology and other forms of divination, like many colonial practices that have subsequently been classified as antique, backward, or irrational, played a fundamental role in the development of attitudes toward the future that we now consider rational and modern.[16]

To take one prominent example, consider the aggressive but partial critique of astrology made by Francis Bacon. In *De Augmentis Scientarum*, his early seventeenth-century meditation on scientific method and attempt to create a taxonomy of knowledge, Bacon questioned the current practice of astrology. He found it horribly flawed and lacking rigor. "It is so full of superstition," Bacon wrote, "that scarce anything sound can be discovered in it."[17] But far from jettisoning the core assumptions that supported astrological prediction, Bacon reaffirmed them with vigor. "I would rather have it [astrology] purified than altogether rejected," he concluded. He did not question celestial influence, for example, but held that it should be sought in the positions of the large planets rather than in all of the stars.[18] Once purged of such erroneous principles, Bacon confidently looked forward to a future of finely honed predictions. One of the great minds of the scientific revolution but also a committed man of Christian faith, Bacon himself offered a prediction, forecasting a future in which a more rigorous, refined astrology would allow its practitioners to know in advance "floods, droughts, heats, frosts, earthquakes, irruptions of water, eruptions of fire, great winds and rains, the various seasons of the year, plagues, epidemics, diseases, plenty and dearth of grain, wars, seditions, schisms, transmigrations of peoples, and in short of all commotions or greater revolutions of things, *natural as well as civil*."[19]

Bacon's vision of astrology captured a paradox at the heart of its practice in the seventeenth century. Astrology was at once a science (in the Baconian sense), with precise rules and procedures, and an art, with an essential role for interpretation, inference, and explication. This is a complicated mix that we now understand is true of most scientific knowledge. Given this combination of established techniques and individual interpretation, scholars of astrology have pointed out how important it is to historicize its practice and situate it within the hierarchies of power and knowledge of the time in question.[20]

At the center of the debate over astrology in seventeenth-century Europe and the Americas was the distinction between so-called natural or rational astrology and judicial astrology.[21] Natural or rational astrology designated a science of the stars that limited itself to discerning the general influence of the heavens, such as patterns in the weather or diseases, the mainstays of the almanacs referred to above. It relied on Hippocratic and Galenic theories of medicine and physiology, which held that four bodily humors (blood, yellow bile [choler], black bile, and phlegm) influenced health and disposition. One's health depended on achieving a balance among the four fluids and their corresponding properties of heat and cold, dry and damp.[22] Astral rays were understood to affect the humors, potentially bringing them in and out of equilibrium, and could thus indirectly influence the health of individual bodies. The humors could also foster conditions conducive to the spread of disease, which in turn positioned astrologers to offer predictions of great plagues and other epidemics.

Few questioned this theory of heavenly influence, based as it was on accepted descriptions of the underlying forces operating in the world and the human body, a medieval and early modern standard model of the physical world. Very early in the colonial period, in fact, the humoral theory of medicine could be found throughout Spanish America and New Spain, from its cities to its frontiers.[23] It did not create any major dilemmas for the Catholic dogmas of free will and divine intervention since at the time most people considered astral influences to be general in nature and thought they could be "opposed by the more dominant forces of mind and spirit."[24]

Though less common in practice than the modest predictions found in most almanacs, natural astrology, with the full support of church authorities, could also be used to predict events on a much grander scale, such as the probabilities of epidemics referred to above but also major inflection points that would affect whole societies, faiths, and empires. For a noted case among many obscure or humble predictions, consider Enrico Martínez, or Heinrich Martin, a German cosmologist and printer who lived in Mexico City in the early seventeenth century. Martínez held the first chair in astrology in New Spain and used astrological reasoning to predict a breathtaking range of events and phenomena. In his *Repertorio de los tiempos e historia natural desta Nueva España* (Mexico City, 1606), he predicted the impending collapse of the Ottoman empire, the great world power of the sixteenth and seventeenth centuries that so concerned many in Catholic Europe and troubled the Hapsburg empire in particular. Read against the backdrop of great imperial struggles in the Mediterranean, Martínez's interpretation of the stars led him to predict with great confidence that the Ottoman empire would implode during the reign of its current sultan, Ahmed I.[25]

Judicial astrology, in contrast, offered knowledge of the future in more detail. Those who worked in judicial astrology discerned events on a smaller scale, which, for those involved, could be even more momentous than the collapse of an empire. Whereas the natural astrologer might note heavenly influence on bodily humors or muse about the eventual destruction of a polity, perhaps drawing evidence from astrological signs and celestial prodigies to support his position, the judicial astrologer made predictions that were closer to the ground or offered detailed guidance relevant to an individual or small group. These interventions could include the most common practice of drawing genitures, or figures of the stars as they were positioned at someone's birth, and also inceptions and elections, by which the astrologer interpreted astral influences at the beginning of some important undertaking, such as a marriage or a business venture.[26]

Given its specific predictions, judicial astrology was more powerful and dangerous than natural astrology. As a result, some of its practitioners greedily sought out astral knowledge. At times, their contemporaries described them as addicted to the practice, which was so seductive with its promises of revealed futures. Their newfound knowledge of the future securely in hand, some astrologers pored over their star charts for valuable bits of hidden wisdom, coveting their secret narratives of the future for the flush of power they offered. Others seem to have been reluctantly pushed over the edge from natural to judicial astrology because their clients demanded more detailed and personally tailored guidance.

Grafton, for example, compares the astrologers of Renaissance Europe to recent economists. Both groups were quick to qualify the predictive capability of their respective sciences and were therefore reluctant to provide specific guidance. They often did so nonetheless, given the material rewards that accompanied prediction. While the analogy should not be stretched too far, Grafton's comparison highlights the problem of imprecision that haunted the practice of judicial astrology as well as most forms of prediction, given that forecasts were always subject to scrutiny after the fact. Did the astrologer get it right? If not, what did the failed prediction say about his techniques or motives? But the comparison between astrologers and modern forecasters also emphasizes the exchange relationship, the desire and market for future knowledge that drove the practice despite its many flaws. Many examples suggest that the relationship between consumers and suppliers of foresight could lead some otherwise cautious astronomers into the practice of astrology, in both its natural and judicial forms.[27] In historians' parlance, this means that those responsible for the shifts in astrological practice—the agents of historical change—were everyday consumers of astrology as much as its theorists and practitioners.

Whatever the motivation behind judicial astrology, this more detailed form of futuremaking created theological dangers. Judicial astrology, like other divinatory arts, such as palm reading, could easily violate fundamental dogmas of the church. Most significantly, if the astrologer held that the future was foretold in the stars (or the lines of the hand or the shape of the face), then both the notions of free will and divine providence were severely undermined. Without free will there could be little hope of salvation since redemption itself depended on one's ability to make voluntary choices unfettered by determining forces, astral or otherwise. This was the position of the Dominican theologian Thomas Aquinas, and it was a foundational concept for Catholics throughout the Reformation and beyond. Yet even Aquinas admitted that the stars could influence human behavior. "The majority of men follow their passions," he explained, "which are movements of the sensitive appetite, in which movements of the heavenly bodies can co-operate; but few are wise enough to resist these passions. Consequently astrologers are able to foretell the truth in the majority of cases, especially in a general way. But not in particular cases; for nothing prevents man from resisting his passions by his free-will. Wherefore the astrologers themselves are wont to say that 'the wise man is stronger than the stars.'"[28] The problem for Aquinas, as for most practitioners and regulators of astrology, was not whether the stars could influence happenings on earth. That was obvious. But how could one discern the details and the limits of that influence? How specific could predictions be without violating church teachings and orthodoxy? What knowledge was good knowledge, and how should it be determined? Could all be trusted with its possession? And, most intriguingly, how clearly could one discern the future without undermining the ability of an individual to operate with some degree of freedom? In this sense, they struggled with a question that has become paramount in our world. That is, does knowledge of the future lead to greater control over events to come and thus instill a sense of efficacy and hope? Or does it simply reveal our inability to influence them, leading to inertia and despair?

The much smaller literature on astrology in New Spain confirms some of this general wisdom from early modern Europe. Above all, as we have seen, astrologers and their clients clearly found it difficult to avoid making specific predictions. In New Spain, as across the Atlantic, this meant the distinction between natural-rational and judicial astrology was of fundamental importance, at least to church officials and Inquisitors, though the boundary was not always easy for officials to define. The problem was both practical, given the many forms of astrology in circulation, and theoretical, considering the common intellectual premises that supported all astrological practice. Since both natural and judicial astrology assumed celestial influences on the earth and its inhabitants, "it was impossible to specify a fixed point separating mere astral influence on the will, by the humors, from outright determination."[29] This was the issue in 1643, when a Mercedarian friar was accused of using judicial astrology to offer guidance to the president of the Audiencia, or regional high court, in Guatemala. He allegedly advised the official to be wary of a volatile, "mercurial man" who might be inclined to do him harm. The accused astrologer, Nicolás de Alarcón, taught theology in the local Mercedarian convent and leaned on Aquinas and other intellectual authorities to defend his predictions. His prognostications were purely conjectural, he argued, and described "inclinations" that were derived from "natural causes." Such conjectural knowledge of future events and human tendencies did not run afoul of the principle of free will, because "man can always overcome the bad inclinations and follow the good."[30]

We have encountered this ambiguous boundary in the theology of Aquinas and also in the example of Martínez, who made bold predictions about future events based on astrological reasoning in his *Repertorio de los tiempos*. Martínez, however, received official approval for his writing and was himself a *familiar*, or lay informant, of New Spain's Inquisition.[31] He intended to bring sophisticated cosmological and astrological thought to a larger, less educated audience. Thus the book was written in relatively accessible language and included not only grand discussions of world history and prognostication but also practical information for merchants and farmers.[32] Such combinations of future news, though in much abbreviated form, could be found in scores of almanacs published later in the seventeenth and eighteenth centuries. This was a compelling mix, one that enjoyed a large audience in New Spain, but it could easily cross the line from natural to judicial astrology.

Fashioning himself a popularizer of astral knowledge would have made Martínez particularly susceptible to censure from Inquisitors, given their concern with wiping out heresy and their assumption that heterodox ideas and practices could spread from one individual or place to another, in much the way we might fear the outbreak of a virulent disease.[33] In the eyes of the Inquisitors, those who might act as vectors for dangerous ideas deserved greater scrutiny and also more severe punishment if they were found to pass on superstition or heresy. Put another way, knowledge about knowledge, and the threat of spreading it, was even more dangerous than knowledge itself. In 1704, in a major case against a physician-healer accused of superstition and practicing divination, including an astrologically based form of palm reading, a functionary of the Inquisition reminded his colleagues that the accused should receive a punishment worthy "not only as the perpetrator of them [the serious offenses], but also as the teacher (*maestro*) that he pretended to be."[34] Martínez was well aware of this dilemma and employed a number of techniques to protect himself from charges of being a judicial astrologer or celestial determinist. He found an interpretive compromise that allowed him to discuss astrology in the context of events that would normally be considered the domain of free will.[35]

Many astrologers worked in this fertile middle ground, making predictions that appealed to those who wanted more precise foresight but generally staying within the boundaries set by the Inquisition. But even in the almanacs that limited themselves to discussing the weather and astral influences on the body, predictions could be quite specific. They foretold things like strong winds and the arrival of spring heat, even down to a specific date. Sigüenza y Góngora offered these sorts of narrow-gauged forecasts, as did most authors of almanacs and lunarios. In his almanac for 1698, to take one example, he predicted that Wednesday, April 13, would see "lots of clouds ... warm and windy." Although the following day marked a good time to plant corn, the stars suggested avoiding the use of cupping glasses or bleedings of the head.[36]

Despite moments of intense Inquisitorial censure that suppressed almanac publication, especially around the mid-seventeenth century, presses continued to publish them throughout the rest of the colonial period and into the nineteenth century. An almanac from Puebla in 1753 offered much the same type of information found in those published a century earlier. On the basis of celestial observations and computations made around the city, the author adapted his predictions to its immediate environs. On January 9, he noted, one could expect "very cold air in the hot county, thick clouds in temperate zones, [and] some freezes in colder regions."[37] By the third week of the month (precisely Thursday the twentieth), "the sun is in Aquarius" and "the sky will be calm and clear in the colder and temperate lands, which will make the sun's rays mild [and] the air dry in the hot country, even in humid zones."[38] This would make the following Sunday "good for irrigating in the hot country."[39]

What should we make of such predictions? The information itself, some of which might seem exotic to us—such as the influence of the heavens on bodily humors and the use of bleeding and other purgatives as medical interventions—would have been quite commonplace and mundane to contemporaries. The writing was not very stylized. In the dominant literary form of the time, now sometimes referred to with the catchall label baroque, authors of all sorts, from poets to preachers, favored dense, elaborate language thick with puns, double meanings, and allusions. The language employed by the authors of almanacs and libros pronósticos, in striking contrast, was anything but baroque. Entries were short, to the point, and repetitive. What made them interesting and an item that people would pay for year after year was not their style or even their content so much as how they situated information in time. A windy afternoon with the threat of hail was ordinary, boring even. But when a learned practitioner of astrology used science to forecast a windy afternoon accompanied by hail and thunder on August 24 of the coming year it became interesting, intriguing, and something of value.[40]

These kinds of statements, though they might be defended on purely technical grounds as a form of natural astrology, given that astral forces could influence the weather, would be read by most as sharp, precise predictions that could have definite effects on individuals. Such statements might not seem all that different from a prediction that foretold a specific event on a specific day. New Spain's Inquisitors thought so. They were especially worried that less sophisticated readers might misinterpret the meaning of the almanacs' predictions, particularly the complicated relationship between (natural) causes and (human) effects. An official reviewing a lunario for 1673 asked that the author produce a more robust account of "the link between comets and the events that they signal," distinguishing carefully between those comets that are of natural origin and those that "God freely chooses" to herald some event. Although such information was unlikely to be misinterpreted by "civilized and well-educated people," the official continued, among the simple, rough folk of the countryside who consult the lunarios the danger of misunderstanding was greater, "and therefore it is all the more important to avoid it."[41] The concern of the censor, in other words, was not just the information contained in an almanac but questions like Who would try to interpret it? How would they use it? Could they safely consume subtle, complicated knowledge?[42] His hand-wringing implies that early modern censorship was not always as simple as the suppression of forbidden knowledge; it was often a question of setting acceptable limits on that information, defining potential audiences, and balancing the possibility of contagion with the promise of value.[43]

In the seventeenth century the Inquisition went to great lengths to define the boundary between judicial and natural astrology and thus to create an authorized domain of astrological practice. As early as 1616 the Holy Office had issued an edict on the matter, proclaiming,

> We let it be known that the prosecutor [*promotor fiscal*] of this Holy Office appeared before us and described that it has come to his attention that a great many and diverse people in our territory, with little fear of God, in grave danger to their souls and consciences, and in scandal to the Christian community ... have given themselves to the study of judicial astrology, and they practice it mixed with many superstitions, making predictions by the stars and their positions about contingent futures and fortuitous events or [about] happenings that are dependent on providence [*divina voluntad*] or the free will of men ... [including] ... events they have experienced in the past or will experience in the future, the futures of their children ... [their] health, illnesses, financial losses and gains.... the way they will die [and] other divinations and predictions of a similar sort.[44]

Although the Inquisition worded this edict loosely, attempting to cast a net over a range of illicit astrological and divinatory practices, throughout the seventeenth century Inquisitors periodically flagged specific lines in almanac manuscripts, usually because they deemed them to violate the principles of free will and divine intervention. This was the issue in the case of a palm reader named Pedro Suárez de Mayorga. In 1583, Suárez, a native of Sevilla but by then a resident of Tepeaca in New Spain, was tried by the Inquisition for superstition. A central piece of the case against him was his alleged possession of an unpublished manuscript in Spanish translation of the *Opus Mathematicum* by the Flemish Johannes Taisnier. The Taisnerio, as it was referred to in shorthand, was a treatise on chiromancy and physiognomy (the art of interpreting facial features) that circulated widely in sixteenth-century Europe. In their careful reading of its contents, New Spain's Inquisitors found the Taisnerio problematic, not because it somehow violated the dogma of divine intervention but because it allowed the chiromancer and his clients to claim knowledge that was the exclusive domain of God. Interpreting the palm's "life line" (*la línea vital*) allowed one to peer into God's will. Even if the chiromancer prefaced his work by recognizing an all-powerful God, as Taisnier did, the very notion of a life line etched in flesh suggested a strong determinism or even predestination, which in turn undermined the concept of free will, as the lines of the palm clearly anticipated future events.[45] The Inquisitors' analysis of the Taisnerio highlighted one of the central problems of divination and many other forms of futuremaking, including those that would later come wrapped in the mystique of a more secular, scientific epistemology, such as probability, risk analysis, and big data. The problem they grappled with continues to be a cruel paradox of the human condition: peering into the future at once opens it up, since it gives us some knowledge of the yet to be seen, and potentially forecloses it, since the very act of glimpsing the future might reveal our limited ability to influence it.[46]

Even a figure as prominent as Sigüenza was not immune to this type of review. He repeatedly found his manuscripts returned to him for revision because he had made predictions that drew too strong a link between astral forces and particular events or that described with certainty what was in fact contingent. In the original draft of his *Lunario y pronóstico de temporales* for 1675, which drew multiple rebukes from the censors, Sigüenza noted that celestial positions should make "everyone in the streets walk carefully and warily." The stars also foretold that "an important person would die." The censors found these statements highly problematic. As one noted, "I take both of these to be formally judicial and divinatory propositions. The first [because] thefts are the free [choices] of the thief. The second because God [possesses] absolute control over the death of any particular person.... Though astronomical influence can even cause plagues or the death of whole groups [of people], it can't determine [the death of] individual people, and much less their particular social status."[47] This was similar to a criticism made by Inquisitors two years earlier, when Sigüenza had predicted "sudden deaths and illnesses of nobles."[48]

Publishing in the late seventeenth century, Sigüenza encountered an Inquisition that had ramped up its efforts against judicial astrology some decades earlier. In 1647 the Holy Office in Madrid had issued an edict that attempted to clarify the boundary between judicial and natural astrology. On one hand, it noted the danger of publications that included "material related to judicial astrology and prognostications, horoscopes, interrogatories and elections," in part because "simple and ignorant folk, and those lacking good judgment or [being] naive take for truth the content of said almanacs even though the pronouncements made in them depend on human choice and free will." In an attempt to distinguish between those things that were the cause of natural forces (including the stars) and those that depended on free will, the edict limited such publications to those that dealt exclusively with navigation, medicine, agriculture, and those focused on the weather and had a clear connection to natural events, such as eclipses, rains, or plagues.[49] In short, it reaffirmed the long-standing prohibition against judicial astrology while supporting the orthodoxy of natural astrology. In epistemological terms, it limited predictions to those derived from natural causes and those that did not venture into the province of free will or divine intervention. In so doing the edict kept open the possibility for future knowledge that individuals could act upon, so long as the source of that knowledge was acceptable.

New Spain's Inquisitors seem to have responded to this prodding from Madrid but also to their own misgivings about the spread of judicial astrology in New Spain. As a result, we have a number of high-profile, detailed cases from the period. Inquisitorial zeal is not a clear sign of increased astrological activity, but these cases reveal a substantial market in futuremaking, in both its orthodox and unorthodox forms, whether or not they were a product of stepped-up investigations or more general interest in astrology.[50] On closer inspection, indeed, the spike in Inquisition records related to astrology and divination around the middle of the seventeenth century suggests more of a steady stream of divinatory practices over the previous half century rather than a sudden surge. A rash of denunciations of chiromancy in Cholula in 1650, for example, turns out to include not only allegations against local palm readers—some dating back a number of years and most dealing with deceased offenders—but also a denunciation by a woman who described a reading she had received decades earlier while a girl in Mexico City.[51] In the same year, a similar situation occurred in Zacatecas, where, after hearing an edict of the Inquisition, individuals recounted earlier readings and other divinations, including one going back some twenty-five years; again, the alleged chiromancer was already dead.[52] Historical records like these thus give us a side-ways glance at a much broader swath of practices than those that are in the foreground of the document.

The Inquisitors' subsequent investigations also call attention to the difficulty of their project, given the sometimes fuzzy distinction between natural and judicial astrology, the narrow pathway be-tween the two for their practitioners, and, above all, the desire of so many to peer into the future. Driven by the human urge for knowl-edge, subjects in New Spain, like their European contemporaries, chased foresight. They looked eagerly for individuals—including astrologers but also palm readers, diviners, and soothsayers of vari-ous sorts—who professed to be able to read and interpret the fu-ture. Frequently, judicial astrology and other forms of divination were part of the same practice, and the varying techniques could support one another: knowledge of Latin and books of astrology gave an air of science to other arts that required less formal educa-tion and, conversely, the practices of the "unsanctioned domain," such as the use of Indigenous hallucinogens, afforded a mystique of hidden wisdom and power.[53] In most cases, practitioners and their clients tried to establish some authority for the information they produced and consumed, referring to intellectual pedigrees, con-nections to other astrologers, remarkable personal characteristics and prodigies that signaled power, or simply the efficacy of their advice and predictions.[54] Diviners referred to as *zahoríes* or *zahori-nas*, adept at locating concealed or lost objects, were consistently described as having similar characteristics, which established them as part of this divinatory tradition and in turn bolstered their claims to have foresight. In many locales and times such diviners were said to have the mark of a crucifix on their back or the roof of their mouth, to possess powers that tended to be strongest on a particu-lar day (usually Friday), and to enjoy a special gift for seeing under-ground. Above all, they were known to have uttered audible cries while in the womb.[55] Other diviners said their power was autho-rized by the Inquisition or was a gift from God, such as the mestiza midwife Juana, who read palms in Mexico City and claimed to have a license from the Holy Office to predict the future.[56] Even many zahoríes and zahorinas asserted that God gave them their power.[57] Such attempts to establish the authority of the practitioner are consistent with other instances of popular divination documented in New Spain and elsewhere.[58]

A demand for future knowledge that had some credibility, authority, and quality drove the market for prediction in all of its diverse forms. This was true even in the published almanacs. Again, Sigüenza illustrates the broader trend. A renowned intellectual, this Creole from Mexico City spent his life pursuing scientific and literary interests in the viceregal capital. His projects ranged widely, and he distinguished himself as an antiquarian, poet, mathematician, and astronomer, eventually securing a university chair and the title of royal cosmographer. He sat at the center of intellectual life in the capital and was part of knowledge communities that crossed the Atlantic. He enjoyed a close friendship with the other great Creole intellectual of the period, Sor Juana Inés de la Cruz, who, like Sigüenza, melded literary and scientific pursuits within an intensely spiritual personal and cultural context. Sigüenza was also an astrologer, and as we've seen, in the later seventeenth century he regularly published almanacs and pronósticos.[59] These works contained the usual predictions of future weather and astral influence on bodily medicine. Yet, as discussed earlier, on multiple occasions he stepped across the boundary of natural astrology into predictions that were so specific and related so manifestly to individual free will that the Inquisitors censored the materials and gently reprimanded the author.

Sigüenza's occasional brushes with the Inquisition are a bit surprising, given the number of times he disavowed the predictive capabilities of astrology and even ridiculed its practice. The most prominent of these comments came in a semipublic dispute with a learned Jesuit on the question of celestial prodigies. The appearance of a comet in 1680 had caused great consternation on both sides of the Atlantic. Many feared it signaled some imminent catastrophe. Stepping into the fray, Sigüenza noted that while comets are certainly the work of God, one cannot determine with certainty the meaning of such events. In claiming incertitude, he refuted the position of Eusebio Kino, an Austrian Jesuit recently arrived in New Spain, who had aggressively reaffirmed the conventional wisdom of the day, which held that comets portended great calamities and afflictions.[60] Sigüenza, in contrast, urged caution and questioned the predictive capabilities of astrology. In the absence of a clear causal relationship between the comet and worldly events, he argued, we must trust in observations and limit our predictions.[61] "I also am an Astrologer," Sigüenza noted, with perhaps a hint of irony, given that he held a university chair in the subject, "and I know very well on which foot Astrology limps, and upon what exceedingly weak foundations its structure is reared."[62]

Sigüenza's disparaging remarks about the "exceedingly weak foundations" of astrology and his colloquy with Kino led earlier historians, most notably Irving Leonard, to characterize him as a precocious modern. Like Sor Juana, Sigüenza was fundamentally a rational thinker, Leonard argued, one whose critical approach to knowledge, questioning of inherited truths, and embrace of empiricism made him chafe against the obscurantism and scientific dogmas of his time. Such qualities prompted Leonard to describe Sigüenza as a "modern spirit lighting up the darkness of neomedieval thought."[63] While it is true that Sigüenza and Sor Juana famously pushed back against many received wisdoms and offered biting critiques of some defenders of social and intellectual norms, Sigüenza and other refined astrologers were embedded in the epistemologies and practices of their moment. If we take Sigüenza to be a precocious modern, a rational mind out of place in tradition-bound "Baroque Mexico," we bring one facet of his life into view, but we miss the ways in which his ideas, even when they clashed with those of some of his contemporaries, can be best grasped as a product of his time.[64]

Despite his misgivings about astrology and his public disavowal of its predictive capabilities, for example, year after year Sigüenza brought his lunarios and pronósticos to Inquisitors in manuscript form, seeking approval for publication. What are we to make of this? Many of Sigüenza's published works undoubtedly responded to the market for astrological knowledge and his need for income. He admitted as much when he noted wryly that an author of almanacs "lost more in reputation than he gained in income."[65] More important, the market for foresight and its regulation in New Spain in fact produced the very critiques of its own excesses. These were arguments Sigüenza would deploy famously in his dispute with Kino over the 1680 comet. When Sigüenza attacked those who

defended the position that comets presaged some affliction from
God, such as Kino, he did so via a critique that the Inquisition had
long used against almanacs that slipped from natural into judicial
astrology, namely, that astrological predictions should be limited to
those instances in which one can draw a clear causal link between
astral forces and their terrestrial influences. Without such certainty,
Sigüenza argued, one must err on the side of discretion and hold
back further interpretations. This was precisely the argument made
over and over again by Inquisitorial censors, including in their review of Sigüenza's work. It was also deployed more than a generation earlier by another Creole intellectual, Diego Rodríguez, whose
connection to astrology was much stronger than Sigüenza's.[66]

Rodríguez was a Mercedarian friar and Creole who, like
Sigüenza, pursued a variety of intellectual and professional interests, including engineering and astrology. Among other projects,
Rodríguez worked on the grueling, multigenerational effort to
drain waters in the Valley of Mexico and defend the city against a
perennial threat of floods; he also helped engineer a system for
raising and installing a new set of massive church bells in the ongoing construction of Mexico City's enormous cathedral. In 1637 he
was named to the university chair in mathematics and astrology,
the post later occupied by Sigüenza. Also like Sigüenza, Fray Diego
published almanacs with astrological content.[67]

Rodríguez occupied a prominent place among the capital's
scholarly community. He founded a salon of intellectuals, some of
whom seem to have engaged in judicial astrology. Gathering in the
large Mercedarian convent in Mexico City, the salon met regularly
from the 1630s into the early 1650s and was an intellectual hot-
house of the capital. As the Mexican historian of science Elías
Trabulse notes, the group formed a kind of "semisecret confraternity" dedicated to knowledge. If Rodríguez dabbled in some unauthorized forms of astrological thought, which seems quite likely,
it shouldn't be taken as a mark against his status as a scientific
thinker, for luminaries of early modern learning like Tycho Brahe
and Johannes Kepler also practiced judicial astrology.[68] Instead, the
history of Fray Diego and the network of astrologers surrounding
him points to the ways in which astrological thought was lodged
deeply in the imaginaries of many people in seventeenth-century

New Spain. A belief in astral knowledge as opening a window into the future permeated this world. The picture that emerges from the documents surrounding Rodríguez is one of a community of astrologers that crossed traditional social indicators of education, wealth, and other markers of social status. It was a group whose members yearned for new knowledge, and one in which religious devotion and scientific pursuits were tightly intertwined. Fray Diego, for example, argued with great sophistication and contemporary credibility that the heavenly influences on New Spain were advantageous, in part because they were sheltered by the Immaculate Conception and Our Lady of Guadalupe.[69] Like other forms of colonial future-making, the practices and ideas related to astrology formed a subtle and intellectually productive mixture; only much later would they be artificially separated like liquids in a centrifuge and then labeled traditional and modern.[70]

Although the Inquisition never tried Rodríguez, he was called to testify in proceedings against individuals who had some connection to him and his salon. Most famously, a mason and architect named Melchor Pérez de Soto, who also took part in the competition to solve the problem of hoisting the cathedral's church bells, was investigated and jailed by the Inquisition for a variety of alleged offenses, including the practice of judicial astrology and chiromancy. A Creole who lived and worked in Mexico City, Pérez de Soto was apparently introduced to the practice of astrology while on a maritime expedition to lower California in 1643. Over the next decade he became deeply attracted to astronomical and astrological knowledge, in both their authorized and unauthorized forms, including the casting of horoscopes. In late 1654 and early 1655, the Inquisition moved against the builder and astrologist after he was repeatedly denounced for possessing and trafficking in forbidden astrological texts. The denunciations began in 1650, when Gaspar de Rivero Vasconcelos, a mulatto and native of Tangiers who was studying canon law in the capital and was himself being investigated for practicing judicial astrology, claimed that Pérez de Soto had hired him to translate a number of astrological texts from Latin. In subsequent years two other translators made similar allegations. After being taken into custody by the Inquisition, Pérez de Soto endured an intense investigation. At one point he contended that

Fray Diego Rodríguez had guided his study of astrology, though other witnesses rebutted this claim and said that Rodríguez rejected the celestial determinism that Pérez de Soto embraced. Before his trial reached a definitive conclusion, Pérez de Soto died in one of the more hideous tragedies that unfolded in the Inquisition's secret prison. Suffering from deep depression, he was given a cellmate by the Inquisitors, supposedly to keep him company. The man soon bludgeoned Pérez de Soto to death and said he had acted in self-defense.[71]

Pérez de Soto's life was as remarkable as his death. Most astonishing of all was the enormous collection of books the Inquisition's functionaries discovered at his house. This middling professional owned perhaps the largest library in New Spain. Amassed over many years, the nearly sixteen hundred books ran the gamut from the purely spiritual and devotional to the primarily secular and scientific. Among many other subjects, the collection contained works of literature, history, poetry, short stories, and philosophy as well as grammars, dictionaries, and handbooks on navigation, mining, the manual arts, and religious meditation. It also housed many of the most important treatises on cosmography, astronomy, and astrology, not only classic works from Europe but also those of New Spain, such as Martínez's *Repertorio de los tiempos*.[72] Among many texts touching on aspects of astrology, Pérez's library numbered some fifty-seven lunarios.[73]

He stalked astrology and forbidden knowledge tenaciously, and it brought a severe response from authorities. Compared with most residents of the capital, his relationship to refined knowledge and astrology in particular was dramatic and exceptional. But what does his singularity have to say about astrology and other dangerous knowledge he desired? First, his huge trove of books were written in many languages—in addition to Latin—that he could not read or, at best, could only muddle through, hinting at a kind of obsessive quest for knowledge. Many of his texts must have sat on his shelves like so many tightly sealed casks of wisdom. But he also wanted access to that material. His books of astrological practice were more than mere talismans; he knew the information they possessed was practical and potentially accessible. Pérez's use of translators and his participation in the intellectual circle associated with

Rodríguez were two of the many ways he tried to gain access to that information. He exchanged texts with the inner circle of Rodríguez's salon and others with whom he was only casually associated, among them the scribes and translators who later testified against him. These connections give a sense of the ways in which knowledge could circulate across boundaries of social and educational status. His network was not unlike that described by Nicolás de Aste, the young man found guilty of practicing judicial astrology in 1617, who claimed that none other than Enrico Martínez had taught him the art; or by Juan Beteta from Granada, who denounced himself as an astrologer to the Inquisition in Mexico City in 1582 and told of other practicing stargazers he knew in the city, including Bartolomé de Argumedo, who, in the trial of Suárez de Mayorga, was soon implicated as one of the translators of the *Opus Mathematicum*.[74]

Indeed, astrological practices in New Spain bring up many of the interpretive challenges I discussed in the introduction. Astrologers and those seeking their services came from diverse backgrounds and occupations. While some of the more learned practitioners limited themselves to the sanctioned version of astrology—that is, the natural-rational astrology that discussed broad astral influence on the natural and social world—others worked deeply in the unsanctioned form of judicial astrology; many dabbled in both types or interpreted the stars in ways that made the formal distinction quite hazy in practice. For the most part, later scholars studied the elevated astrology of the almanac authors and the astrological practices of the street and countryside as separate domains when in fact they formed part of a robust market for future knowledge that moved beyond astrology, narrowly defined, and included many other divinatory practices. The market for future knowledge demanded both its sanctioned and unsanctioned forms, and, as we have seen, the two were often conflated. The Inquisition considered this body of knowledge powerful, dangerous, and in need of close oversight.

But by the middle of the eighteenth century these circumstances had changed quite dramatically. For one thing, the status and influence of judicial astrology had declined considerably, and New Spain's astrologers / astronomers would be far less interested in pursuing it. In the sixteenth century and the seventeenth, individuals like Martínez and Fray Rodríguez were at the forefront of knowledge production and held positions of great authority, yet still stepped into the realm of judicial astrology or formed part of networks connected to it. By the turn of the eighteenth century, in contrast, figures like Sigüenza were no longer invested in its practice or epistemological status. And, remarkably, neither was the Inquisition. Whereas for much of the previous century Inquisitors had tenaciously pursued alleged astrologers like Guillén de Lombardo, Pérez de Soto, and Rivero Vasconcelos and fretted over the misinterpretation of astrological information on the part of the less educated, by the eighteenth century they had left most of those concerns behind.

This is not to say that the market for this sort of future knowledge disappeared in the eighteenth century. The Inquisition still investigated the occasional case of a diviner or astrologer, but nothing compared with the many cases of judicial astrology, chiromancy, face reading, zahoríes, and other forms of popular divination the Holy Office had brought over the previous two centuries. Neither did the market for printed works related to astrology diminish. For example, astronomers and publishers continued to produce yearly libros pronósticos throughout the eighteenth century and beyond.[75] Fragmentary evidence suggests that some almanacs with judicial content may have been in circulation, and the licensed pronósticos still included information about the weather and medicine that could be quite precise. But, as was the case with judicial astrology and popular divination, in the eighteenth century the intellectual and practical consternation over this market for future knowledge had largely abated.[76]

In 1711, for example, the Inquisition investigated a professor of mathematics for writing a manuscript that drew on the prophecies of Nostradamus. They found him to have predicted "contingent" futures, a clear sign of astrology that moved from the natural into the judicial. Yet rather than pursuing a lengthy investigation and trial, the Inquisitors suspended the proceedings and let the accused off with a warning to avoid such predictions in the future.[77] The denunciation of a zahorina in Querétaro in 1795 didn't create much of a stir in the Holy Office either. Although the zahorina was reported to have located a woman who had fled her husband, using nothing more than some bits of the woman's hair, one of her old shirts, and the calls of one of her children, again the Inquisition decided not to probe further.[78]

Most telling of all was the Inquisition's review in 1758 of a manuscript by another mathematician, Don Joaquin González del Pliego. In the text, titled *El antipronóstico perpetuo*, González made a scathing attack on the intellectual foundations and social dangers of judicial astrology. We might expect the Inquisitors to have celebrated a text of this sort; after all, the Inquisition had long attacked judicial astrology itself. Yet González found *himself* attacked by the Inquisition and his argument rejected by the second censor asked to examine the text. Fray Antonio Casimiro de Montenegro, a censor for the Inquisition, found nothing objectionable in the theoretical position staked out by González but questioned the proposed publication on the grounds that it presented a distorted picture of astrology as it was actually practiced in eighteenth-century New Spain. Drawing on the Spanish Golden Age playwright and poet Pedro Calderón de la Barca, the censor wrote, "He who wins without an opponent / can't be said to win." The author, in other words, had erected a kind of straw man, so the censor complained, since judicial astrology was not to be found in "Our Mexico." Neither should the author call for the suppression or censoring of legitimate libros pronósticos, even if the ignorant masses might misuse the information they found in them. The fact that men kill one another, the censor concluded, should not be grounds "to outlaw making swords, knives nor blunderbusses."[79]

How had the Inquisition reached these conclusions? Why was there now such a different attitude about the place of judicial astrology in New Spain? It might seem logical to explain these changes with recourse to contemporary developments in Europe or British North America. And, in fact, the decline of judicial astrology over the course of the seventeenth century is a point of consensus in the scholarship. Keith Thomas, for example, situates judicial astrology in a broader story about the diminished hold of magic on the populace of seventeenth-century England, especially among the elite. He notes how new technologies, such as improved shipping, insurance, and firefighting, among others, made life more predictable and magic less necessary or viable, as did urbanization and new ideas related to the scientific revolution, including empiricism and the repudiation of Neoplatonic and Aristotelian models of the physical world. He places most explanatory weight on a shift in "aspirations," "a new practical, optimistic attitude" that valued "self-help" and "human capacity," an outlook that itself developed out of some of the previously mentioned factors.[80] For British North America, Jon Butler pegs the decline in occult and astrological practices on a variety of factors. These ranged from a decline in the number of texts in circulation to the belief systems of evangelical Christianity and Calvinism, which in very different ways competed with the promise of astrology to solve everyday problems or reveal the future, to the enforcement of orthodoxy by church leaders and government officials.[81]

Save for the last, however, none of these factors were of any importance in seventeenth-century New Spain. And though it is often trotted out in the study of late Spanish America and other colonial societies, the notion of an intellectual or cultural ripple effect—whereby change occurs in a putative center, such as Britain or France, and then travels out to the colonial peripheries—is not very appealing.[82] For while we should neither discount the importance of a rising transatlantic empiricism among scientists (and here the case of Sigüenza can be seen as a harbinger of sorts) nor dismiss the later influence of Enlightenment thought, the evidence we have examined from New Spain itself points toward a very different course of events. It is a story of common people and consumers of astrology as co-agents of change, alongside the more traditional narrative described by Butler and Thomas, wherein popular practices are confronted with outside forces like new technologies, new socioeconomic factors, new attitudes on the part of an intellectual elite, top-down reform projects, and so on. As noted earlier, although astrology and the information it produced drew upon universal traditions and techniques, it was also a very local affair in that, like other forms of divination, it spoke to specific and individual concerns.[83] But in New Spain so too was the critique of that knowledge in part a local matter. In seventeenth-century New Spain a dialogue between two forms of empiricism developed. One grew out of Catholic theology and the regulation of the

Inquisition. The other was a popular empiricism that drew upon the ideas of the church and its defenders of orthodoxy and then used that information to evaluate the knowledge being produced by New Spain's many astrologers and diviners.

Surprisingly, New Spain's Inquisitors provided part of the impetus toward a more empirically grounded and precise form of futuremaking while policing the boundary between authorized and unauthorized forms of astrology. The Inquisition censored those drawing horoscopes and publishing almanacs in part to defend the Catholic dogma of human free will and its paradoxical partner, divine intervention. As part of this project, they rebuked astrologers of all sorts, not only for their errant practices or heterodoxy but also for their lack of precision and clarity. In the case of almanac publishing, this defense of dogma and tradition was also a critique of knowledge because it pushed astrologers to offer more concrete evidence and more explicit causal linkages to support their prognostications. This led one seventeenth-century censor, Father Antonio Núñez de Miranda, to warn almanac authors to use exact language, to avoid misleading generalizations, and to keep their predictions "within the philosophical and physical limits of their field."[84]

Yet we should read such criticism neither as a simple adoption of ideas or skepticism emanating from Europe nor as Enlightenment rationality avant la lettre. Far from it. The increasingly precise regulation of knowledge came from a very different origin point, one that on its face could be taken as an example of hidebound tradition. When censors rejected *El antipronóstico perpetuo*, for example, they criticized not only its supposedly distorted descriptions of New Spain's astrology but also its reliance on the Copernican model and the way it brushed aside Old Testament passages that supported heliocentrism.[85] Thus, as Trabulse notes, the emergence of new, empirically driven epistemologies needs to be examined not only earlier in the seventeenth century and in other, less celebrated figures than Sigüenza but also in relation to religion and tradition, not simply in opposition to them. Censors like Núñez de Miranda and others who followed in the eighteenth century pushed for more finely tuned information and fresh knowledge but demanded that it synthesize seamlessly with established teachings.[86]

Yet we need to go beyond the market for almanacs or the regulation of the Inquisitors to explain these developments. In the popular practice of astrology and related forms of divination a critical epistemology was also at work. It was full of inconsistencies and contradictions, as one would expect, but in concert with the investigations of the Inquisitors, the clients of astrologers and diviners demanded precision and efficacy in the future knowledge they received. It seems fair to read these voices and those of the accused, both of which formed part of Inquisition case files, as representative of widely held attitudes and perspectives, insofar as the slew of denunciations against astrologers and diviners comprised many individual, often unsolicited acts.

In case after case individuals denounced astrologers and diviners to the Inquisition and in the process revealed themselves to be critical, discerning consumers of the information they received and of the individuals who supplied it. Part of their critique developed out of a sophisticated understanding of the theological issues surrounding astrology and divination, a knowledge shared by the practitioners of these arts. Informants or accused astrologers and diviners from diverse backgrounds employed this vernacular theology. As we've seen, it proved quite effective when alleging faulty or ineffective astrology.

A command of vernacular theology could also be used to defend oneself from being implicated in an investigation. Now, we might expect that a lecturer of theology who was alleged to have practiced judicial astrology, as Nicolas Alarcón was in 1643, would defend himself through a detailed examination of free will and divine intervention or "certain knowledge" versus "conjectural knowledge" of the future.[87] More surprising was when a soldier in seventeenth-century Santa Fe, on the far reaches of New Spain's northern frontier, self-denounced to the Inquisition, describing a number of astrological readings he had given in the area. After recounting the detailed futures he had predicted—from serious illnesses to the birth of a child—he asserted, "I always understood and believed that all was beholden to the will of God and I always made that clear to all those I worked with."[88] This defense was quite like the palm reader in Zacatecas in 1613, Leonardo Bernabé, who reportedly predicted the violent death of a traveler and claimed to be able to find the location of silver deposits. Yet, according to one informant, Bernabé asserted that palm reading "was a science, but that God controlled all."[89] Or consider the logic of Don Baltasar Mosquera y Valerio, who by his own admission had been a prolific client of a palm reader while serving as the *alcalde mayor*, or district governor, in a northern mining town. In his denunciation to the Inquisition, however, he claimed never to have really believed the predictions. "Although the stars influence things indirectly," he explained, "which can be discerned by Astrology and other sciences, whether licit or illicit, these [predictions] were fallible and contingent, and like all things subject to the will of the Lord."[90] Astrologers and palm readers likewise held that their advice was consistent with the notion of free will because they claimed to reveal tendencies and potential futures that their clients could act upon given sufficient foresight, thereby changing the course of the future and, ironically, invalidating the original prediction.[91]

Informants were also careful, in some cases obsessively so, to report the quality of the information produced by the astrologer or diviner. The alcalde mayor Don Baltasar, for example, listed in great detail the correct and incorrect predictions of his family's palm reader, documenting a relationship that lasted over a decade.[92] In some instances, this seemed to allow an informant to excuse her or his role as a consumer of divinatory knowledge.[93] In others, it justified a denunciation, since showing the efficacy of the predictions suggested that something dangerous, perhaps even diabolical, was at work. Conversely, in cases where predictions proved false, frustrated clients used the Inquisition as a kind of market regulator or arbiter of the quality and authority of knowledge, putting the Inquisition on the trail of alleged charlatans and those not trafficking in reliable information.[94]

Such critical evaluation of information, albeit partial and at times at odds with itself, developed in the context of religion and in contests over orthodoxy and tradition, not in simple opposition to them. The critique relied on a conversation between astrological and divinatory practitioners, their clients, and the church officials charged with monitoring these activities. The many cases of accused diviners and astrologers raised questions similar to those asked in the almanac market: Was future knowledge precise enough to be

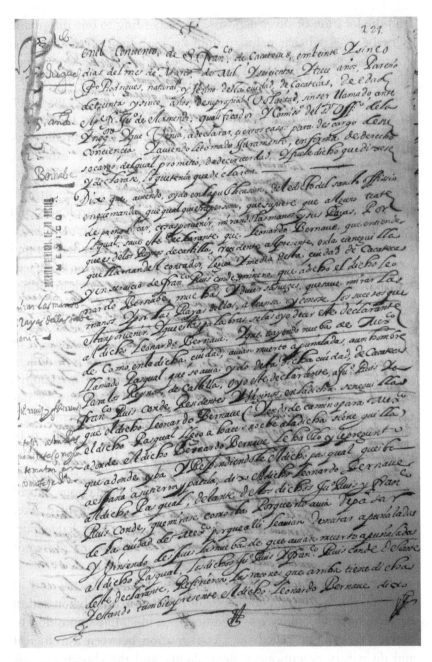

Figure 5. The Inquisition investigates Leonardo Bernabé, an alleged palm reader, in early seventeenth-century Zacatecas. (AGN, Inquisición, vol. 298, exp. 13, "Proceso contra Leonardo Bernabé por quiromántico," 1613.)

useful? Was it supported by some natural explanation? Was it so precise that it violated the notion of human agency or free will? Did it peer into the future with such exactness that it produced knowledge that was the domain of God? The outcome of this dialogue between regulators and consumers of future knowledge gradually eroded the authority of judicial astrology but left open the possibility that information about the future could be specific, useful, and practical for those who desired it.

CHAPTER FOUR

Money

IT MIGHT SEEM APPROPRIATE that theological debates and religious policing shaped the history of astrology and divination in New Spain, but similar concerns, and a similar process of change, revolved around things we would now call economic practices and market relationships. Once again, a conversation developed that crossed boundaries of education, status, and casta. Most subjects in New Spain understood that the stars influenced human behavior, even if only in a general way, and with the correct interpretation the heavens opened a window into future events. So too did many come to realize that money and credit had a force of their own and could shape the future. They were alluring for the power and opportunities they presented but potentially quite dangerous, given the influence they could have over the future, not unlike the sway of the stars and the events revealed by judicial astrologers.

Most notably, money and credit offered ways for individuals of diverse backgrounds to approach and control time. Access to capital—whether in the form of currency, goods, or credit—shaped business opportunities, purchasing power, social mobility, and, in a society where money was used to promote spiritual activities, it even influenced one's fate in the afterlife and the quest for redemption.[1] Money, in short, altered the future, even the forever future of salvation. In this respect it shared a great deal with the predictions of the yearly almanacs, an adept reading of the palm, or the visions of a true *zahorí*.

As in the case of these other future-oriented activities, New Spain inherited key ideas about money and its role in society from the European tradition. A number of these guiding concepts could be found in Catholic theology, yet others originated in early modern economic and political thought that was not directly tied to the church. Between the sixteenth and eighteenth centuries some of these received ideas changed radically in Europe itself. But just as we saw in the case of astrology and divination, the innovations that emerged during the colonial period in New Spain were largely a result of local developments, creative interactions in the Americas, and pragmatic adaptations rather than of concepts imported from overseas. Ideas and practices related to money that arrived from the Spanish metropole or Europe generally interacted in surprising ways with local forms of economic life and the knowledge that supported them, creating a culture of credit and money unique to the colonial world. In turn, some of these new attitudes, ideas, and practices would reverse sail and travel across the Atlantic in the other direction, shaping subsequent European and even global attitudes about money and the economy.

As we've seen, beginning in the late seventeenth century and continuing into the eighteenth, many subjects in New Spain adopted a more critical attitude toward the knowledge offered through astrology and divination. The role of money in New Spain also changed during this period, leading to a far more flexible system of credit and trade. By 1800 an increasingly liberal market for credit and a new attitude toward risk and just pricing could be found throughout much of New Spain. We find evidence of this shift in its major ports, urban areas, and mining centers and in small-scale agricultural production and trade in the countryside as well. Yet tradition strongly influenced these innovations, as it did in the emerging culture of empiricism that surrounded astrological forecasting. The economic environment became more heavily oriented toward the future and the calculation of risk, but it was also a system in which traditional theological and political rudders set the parameters of this new course. Such a mixture of old and new opened pathways for innovation but placed important limits on the evolution of financial and economic thought and practice in New Spain and, later, republican Mexico.

These colonial innovations, then, cannot be explained solely by eighteenth-century developments, nor can they be reduced to the influence of similar shifts in the European context. Their roots stretch back over centuries in the Catholic tradition but were fertilized by the unique environment that emerged in colonial Spanish America and New Spain in particular. They were colonial or American developments, shaped by the exchange of practices and ideas across the Atlantic and within New Spain itself.

In the sixteenth century, for example, inherited ideas about money and credit markets were already changing. This development was as apparent in the newly conquered territories of the Aztec empire, what was becoming the Hapsburg viceroyalty of New Spain, as it was in Spain itself and other parts of Europe. Due in large measure to the boom in precious metal production that followed the Iberian expansion into the Americas, individuals throughout this newly globalized network of trade began to describe money in new ways. Evidence of this shift can be seen from Spain to Mexico to China. People noted that money, previously thought to be static and unchanging, was, in fact, quite unstable. Its very essence, its worth, changed over time and from place to place. Yet, although individuals were beginning to recognize the uncertainty of money, the world of credit and debt remained highly regulated and quite rigid in Europe and Spanish America. It also rested on a medieval tradition in theology in which the church acted as a protector of the poor and in which in theory, if not always in practice, its regulatory authority over economic transactions ensured some basic level of market justice.[2]

In the eighteenth century, in contrast, a more flexible attitude toward money—whether the accumulated money of profit or the market for money in the form of credit and debt—took hold throughout New Spain, from its cities to its villages. Above all, different ideas had emerged about what constituted fair economic practices and an individual's or group's economic rights. Not surprisingly, these attitudes could be found among the economic elite of New Spain, as some well-positioned Spaniards and Spanish

Americans, for example, argued for major reforms to the highly regulated, monopolistic trade policies that, on paper, were the only link between Spain and its possessions in the Americas. These were lofty conversations, many were transatlantic in scope, and they took place in the upper echelons of the royal bureaucracy and the church hierarchy.

But as in the popular epistemology that developed around astrology and divination or the intensive focus on the individual that emerged in New Spain's eighteenth-century confessionals, the new orientation toward money, profit, risk, and credit evolved pragmatically and in many local interactions. People of diverse backgrounds adapted ideas and financial practices to economic settings where much less capital was in play. In the process they demonstrated a sophisticated understanding of the relevant laws and theology, quite like the vernacular theology surrounding confession and divination, and they were quick to use them in legal and financial disputes. In this new economic world it was not at all surprising when, in the mid-eighteenth century, small-scale sugar traders and producers in the mostly Indigenous region of the Huasteca defended their decisions to enter into futures and credit contracts based on their freedom to take risk and reap profits. Using financial instruments that the church and other authorities had previously considered usurious and sinful, they argued that such tools were now economic rights and essential to their well-being.

This shift had enormous implications for how colonial subjects experienced time, especially the future. Money was previously thought to be something fixed and sterile. It could not change or reproduce itself with the passage of time. Theoretically speaking, it sat outside the flow of time. It was literally *timeless*. By the eighteenth century, quite the opposite was true: the value of money could and did change over time; and, in the absence of other factors, money reproduced itself in all sorts of unusual ways. In turn, residents of New Spain, from silver magnates to sugarcane farmers, knew that money could easily influence time and the future, whether the ability to finance next year's crops, to receive payment for future deliveries, or to endow the celebration of Masses to help save one's soul. In very tangible terms, time was money and money was time. Over the arc of the colonial era, this relationship became more widely understood and accepted, and it allowed individuals from diverse backgrounds and social positions to use credit and economic language to project themselves into the future in novel ways. The future became more expansive albeit full of risk and uncertainty.

To see how this process unfolded, let us step back into the sixteenth century, itself a period of colossal change on both sides of the Atlantic. In contemporary historical memory, the sixteenth century in both Europe and the Americas is most readily associated with great political, religious, and social upheavals, whether the Protestant Reformation and Catholic Counter-Reformation, the bloody intra-continental struggles among European powers, or the dramatic over-seas expansion of the Iberian-based empires, with all of their horrific consequences for Indigenous peoples. Sometimes these are framed as cultural or intellectual events, such as the rejection of theologies and dogma of the Roman Catholic Church in movements associated with the Reformation and the resulting shift from a more communal notion of salvation to a spirituality that emphasized the individual's role in redemption; the aggressive campaigns to extirpate native spir-ituality and ritual in the Americas and replace it with Christianity; or the early moment of *mestizaje*, the mixture of peoples, ideas, and cus-toms in the emerging colonial world.

Yet this period was also a time of massive economic change in Europe, Spanish America, and many other regions, all of which were becoming more closely tied to one another. Many historians characterize it as the first moment of globalization. Contemporaries were beginning to see it that way, too. In 1569 a Spanish Dominican friar, Tomás de Mercado, who had spent time in New Spain, reflected on the dramatic changes to trade over the previous fifty years. Powerful merchants, Mercado wrote, now traded "in all parts of the world." A world, he continued, in which "everybody de-pends on everybody else."[3] In Mercado's Europe, traditional modes of production were now embedded in a system of expanded trade networks and nascent capitalism. This process had begun in ear-nest in the fourteenth century yet quickened remarkably alongside the sixteenth-century Atlantic explorations and invasions and the subsequent trade relationships that linked Europe, Africa, and the

Americas. In the locations of imperial expansion, existing economic models and their accompanying social hierarchies were replaced or linked to new techniques of labor exploitation and trade. Most important with regard to the question of money and its relationship to time and the future, the economies in the core regions of Spanish America—the central part of the Viceroyalty of New Spain and the highland Andean zones of the Viceroyalty of Peru—became engines of the production of vast amounts of precious metals, especially silver.

These economic engines required fuel of various sorts, most important, human labor. Peoples of African descent and Indigenous Americans supplied most of this toil, sometimes voluntarily but more often as a result of some form of coercion, including forced labor drafts and chattel slavery. Over time, certainly by the seventeenth century, labor regimes in much of the core regions and especially in the mining zones shifted toward wage labor. But the appetite for labor and other inputs remained voracious.[4] The internal economies of both New Spain and Peru developed around the mining centers, providing the essential inputs for the boom in silver production. These inputs included not just human labor but animals, foodstuffs, clothing, timber, tools, and so on. From these ingredients emerged robust, complex economic systems.[5] They generated a mammoth increase in the production of precious metals and an unprecedented surge in coinage and money supply in Europe.

The flow of this bullion, or precious metals in bulk form, to the royal treasuries in Mexico City and Lima and then across the Atlantic to Spain boggles the mind with its size and rapid expansion. In the first decades of the sixteenth century the initial plunder of the native societies of the Caribbean and, later, the Aztec and Inca empires on the mainland combined with ubiquitous placer mining to produce an impressive flow of precious metals to the royal treasury in Spain. As early as 1534 an official of the treasury in Seville exclaimed, "The quantity of gold that arrives every day from the Indies and especially from Peru, is quite incredible; I think that if this torrent of gold lasts even ten years, this city will become the richest in the world."[6] The treasurer made these remarks just after the ransoming of the Inca emperor Atahualpa by the Spanish conquistador Francisco Pizarro, when the Inca famously made good on his promise to fill a room with gold and silver to secure his release. The fall of the Aztec empire and its enormous plunder had come just a decade before. From the perspective of most Spaniards, both were truly wondrous events, confirmed by the flow of riches back to Spain. The conquest and spoils were so remarkable, in fact, that they seemed to exceed the ability of language to describe them.

Even though the treasurer filled his assessment with superlatives, he set his sights far too low, it turned out. His torrent of gold would soon become a deluge of silver. By the final decades of the sixteenth century the flow of precious metals across the Atlantic, especially silver, reached prodigious levels. This surge in production followed numerous midcentury discoveries of ore in central and northern New Spain and the mammoth silver strike in 1545 at the *cerro rico*, or "rich hill," of Potosí in Peru (now Bolivia). It also followed the introduction of technical advances in mining and metallurgy, most notably the use of mercury amalgamation to extract silver from ore.

Amalgamation fundamentally shifted the style and size of silver production. Brought to the Americas in the 1550s, after being developed in Hapsburg territories in Germany, silver amalgamation was one step of a new production process that exploited economies of scale and demanded greater labor specialization. The method began with the transport of raw ore to increasingly large production facilities that included a refinery, referred to as an *hacienda de minas* or *hacienda de beneficio*. Strategically located near the mines, the haciendas contained water-powered stamps or, more often, given the arid environments of many of the mining regions, mule-powered devices that crushed the chunks of ore into a powder. Engineers and refiners then mixed the crushed ore with water, salt, copper pyrite, and other reagents, most important, mercury, to create a pasty substance. Workers spread the paste into a thin layer, a so-called *torta*, or "cake," that was then left outside to dry in huge, open-air patios. Once engineers and supervisors had determined that the desired chemical reactions were complete, whereby silver and mercury amalgamated, or bound to each other, laborers heated pieces of the dry torta to burn off the mercury and other impurities. While exposing workers and the surrounding environment to the dreadful and not entirely understood dangers of chemical contamination and industrial pollution, the process worked remark-ably well, and, after the final burn-off, it left something very close to pure silver.[7]

Sometimes referred to simply as the patio process, in reference to the open-air drying of the torta, the use of amalgamation on a mass scale led to a rapid and sustained increase in silver produc-tion. As a result, total production of precious metals in Spanish America reached some 21.6 million pesos in the five-year period from 1571 to 1575. By the end of the century, five-year production was in the range of 60 million pesos. After dropping off in the first years of the seventeenth century, it then reached a peak of nearly 78 million pesos for 1621–25. Although these figures reflect total output—the official receipts of bullion by the Spanish crown were lower—the general trend in Spain's royal coffers mimicked the fig-ures above, and in the late sixteenth to early seventeenth century the royal treasury received something in the range of 40–60 mil-lion pesos' worth of precious metals from the Americas every five years. The total amount of American silver that made its way to Europe between 1500 and 1650 is estimated to have been in the range of 16,000 tons.[8]

Table 1. American Precious Metal Production and Registered Receipts in Spain, 1571–1630 (in millions of pesos)

Year	Production	Registered receipts (Spain)
1571–75	21.6	19.7
1576–80	44.4	28.5
1581–85	49	48.6
1586–90	61.5	39.4
1591–95	59.3	58.2
1596–1600	51.6	57
1601–5	39.5	44.9
1606–10	43.1	52
1611–15	61.6	40.6
1616–20	63.1	49.8
1621–25	77.9	44.7
1626–30	48.9	41.3

Source: Stein and Stein, *Silver, Trade, and War,* 24.

According to mercantilist theories that dominated economic thinking at the time, this windfall should have augured well for the Spanish crown and its subjects on the Iberian peninsula. Mercantilists believed that "gold and silver were the substance and the definition of private and national wealth." These metals were a dependable store of value and an almost universally recognized form of money that could be used to purchase property, labor, and loyalty.[9] As the Dominican Mercado put it, "One of the principal requisites for the prosperity and happiness of a kingdom is always to hold within itself a great quantity of money and an abundance of gold and silver, which are in substance all the temporal riches of this life, or, at least, which come to embrace them all. A kingdom which has money in some sense has all things."[10] The real weight of bullion, in short, came from its density of power. Mercantilists wanted to capture as much of that economic power as possible within the imperial treasury and the local economy because the world supply of metals was limited. If not a zero-sum game, in other words, most early modern economic theorists described the quest for precious metals as a contest with substantial limits on the overall riches to be won. They emphasized that wealth creation was really not a process of generation at all but a kind of hoarding, a competition for slices of a limited pie. The pie could be conceived of as wealth, power, or even slices of the future, given the permanence and timelessness of money.

The transport of royal bullion back to Spain reflected these assumptions. Carefully orchestrated tax collection funneled the crown's share of mining proceeds from the production zones of New Spain and Peru to the American treasuries and mints in Lima and Mexico City and then to the small number of authorized trading ports in the circum-Caribbean. The system culminated in the Carrera de Indias, or Indies run, a yearly sailing of a single, authorized treasure convoy to southern Spain. After the fleet made the westward crossing of the Atlantic and unloaded its cargo of European exports in Veracruz and Cartagena de Indias, dockworkers reloaded the ships with American goods, above all, the current year's remittance of bullion. The fleet reunited in Havana and, after waiting for favorable winds, made its way back across the Atlantic in early summer. Spanish officials designed the entire process, especially the sailing of the fleet, to be rigid and controlled from the top down. They intended the Carrera de

Indias not only to provide some safety in numbers to counter the increasingly aggressive piracy of other European powers but also to ensure a careful accounting of remittances of bullion to the crown. It was also meant to limit intracolonial trade, since mercantilists sought to create a trade surplus between Spain and the colonies, which they believed would lead to a net increase of wealth for the metropole.[11]

But what became of those carefully guarded shipments of metal? What were they used for and where did they go? For a variety of reasons, much less of it remained in Spain than one might expect. Historians have long established the ways in which the tight regulation of silver production, taxation, and shipment had the unintended effect of creating a large contraband economy around the export of unregulated silver.[12] In addition, much of the regulated silver slipped quickly out of the hands of the royal treasurers in the form of debt servicing, as the promise of American metals led to aggressive spending and borrowing by the crown. American silver funded a long list of military engagements of the Hapsburg monarchs, from ongoing battles against the Ottoman Turks in the eastern Mediterranean to Charles V's successful but hugely expensive and bloody campaign to become Holy Roman Emperor to the unsuccessful but equally costly effort to keep the Dutch territories under Hapsburg control. As a result, much of the silver that traveled from the highlands of New Spain and Peru rested only momentarily in Seville and Madrid before continuing its journey across the Pyrenees to creditors and banking families throughout Europe. The broadest of these rivers of silver flowed between the Spanish treasury in Seville and the Fugger banking house of Germany, which underwrote Charles V's bid for the title of Holy Roman Emperor and many other imperial adventures on the Continent and beyond. Other German bankers also substantially supported the crown, as did financial concerns in Genoa, Florence, Antwerp, and elsewhere outside the peninsula, the Genoese, especially, taking on a large share of crown debt later in the sixteenth century. The interest servicing alone on these obligations of royal debt sped the movement of American treasure from Spain to other parts of Europe.[13]

The river of silver branched off in other directions as well. Recently, a globally oriented historical scholarship has demonstrated that India and, above all, China were the final destinations of much of the precious metal wrested from the mountains of Peru and New Spain. Chinese demand for silver played the key role in the process. After the collapse of government-issued currency, the Ming dynasty eventually gave up on paper money and normalized what had become the informal practice of using silver as a unit of currency. Kenneth Pomeranz describes this as a "remonetizing" of the Chinese economy, by which "silver was becoming the store of value, the money of account (and often the actual medium) for large transactions, and the medium of state payments."[14]

As Pomeranz notes, however, one needs to be careful not to think of silver *only* as money since doing so makes it seem far more of a neutral substance than it actually was. It was not just a unit of exchange or a way of paying for a trade deficit in Asian luxury goods. Instead, he writes, "we need to see silver itself as a good: a refined product with a mineral base, which was well suited to an important function and which the West could produce far more cheaply than any place in Asia."[15] Silver understood as a good means taking into account its more complex process of production, its use as money, and how fluctuating forces of supply and demand could shift its price. It means considering it, much as sixteenth-century individuals were beginning to do, a dynamic product in the world, one full of uncertainty.

Along with an expanding economy and population, China's return to metal currency meant that from the sixteenth to the eighteenth centuries the empire developed a nearly insatiable appetite for American silver. Chinese hunger for silver was sated by the transpacific trade between Peru and New Spain and Chinese ports, through the Spanish territories of the Philippines, and also from transshipments of silver to China via European merchants and bankers. The famed Manila galleons, for example, which sailed from the Mexican port of Acapulco to the Philippines, satisfied not only the desires of Americans and Europeans for goods but also a long-term Chinese demand for money as Chinese silks, porcelain, and regional spices were exchanged for Peruvian and Mexican silver.[16] As in the case of the Atlantic trade, silver moved across the Pacific and through Europe in staggering quantities. Though estimates are hampered by the sizable amount of unregistered trade, between

1550 and 1800 perhaps fifty thousand tons of American silver made its way to China.[17] This silver boom was truly a bonanza for some, especially the Chinese merchants of the southeastern provinces and the mining and shipping magnates of New Spain and Peru. It also underwrote the cultural production and aristocratic opulence of the Spanish Golden Age and, for a time, propped up the Spanish economy as a whole.

Although historians have debated at length what the long-term effects of these factors were on the economic health of Spain, the consensus leaning toward their tendency to undermine Spanish domestic production and industrialization, two short- and medium-term outcomes are quite clear. First, the military, political, and resulting fiscal overextension of Hapsburg Spain led to a series of five royal bankruptcies from the second half of the sixteenth century into the mid-seventeenth century, ironically at the precise time silver production increased dramatically in the Americas. As has been the case in many more recent defaults of sovereign debt, these bankruptcies between 1557 and 1647 changed the terms of the Spanish crown's credit, consolidating and extending the terms of the loans, but did not signal the end of the creditor-debtor relationship. The cycle of credit, debt, and overspending continued.[18]

Second, the expansion of bullion in circulation eroded its value in Europe. When coupled with other local factors, such as the expanded government debt and increased demand for foodstuffs, it led to an extended period of monetary inflation that ran from the middle of the sixteenth century until well into the seventeenth century. With the benefit of hindsight, later observers would label this a price revolution, a period when, between 1500 and 1650, prices rose at an average of 2 percent annually throughout much of Europe. Many working people, in turn, saw their real wages decline considerably. While such levels of inflation might seem modest and controlled from our perspective, given the historical context, when in previous generations the value of silver and gold remained relatively flat and prices relatively stable over the long run, this steady increase in the cost of goods was unprecedented.[19] Most contemporaries, especially laborers and peasants, experienced the price revolution as a change more retrograde than revolutionary. It was a turn of the economic wheel in the wrong direction, one could say, since the rising price of staple goods compressed purchasing power, led to a decline in living standards compared to those enjoyed by previous generations, and created subsistence crises for the marginalized.

When these unsettling effects of money were coupled with the fiscal disasters of the Hapsburg crown, Spaniards began to view the silver produced in New Spain and Peru as something awe-inspiring, strange, and otherworldly. As a result, the Indies became associated in Spanish and European minds with wealth, even *as* wealth itself.[20] For potent examples, we have the fanciful visual and textual representations of the mines at Potosí. Set at thirteen thousand feet in the Andean highlands, in reality a bitterly cold and dry place, some Europeans imagined Potosí as archetypically American, a strange melding of tropical flora, exotically clad natives, and fantastic wealth, all produced in a brutal social and economic hierarchy. Europeans, it seems, were struggling to place the wellspring of this new money in a physical landscape but also within a mental framework. Where did this wealth come from? Why now? What did it mean?[21]

Many Spaniards interpreted these events through spiritual frameworks. They felt that only divine intervention could explain the grandeur of American silver and of Potosí in particular. They considered American wealth and its sudden appearance during the reign of Charles V as a clear sign of Providence—the hand of God—working in the world. And why not? The initial strike at Potosí came just over ten years after the defeat of the Inca empire, when, according to legend, an Indigenous man named Gualpa stumbled upon a glinting silver lode that was thirteen feet wide and stretched for hundreds of feet.[22] "This is the way in which Potosí was discovered," wrote the Jesuit chronicler José de Acosta, "Divine Providence decreeing, for the good of Spain, that the greatest treasure known to exist in the world was hidden and came to light at the time when emperor Charles V, of glorious name, held the reins of empire and the realm of Spain and seigniory of the Indies."[23] For a committed man of faith like Acosta, who had dedicated his adult life to serving the missionary church in the Indies, such a wondrous event could not be conceived of outside of its evangelical implications. After calculating the vast wealth already produced for the

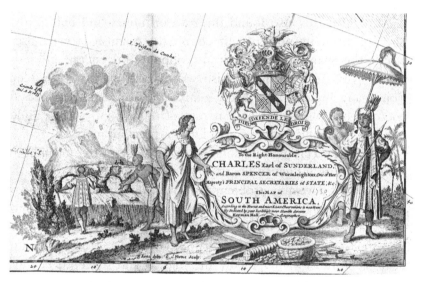

Figure 6. A fanciful vision of American silver wealth, from a cutting-edge map of South America created in London in the early eighteenth century. This representation of Potosí was based on a seventeenth-century Dutch image of the cerro rico, *which had imaginatively added palm trees and windmills to the stark landscape of the Peruvian* altiplano. *(Herman Moll, cartographer,* To the Right Honorable Charles Earl of Sunderland and Baron Spencer of Wormleighton . . . Map of South America *[London: I. Bowles, T. Bowles, and P. Overton, ca. 1709–20]. Courtesy of the John Carter Brown Library at Brown University.)*

crown by the Peruvian mines, Acosta concluded, "We must believe that this has occurred through the special providence of our God, for the good of those people who live so far distant from their head, who is the pope of Rome, vicar of Christ Our Lord, and also for the defense of the Catholic Faith itself and the Roman Church in these parts, where the truth is so much resisted and persecuted by heretics."[24] Decades later, in 1630, another Spanish cleric offered a similar assessment: "Potosí lives in order to serve the imposing aspirations of Spain: it serves to chastise the Turk, humble the Moor, make Flanders tremble and terrify England." Here Potosí stood as an emblem of money but, in addition, as its actual source, and money meant a powerful future for the composite Hapsburg empire.[25]

But Spaniards also found the rush of money and bullion disturbing, given its perverse effects on the Spanish crown's fiscal health, the Spanish and American economies in general, and individual lives. As a result, Spanish writers examined this problem from many angles and in every genre, from economic treatises to poetry. They placed the very nature of money and wealth under scrutiny, including their essential form as precious metals.

The times certainly demanded taking stock of the meaning of money and its influence on the world. Those living through the period faced a vexing problem, one that remains familiar today: riches, it seemed, produced not only wealth but also economic pain, even misery. How so? Previously, precious metals were thought to be the most stable form of currency, a true and unambiguous store of value. Yet by the mid to late sixteenth century, given the inflationary pressures of the previous years and their coincidence with the arrival of American silver, some began to question this received wisdom. Travelers to Spain often remarked on the sudden increase in prices and, therefore, the decline in the value of precious metals. "I learnt a proverb here," remarked a French visitor in 1603, "everything is dear in Spain, except silver."[26] Spanish intellectuals made the most pointed causal linkages. Half a century earlier Martín de Azpilcueta was the first to connect these two phenomena in his *Comentario resolutorio de usuras:* "We see by experience that in France, where money is scarcer than in Spain, bread, wine, cloth, and labour are worth much less. And even in

Spain, in times when money was scarcer, saleable goods and labour were given for very much less than after the discovery of the Indies, which flooded the country with gold and silver. The reason for this is that money is worth more where and when it is scarce than where it is abundant."[27]

Writing in 1556, Azpilcueta, a specialist in church law, had reached a radical conclusion: money, including its most pure form as precious metal, was not stable and therefore not inherently valuable. Instead, it was becoming increasingly clear that the value of money was not intrinsic to the object but changed across space, over time, and depending on external conditions.[28] "All merchandise becomes dearer when it is in great demand and short supply," wrote Azpilcueta, "and [given] that money, in so far as it may be sold, bartered, or exchanged by some other form of contract, is *merchandise*, and therefore becomes dearer when it is in great demand and short supply."[29] He would soon be followed by others, such as Tomás de Mercado, whose ideas we have encountered already. After the initial plundering of the Caribbean, Mexico, and Peru, Spaniards had witnessed shifting valuations whereby the value of gold, silver, and other precious objects fluctuated from previous levels, as it did later between the Old World and the New. It became an even greater source of concern as a result of the emerging price revolution in Europe. In 1556 a Spanish official in Peru, Andrés Hurtado de Mendoza, reported to his superiors an observation that in previous generations would have seemed nonsensical: "Money is worth very little." But it now made perfect sense. A few years later one of his colleagues noted that even between the silver-producing highlands and the coastal city of Lima prices fluctuated wildly.[30]

In the same period new forms of state debt grew rapidly and exacerbated uncertainties about the effects of American bullion. While Europeans, above all Spaniards, grappled with anxieties about apparent fluctuations in value, for example, credit markets were also expanding dramatically, the Spanish crown taking a prominent role in the creation of government bonds, often referred to as *juros*, an innovative, nimble form of public debt. The massive issuing of promissory notes and government debt was both a product and producer of the Spanish expansion into the Americas. Not only was much of the Spanish conquest paid for by credit and the promise of future payment, but when those explorations and invasions reaped treasure, they funded additional borrowing and thereby created positive feedback that increased the sale of debt by the Spanish crown.

Many found the dramatic expansion of large-scale credit just as disturbing as the uncertainty surrounding the value of money in that it produced pieces of paper—the debt contracts, promissory notes, and government bonds—that could circulate as money. In the second half of the sixteenth century the use of such paper as currency led Mercado to refer to regional trade fairs as "veritable factories of [credit] certificates."[31] Similarly, if some considered the sudden arrival of American treasure and bullion otherworldly, the relentless expansion of money and promissory notes in the form of government debt also appeared mysterious, since by issuing new credit contracts bankers seemed to be conjuring money from nothing, like an alchemist making gold from straw. As we will see, critics of such financial sorcery could find support in medieval theories of usury which held that money was a sterile thing and should not reproduce itself.[32]

All of these uncertainties about the essence of gold and silver led Spanish scholars associated with the School of Salamanca to begin redefining the meaning of precious metals in relationship to space and time. No longer could gold and silver be considered utterly unique, different from most other goods. Following the work of the famed theologian Francisco de Vitoria, these scholars increasingly viewed gold and silver as commodities, not unlike a cartload of grapes or hides. Their price could be expected to fluctuate with the passage of time. Once timeless, precious metals and money had become temporal substances, captured by the march of time.[33]

What did the new understanding of money mean in regard to people's relationship to the future? As we've seen on both sides of the Atlantic, the rapidly changing values of goods and money in the sixteenth century stood in stark relief to the more gentle changes of prices in previous generations. Although economic conditions in previous eras could still be chaotic and unpredictable on many levels, the relative stability of monetary values eased some of this economic uncertainty. It made the future more predictable. It allowed

individuals, families, and communities to plan for their financial futures with some minimal degree of confidence. Economic turbulence, on the other hand, especially uncertainty over the value of
money, tends to have the opposite effect, making the present over-
whelm the future. Describing a more recent episode of Mexican
economic turmoil, Claudio Lomnitz calls this condition a "present
saturation," wherein individuals become so consumed with current
conditions, anxiety, and hopelessness that the future withers away or
recedes into itself. Largely as a result of the crisis of currency valuations, one's ability to produce usable images of the future is de-
stroyed.[34] Many of the voices that spoke on the subject of money in
sixteenth-century Spain and Spanish America echoed this sentiment.

Yet there were forces pushing in the opposite direction, creating other economic pathways to the future. The same individuals
who described disturbing price changes were also living through a
time of great innovation in financial instruments and credit practices. These new ideas and techniques contributed to the economic
uncertainty of the present, as we encountered in the case of juros
and the expansion of government debt, and some scholars impli-
cate them in the price revolution itself. But they grew as well out of
a longer-term change in European attitudes toward money that
subjected money to the effects of time and in the process made it
more future oriented. When, in the sixteenth century, Spanish
theologians of the School of Salamanca discussed the nature of
money, they were the most recent voices in a long-running conversation in Catholic law and theology that had slowly reconceptual-
ized the essence of money, with enormous implications for the
ways in which individuals could execute financial transactions, especially credit. Money now meant not just the hard currency of
precious metals but the soft currency of promissory notes, juros,
and credit, and, whatever its form, it was clearly situated in time
and subject to fluctuations in value.[35] The result was a new set of
credit instruments that formed the backbone of the rapidly expanding economies in Spanish America.

These financial devices and their unique versions in the
Americas and New Spain grew out of a political, economic, and
theological tradition that produced attitudes to trade, investment,
and credit that were quite different from our own. The theological

and legal concept of usury, or the prohibition against receiving payments for a loan beyond the original principal, explains many of the peculiarities of finance, credit, and contracts in early modern Europe and in those parts of the Americas that experienced European imperialism.[36] As was the case with so many other key topics, the writings of Aquinas were a point of departure for the analysis of usury in late medieval and early modern Christendom. Aquinas's position on the matter was quite clear. Like other scholastic writers, he argued that to charge interest on a simple loan amounted to usury—something to be avoided and also a cause of sin.

What exactly was wrong with charging for a loan? For us, interest is a given, a truly natural part of our economic world. Credit is something that many people need, that a smaller number have to offer, and it thus seems reasonable that parties from each group would enter into transactions with each other. It appears logical they would charge a price (interest) for the thing being exchanged (money).[37] A current textbook of economics would frame interest in terms of supply and demand, their fluctuations over time, and the changes to price that result from the interaction of money supply and demand in the marketplace. Interest, conceived of in this way as the price of credit, should go up when the supply of credit is low and demand for it is high. Conversely, weak demand for loans and an ample supply of capital available to be lent should make the cost of loans decrease. Credit has a price, in other words, and it should be expected to change over time. Its value can expand and contract in the marketplace, independent of its essential qualities. The result is fair value, a market-derived price of money.

While commonsensical when framed in the terms and assumptions of contemporary economics, such statements would have been rejected as utterly illogical and absurd by medieval or early modern theologians and legal scholars. Their view of the world helps explain the evolution of money and its relationship to the future in New Spain. To them, interest on a simple loan, whatever the price, far from being the just price of money, amounted to a great *injustice*. "To take usury for the loan of money is in itself unjust," Aquinas wrote, "because it is selling what is not, by which an inequality is manifestly constituted, which is against justice." "Selling what is not" is a curious phrase that referred to money's natural use: its consumption through exchange; that is, through parting with it. Money was for spending. But if money had to be returned *and* a price paid for its use, then the money wasn't really being sold or consumed at all, which was unnatural. What *was* being sold in a usurious transaction? Time or, rather, the future.

This led medieval moralists to describe usury as a particularly insidious form of sin, since lenders sold time, which was the property of God. To sell someone else's property amounted to theft, hence the description of usurers as "thieves of time."[38] And, unlike most sins, usury never stopped. In an imagined dialogue between a monk and a novice written in the early thirteenth century, the novice observes, "Usury seems to me a very grievous sin, and one most difficult to cure." "You are right," the monk replies. "Every other sin has its periods of intermission; usury never rests from sin. Though its master be asleep, it never sleeps, but always grows and climbs."[39]

This radically different opinion emerged quite rationally from what these two religious understood to be the nature of money. Along with other thinkers at the time, Aquinas considered money a sterile thing, something that should not be expected to reproduce itself in the absence of other factors. "In evidence of which," Aquinas wrote, "it should be recognized that the use of some things is in their consumption: for instance, wine is consumed when used as a drink, and wheat when used as food. In such cases the use of a thing cannot be reckoned separately from the thing itself, so whenever a thing's use is granted to anyone, the thing itself is given at one and the same time." He went on to discuss other sorts of goods, such as a home, where the use and consumption of the thing should be thought of as separate actions. This was not the case with money, he noted, which was more like wine and other items whose consumption was intrinsic to the object's use. "Money . . . has been invented for the making of exchanges; and thus the proper and principal use of money lies in its consumption or in parting with it, according to its expenditure in exchanges. For which reason, then, it is unlawful to charge a price for the loan of a sum of money, which is called usury."[40] In making this critique, Aquinas drew on an intellectual condemnation of usury going back to Aristotle. In the passage above Aquinas references Aristotle's criticism of usury as an utterly unnatural act, for it used money (to

produce more money) against its nature (as a unit of exchange).[41]
Money, in Aquinas's thinking, was sterile and therefore should not
be productive in and of itself. His analysis, like those of other early
scholastics, rested on an assumption about money that separates
medieval and early modern usury theory from our conception of
money and lending: that money had an essential value and was in-
vulnerable to market forces or the ravages of time.

Early usury theory differed from our ideas about money in
other ways. For one, it attempted to distinguish interest from usury,
terms that later commentators and our own usage sometimes present as being synonymous.[42] Most of the key thinkers that informed
early writing on usury theory separated the two with great care.
They noted a fundamental difference between interest or, properly
put, true interest (*verum interesse*) and payments on top of the principal loan, or what we now refer to as an interest payment. True interest meant that the lender was exposed to some significant risk or
financial damage. If a sum of money was truly subject to loss,
Catholic canon law sometimes allowed the taking of payments in
excess of principal. In the case of a simple loan, in contrast, to do so
was usurious and sinful.[43] Aquinas, following Augustine and other,
earlier commentators quite closely, put it simply: "To take money
as the price of money lent ... the price for use, that is called
usury."[44] The distinction between true interest and usury could be
quite difficult to make in practice and required interpretations and
rulings based on changing economic institutions, trade relationships, and so on. Thus, as in the law and theology related to prediction and astrology, some flexibility was built in to the ideas that
governed economic relationships and financial instruments.

Financial innovation in early modern credit markets developed
within these areas of theological and legal uncertainty. To overcome the prohibition against usury, for example, pre-Reformation
Europeans had developed a number of instruments and accompanying legal and theological defenses that permitted the transfer of
capital from one party to another with a promised return of principal plus some additional payment. In essence, these techniques
amounted to what we would call a loan at interest, but one that
could be defended as non-usurious and that was subject to general
moral and theological constraints of usury theory.[45]

Sixteenth-century New Spain inherited these forms of credit, and they became pillars of the colonial economy. The most important of these was an instrument known as the *censo*. In essence, the censo (from the medieval Latin *census*) was a contract of sale rather than a loan. The censo contract promised a payment of annual annuities "from fruitful property," such as an agricultural estate, in return for a transfer of funds to another party.[46] The person buying the censo—the lender, or *censualista*—gave cash to the counterparty, the debtor, or *censuario*. By wrapping the transfer of capital and its reimbursement in a sales contract, rather than in a loan, the censo contract circumvented the problem of usury; or, as Aquinas put it, simply taking money for money lent—that is, "the price for use." Structured as a purchase contract, the censo bound together a debtor and creditor. It then exposed the owner of the contract (the lender) to losses in a legal and theologically sanctioned way. The lender now possessed verum interesse, or true interest, in the eventual return of the capital. This exposure to loss authorized the annuity payments, over and above the amount required to return the original principal, without creating a usurious transaction. Moreover, unless the censo was for a fixed term (most were not), the contract did not require the borrower to return the original principal but simply to keep making the annuity payments, which further distinguished the censo from a simple loan at interest.[47]

This intellectual development and legal construct had the deepest of roots. Under the general rubric of interesse, a concept that stretched back to Roman law, scholastic theologians and jurists examined some conditions of contracts and risk exposure that allowed one to charge for a loan. By the thirteenth century these specialists in canon law had revived the category of interesse to refer to the damages or losses when one party in a transaction failed to honor its commitments. As a result, they considered interesse separate from the loan itself and a way to compensate an aggrieved party in a broken contract.

Shortly thereafter, Aquinas built on this idea and placed the loss of *potential* or *probable* profits under the label of interesse, again an idea that could be found in Roman law. This seemingly minor revision to usury theory in fact held major implications for underlying assumptions about the nature of money. It suggested that money was productive and causal. It could create and alter things in the world. Interesse now opened the door to loan payments that were based on what economists would now call future value, in that the payments indexed a theoretical or imagined sum of money to compensate for the loss of future profits.

Under this model, money had some force independent of the person who possessed it. As John Noonan notes, "In the *Summa* [of Aquinas], money is conceived as containing profits, as a seed contains harvests." Clearly this would contradict Aquinas's own statements and the accepted position of other theologians and legal scholars about the sterility of money.[48] Indeed, Aquinas himself qualified this assertion, and it would be some time before consensus emerged around the question of compensation for potential losses—or the inverse, being unable to reap potential profits because money was loaned rather than used for some other purpose, an economic condition now referred to as opportunity cost.[49] Although these early debates over usury and lending were quite technical and arcane, they were part of an increasingly widespread conversation about the nature of money and the acceptability of certain kinds of profits in the later medieval and early modern period.

The debate about the meaning of "interesse" and its relationship to the concept of usury would continue for centuries. Spanish jurists and theologians revisited the issue in the sixteenth century, for example, but over time the qualifications posited by Aquinas eventually became broadly accepted. Under the categories of *lucrum cessans* (lost potential profits) and *damnuns emergens* (losses incurred by a lender as a result of the loan), this shift among scholastic thinkers allowed for some compensation on top of a loan's principal. It opened the door, in other words, to a model of loan making that is much closer to our own understanding of interest, at least if we think of interest as compensation for a loan. Yet, as we will see, it remained embedded in a web of economic thought and practice that was far from our contemporary notions of interest as the price of money determined by market forces. The tension between these two forces, market versus moral, would shape the credit markets that developed in New Spain in the sixteenth century and evolved throughout the colonial period.[50]

This revised conception of money and its relationship to productivity also suggested a different understanding of worldly time.
Under this emerging relationship of money and credit, one could
more easily imagine a future material life and not just an imagined
afterlife. These ideas and their practical application in trade and
lending offered a different pathway to a future in the world, since
they created a legal and theological foundation for more robust
credit markets. In practical terms, more and more people realized
that money changed over time. Money was not sterile but alive. It
was infused with social relationships, expectations and trust, and
hopes about the future. The shortage of currency and the importance of credit in New Spain sped this process along and made the
shifting value of money quite obvious to those in the region. From
direct experience they now understood that it was normal, even
natural, for money to fluctuate in value. Time warped the value and
meaning of money, yet money changed one's experience of time.

Developed in the context of usury theory and shifting ideas about
the meaning of money, diverse versions of the censo could be
found in sixteenth-century New Spain. Until the rise of new,
shorter-term instruments in the late seventeenth and eighteenth
centuries they were the most common method of structuring formal loans in the colonial period.[51] Before turning to these later innovations in lending, I want to consider the adaptation of the censo
to the nascent colonial economy. On one hand, the quick spread of
censos in sixteenth-century New Spain demonstrated a strong local
demand for credit. On the other, it revealed how the early colonial
financial environment, with the censo at its center, limited the ability of individuals to shape their futures through credit.

The censos of New Spain functioned much like the late medieval versions described above that became common in fifteenth-
century Europe and were approved multiple times by the papacy.
Parties structured the agreement as a contract of sale in order to
bypass the church's prohibition of usury. The censuario, or purchaser of the contract, offered a sum of money to the censualista,
or seller, usually backed by a lien against a property but in some
cases through cosigning of guarantors. The purchaser then trans-
ferred a sum of money to the seller of the contract. The censualista

(contract seller or debtor) was legally obligated to make regular payments (*réditos*) to the purchaser, usually quarterly, which we might think of as interest. In New Spain the most common rate for such payments was 5 percent annually, though we have substantial evidence of much higher rates earlier in the sixteenth century. They were generally long-term instruments, held for decades or, in some cases, even centuries. While certain types of censos could be redeemed by the debtor—that is, by paying off the principal—many were perpetual, meaning the contracts and payments continued indefinitely.[52] In any case, scholars have shown that even the redeemable contracts tended to stay in effect for long periods. In sum, censos were long-term, relatively stable sources of income for creditors and one of the few types of formal credit for debtors.[53]

The credit instruments described so far often involved a transaction whereby the church served as one of the parties, and in the seventeenth century the church became the most important source of credit, a position it maintained throughout the rest of the colonial period. Although other creditors played central roles from early in the sixteenth century, even then the church's position on usury provided a framework for credit relationships.[54] Outside of church institutions, for example, middle- to large-scale merchants served as major sources and consumers of credit. As was the case for so many in New Spain, merchants' economic lifeblood pulsed with loans. A survey of the accounts of prominent merchants in Mexico City in the first half of the seventeenth century found individuals with total debts that could range from five thousand pesos to well over two hundred thousand pesos, with similar amounts extended as credit. Such financial leveraging was also common in Spain and other trade centers in the Americas. A mid-seventeenth-century document from the *consulado* of Seville reported that "the merchant more often uses credit than cash, and if he has 10,000 ducats on hand he can invest 200,000 pesos on credit."[55] While the entries on these ledgers could represent debts in kind, they often referred to transactions similar to the censos. Merchants, for example, sometimes structured loans in the form of sales contracts to avoid the appearance of usurious lending, even if the actual transactions violated the spirit of the agreement. "The contract would state the terms for such a sale," notes Louisa Hoberman, "but all that transpired was that the lender gave the borrower a sum and received a higher repayment, which included the illegal interest passed off as charges due to costs and risk."[56]

Credit also flowed informally, whether in the form of goods sold on promise of later payment, advance purchase of products, or simple loans that technically ran afoul of the church's restrictions against usury. In these transactions, as in the case of merchant credit, interest rates sometimes floated well above the 5 percent charged on most church loans and annuities. Yet even then the standards and framework established by the church provided a moral and legal reference point; we know about such cases primarily through the lawsuits or Inquisitorial investigations that challenged high rates of interest under the charge of usury.[57]

Most economic historians agree that the system of credit in sixteenth- and seventeenth-century New Spain functioned surprisingly well, yet it carried a number of important limitations. For one, New Spain lacked a formal banking system. Most authorized credit was supplied by various arms of the church, from convents to dioceses to the Holy Office of the Inquisition. These church lenders were generally risk averse. Given that usury theory placed a ceiling on credit prices, they quite rationally preferred confidence of repayment over potential return and thus favored potential creditors with strong reputations and social connections. Even when lenders were not associated with the church, as in the case of merchant creditors, they rarely acted as financial intermediaries, that is, serving as go-betweens for providers and consumers of credit. Instead, most creditors lent directly and therefore relied heavily on personal relationships or networks when judging credit worthiness.

Second, New Spain suffered from chronic shortages of currency, as did much of Spanish America.[58] There were many reasons for this long-term cash shortage in New Spain: outflows of silver bullion and minted coins to the Spanish metropole and other parts of the empire; demand for silver in China and American demand for Asian luxury products; an accumulation of cash by large-scale merchants; and an undersupply of low-value currency.[59] As a result, it was often hard to secure coinage in one of the world's biggest producers of silver coins. The scarcity of cash made debt and credit the true, if virtual, coins of the realm and fostered a culture of inventive credit

relationships, both formal and informal. As early as 1558 the shortage of currency led one Spaniard, Antonio Mateos, to call New
Spain "the most cash poor place there is," which, he continued, was
the main reason for the elaborate credit systems already in place, just
a generation after the conquest of the Aztec empire.[60] This was true
of wealthy merchants and landowners, such as those discussed above,
and also of individuals of modest means. In a legal proceeding from
late seventeenth-century Mexico City, for example, a master shoe-
maker, Salvador de Cañas, meticulously listed some thirty-seven individuals who had outstanding debts with him, most of them small
loans in the range of one to twelve pesos. Such arrangements were
common, even the norm, as Douglas Cope has demonstrated, and in
New Spain credit was truly "an integrative mechanism, [part of] the
daily process of give and take, borrow and repay, promise and fulfill,
that linked artisan to merchant, producer to consumer, and patron to
client."[61] Data from the ubiquitous censos sharpens this view from
the artisan's account books: more than 80 percent of sixteenth-
century censos were valued at less than two thousand pesos and people of lower social rank also took advantage of the censo as a source
of credit.[62] At all levels of colonial society access to credit was essential for the smooth functioning of the economy, for individual economic success and social mobility, and, quite often, simply for
survival in a world with far fewer social safety nets than our own.

Not surprisingly, given the explosion of silver production and
credit in the late sixteenth century, by the seventeenth century
money and wealth were topics of great concern in Spain and its
American possessions. We've already seen how the anxiety that accompanied the Indies question and the ongoing price revolution in
Iberia and Europe raised questions about the role money played in
human affairs. It was becoming obvious, even to poets and play-
wrights, that money was not a neutral, unchanging substance but
one that possessed a force of its own, a power that could work in
strange ways and warp human relationships and time. As a result
of the increasing prominence of money in public debates and individuals' thoughts, seventeenth-century writers on both sides of the
Spanish Atlantic used money as a source of literary material and as
a poetic device, most famously by the Spanish poet Francisco de
Quevedo in his "Poderoso Caballero es Don Dinero." Don Dinero,

as Quevedo put it, embodied the life course of new money: it was born in the Indies, matured in Spain, and put to rest in the trade and credit center of Genoa.[63]

Money figured prominently in the cultural production of seventeenth-century New Spain. In urban areas like Mexico City, the Creole elite operated in an economy that was increasingly independent of Spain, much more robust than that of the metropole, and built on credit and trade. The language of money, credit, and finance appears in the writings of Sor Juana Inés de la Cruz, New Spain's most celebrated seventeenth-century poet. In 1669, around the age of twenty, Sor Juana professed in Mexico City's convent of San Jerónimo, where she remained until her death in 1695. In addition to her well-known literary and scientific pursuits, which led to her fame on both sides of the Atlantic, she served as the convent's accountant for nearly a decade at the end of her life. This was no small task, for San Jerónimo was one of the oldest, most financially secure convents of nuns in the city, having a financial portfolio and history of contracts going back to the sixteenth century. While the records during Sor Juana's tenure as head accountant are incomplete, all surviving evidence points to the varied and complicated economic transactions that she and other administrators at San Jerónimo would have managed. Shortly before Sor Juana entered San Jerónimo, for example, we know that the convent held mortgages against nearly eighty properties in Mexico City and the countryside of central New Spain. The convent's accountants also managed a thick portfolio of rental properties in Mexico City and environs—some estimates put the number of properties at around five hundred—in addition to overseeing the accounts receivable and payable for the convent's internal operations. As was true of much of New Spain's economy, engines of credit powered San Jerónimo's economic activity, linking the cloistered convent to the outside world but also underwriting the spiritual, literary, and other activities that occurred inside it. While bodies were restricted from entering and exiting the convent, credit passed through its walls as easily as conversation drifting across the screen of a receiving parlor.[64]

Immersed in this world of loans, liens, and ledgers, Sor Juana generously sprinkled her poems with references to money and credit. In one of her many sonnets, she used the language of bookkeeping to capture the ambivalence of human hope, the way it cruelly teases us throughout the life course. Hope, she explained, balances the account of our wishes and fears.[65] Similar metaphors of credit and debt are found in her love poems and ballads, such as "Ballad 44," in which an anonymous suitor considers the limits of a gift giving using the vocabulary of debt and repayment.[66]

Although one might expect Sor Juana's literary work to use vocabulary drawn from her many other activities, whether observations of the heavens or an audit of accounts, her frequent use of financial language seems to be part of a shift in the way that some subjects in New Spain and Spanish America understood the link between money and status and even between money and one's sense of self. In this New World of money, distance from the Spanish metropole and other centers of power in Europe was not necessarily an impediment to status. By emphasizing credit practices and economic transactions that generated wealth, Sor Juana and other Creoles cultivated a new mark of distinction from the Old World and "a new form of prestige."[67] The poet as well as other subjects in New Spain considered themselves to be from the place (the Indies, and New Spain in particular) where wealth literally materialized in the form of silver coinage. This attitude was recognized in Europe as well as in the Americas. As Alina Sokol describes it, an early modern correlative property linked the Indies to silver and money. "Seen from Spain," she writes, "the Indies were treasure excavated from the mines of Potosí and Zacatecas, and insofar as this treasure was used in moneymaking, the Indies were also money."[68] Early Spanish Americans, for example, obsessively described the riches of Peru, at times linking Peru to the biblical mines of Ophir and the riches of King Solomon, as a way of promoting an emerging sense of Americanness.[69] Similarly, one's ability to harness this mineral wealth, including through the indirect reins of credit and accounting, was a way to begin distinguishing New Spain and Spanish America in general from Spain itself.

Such attitudes about finance and money might seem at odds with some of our received wisdom of colonial Mexico. Casual observers sometimes think of seventeenth-century New Spain as a place of sleepy landed estates, a rent-seeking elite, and a populace short on economic innovation. Although such perceptions of colonial Mexico have long been debunked in the historical scholarship, they float like a kind of haze over popular perceptions of Spanish America. But it is a faulty perspective, and in adopting it one can easily overlook the creativity and future orientation that characterized colonial spaces like New Spain.

Indeed, it is clear that a changed relationship to the financial future emerged in New Spain during the seventeenth and eighteenth centuries. At about the same time Sor Juana was managing the books of her convents and boldly using financial language in her poetry, economic actors of all sorts began using a form of credit that quickly replaced the censo as the dominant lending instrument.[70] Usually referred to with the rather awkward name of *depósito irregular*, this financial innovation tested the limits of usury in much more aggressive ways than the censo and its variations had. Above all, the depósito irregular expanded the world of short-term credit and made it accessible to those without landed property for collateral.[71] Given this increased flexibility in lending, the depósito raised concerns among some in the church. They argued that it violated fundamental prohibitions against usury.[72] Yet, perhaps surprisingly from our contemporary vantage, the Mexican church eventually embraced the new device both in practice and on paper: it became the most common way the church entered into credit contracts throughout the eighteenth century and until Mexico's independence from Spain in 1821.

What was this new device and where did it come from? The depósito irregular contract shared some qualities with the earlier censos but also differed from the older devices in a variety of ways. Most notably, the depósito offered credit with shorter terms and relatively flexible collateral, which opened the doors of formal credit to different groups of lenders and borrowers. In this way, the new contract contributed to a more time-sensitive credit system but was itself a reflection of a new culture of credit that was widespread throughout New Spain by the time the depósito emerged as the dominant loan type in the eighteenth century.

Though it is rather intricate, a brief look at the internal structure of this form of credit explains part of this shift. The depósito was a contract of sale, much like the censo. Upon signing a contract, the creditor (*depositante*) provided the borrower (*depositario*) with an agreed-upon sum. This "deposit" entitled the creditor to annual payments, which generally amounted to 5 percent of the principal. While similar to the traditional censo insofar as the "purchase" of the right to annual interest allowed the two parties to avoid charges of usury, the depósito irregular reflected the need of both parties to maintain more room to maneuver in their economic futures.

The depósito offered this increased flexibility in a number of ways. First, it was redeemable: the borrower could return the principal at any point and close out the loan; redemptions became a regular occurrence in the eighteenth century.[73] The early return of principal by debtors was in part a result of greater liquidity in the economy as a whole, but the depósitos also contributed to increased availability of cash and fostered a more rapid circulation of money. Second, the contracts tended to be for relatively short terms, usually ranging from two to five years, unlike the censos that often lasted for decades or even centuries. This meant that lenders could recoup their outstanding loans in a reasonable amount of time, which was vital to the merchants who began to play an increasingly prominent role as lenders in the eighteenth century. Third, the depósito was legally tied to the borrower, not to the property that served as collateral. It was a personal loan, in other words, and responsibility for repayment rested ultimately with the original borrower.[74] Finally, the depósito irregular didn't require real property as collateral. Borrowers who did not own land or buildings could secure the loan with livestock, machinery, household goods, and so on. Most intriguingly, the new loans could even be backed by claims against the prospective borrower's future income.[75] In multiple ways, then, the future and the individual figured more prominently in the very structure of these new loans. When compared to the early colonial censos, it was a future of the shorter-term and one filled with greater economic flexibility.

These qualities, including the new relationship of credit to time, led to a debate about the depósito irregular within the church in New Spain. Were such contracts legal? Did they cross the line of usury? Were they sinful? The issue came to a head when New Spain's church officials gathered to discuss doctrine, legal matters, and policy at the IV Provincial Council, held in Mexico City in 1771. This conversation was bound to occur at some point because by the middle of the eighteenth century the depósito had become the dominant credit instrument. As one writer put it, no one could deny that it was a common practice in New Spain "from time immemorial," a common phrase in colonial Spanish America that referred to something deeply embedded in local memory and customs.[76] Furthermore, the contract seemed to have a peculiarly colonial character. Some of the peninsular bishops at the council used other terms to describe the instrument. They confused it with different contracts from the European tradition or noted that they had never heard of such a device before arriving in the Indies.[77]

The council participants disagreed about the legal and theological status of the depósito irregular. Some argued that it resembled a simple loan at interest too closely. The most vocal protest came from a legal adviser to the crown, Don Antonio Joaquín de Rivadeneira, who moreover noted that the particular form of the loan was unique to New Spain. It was a "metaphysical entity," he wrote, an otherworldly device which drew on the qualities of earlier contracts but differed from them all. The result, claimed the jurist, was a "legal fairy known only in the Indies."[78] He found the colonial innovation—this legal sprite—usurious and damaging to the interests of individual borrowers, to those of the crown, and to New Spain as a whole. The contract hurt the fiscal health of the crown, he claimed, because it was not subject to the royal sales tax, or *alcabala*. At the time, the crown was in the process of squeezing additional revenues out of its overseas possessions, including by enacting more aggressive forms of taxation, and, indeed, exemption from the alcabala made the depósito irregular more appealing to colonial subjects chafing under an aggressive Bourbon fiscal policy. In this context, Rivadeneira's argument would have appealed to royal officials charged with implementing such policies and some of the Spanish bishops who supported the Bourbon program. Rivadeneira railed as well against the way loans were attached legally to a person rather than to a piece of property, which he viewed as a form of indebtedness that was particularly dangerous for the way it stalked individuals and their heirs, even long after an original investment might have soured.[79]

Though some of the bishops and other church officials agreed with the points raised by Rivadeneira, in the end the council authorized the contract. The overwhelming picture that emerges from their deliberations is that of an institutional stamp of approval for a financial device that was already approved in practice. They recognized that the depósito was a deeply rooted local practice and had become the backbone of New Spain's financial system. The bishops' decision recognized too the unusually critical place of credit in New Spain's cash-strapped colonial economy and, more generally, the role of commerce in all societies, which they called "the nerve of republics."[80] Another legal consult noted that previous authorities had defended "moderate levels of usury when it is in the interest of society or tradition."[81] In other words, he argued, it was difficult to determine whether a financial transaction was legal in the abstract. Instead, contracts, loans, and other instruments had to be interpreted in some context, whether economic or social.

The attendees at the Provincial Council situated their analysis in the context of their world, or eighteenth-century New Spain. They referred to tradition and custom to support the depósito irregular. They even leaned on the abstract concept of time itself. Their logic headed off in two directions but ultimately ended up in the same place: an argument in favor of financial adaptation and change. One path pointed toward the past: the past was a source of customs, tradition, and implied stability. The very passage of time and the sedimentation of the loan into local practice—its use from time immemorial—helped justify the approval of the depósito.[82] Not only was commerce the "nerve of republics," but, as one Creole theologian put it, without the depósito New Spain's economy would be in a most sorry state: "Commerce would be crippled; fields would lay fallow; buildings wouldn't be built."[83]

Yet their evaluation of the depósito considered a path to the future, specifically the role of time in credit operations. Participants in the debate remarked that the limited redeemability of the depósito—whereby the borrower, but not the creditor, could close out the loan before its term—offered borrowers the full use of the loaned money.[84] This meant, in another way of thinking, that they had the full use of future time, which was part of what they had purchased with their interest payments. The borrowers' (purchased) time couldn't be cut short by an early redemption call by the creditors. Lenders, on the other hand, could justify charging interest by reference to the future, by gesturing to the probability of losses during the time of the loan. This is what we would now call risk, an emerging perspective on the world during the early modern period that gauged the potential dangers of the future, whether in the case of the afterlife or the current life.[85] As these ideas arose out of New Spain's credit practices, time, which had remained technically acausal or powerless in the monetary and usury theory of the sixteenth century, was now clearly understood to be a strong force in the world. Money and time were living things, and they could be hard to tame, even ferocious. The depósito irregular reflected this new attitude toward time. It also crafted a new relationship toward the future. The future, conceived of as a place of economic risk and opportunity, began to shape the present in more forceful ways.

With the advent of the depósito irregular another form of innovation had occurred in New Spain. Drawing on some European models, it pushed the envelope of acceptable credit practices, by adapting loan contracts to the strong demand for more flexible credit in the later colonial period. The depósito irregular also drew heavily on tradition, including a transatlantic history of similar financial maneuvering, and it was regulated by principles of justice and natural law derived from Catholic theology. The legal, theological, and financial traditions that supported the depósito proved critical to its eventual embrace by authorities, including the church, which at the time played the central role as a provider and regulator of formal credit. Somewhat ironically, then, tradition was an engine of innovation.

Yet, as with many of the innovations that occurred in New Spain, these changes cannot be characterized simply as local reactions to imperial reforms or even as the outcome of changes initiated by church or civil officials in New Spain. We have to look beyond and beneath the actions of authorities. A more nimble system of credit, which altered the financial futures of many subjects in New Spain, developed out of the same sort of colonial conversations that shifted ideas about astrology and forecasting. These dialogues spanned time and place in remarkable ways, from the concerns of imperial reformers in Madrid and Seville to the debates among colonial bishops to on-the-ground arguments about economic rights and fair finance in New Spain's cities, villages, and trade fairs.

Let's listen in on one of these conversations, paying attention to the ideas that emerged by 1800 about what constituted acceptable credit and economic practices. We will travel out into New Spain's largely Indigenous countryside, where differing opinions about these issues came to a head at roughly the same time that Spanish and Spanish American authorities were discussing similar questions in the cities. The ideas and demands that drove the move toward short-term credit and adaptive financial practices could also be found in rural areas, even among economic actors that might never have been part of a church-sanctioned loan. These everyday forms of innovation could be found in agricultural market towns, in small-scale commodity transactions, even in remote hamlets. Moving away from the cities and down from the lofty debates of usury theorists and church leaders offers a different glimpse, one of an evolving economic culture in eighteenth-century New Spain. This culture understood access to credit and the ability to engage more freely in market transactions to be indispensable economic rights, yet recognized the social costs of unregulated credit markets.

Consider the investigation of trading practices that took place in 1757–58 in the Huasteca, a region in New Spain's northeast with a large Indigenous population—primarily Nahuas, Otomís, Teenek, and Pame—and a subtropical climate. By the mid-eighteenth century, sugarcane had become an important cash crop and a pillar of the regional economy.[86] Sugar was also a key link in the centuries-old chain of tribute extraction from Indigenous communities by the colonial state, one of the most onerous burdens attached to being designated Indian in Spanish America.[87]

In many ways, then, the unique and particular cultures, linguistic groups, and natural environment in the Huasteca can be thought of as one of many regional variations on an economic theme in colonial New Spain and Spanish America in general. That is, this was an economy that was primarily agricultural and exploited a small number of cash crops. Indigenous peoples and, as in some other locales, enslaved or free people of African descent provided the labor foundation, and Indian tribute remained a key source of revenue for the colonial bureaucracy.[88] All of these activities involved the

Indigenous majority and the institutions of native communities, but also engaged the casta and Spanish minorities in the region. The non-Indigenous minority included individuals in positions of authority, such as civil officials and priests as well as traders, merchants, transport specialists, and other economic actors. The region around Tampamolón fit these patterns, having a large number of Indigenous tributaries, a substantial population of African descent, and a very small number of Spanish and mestizo families.[89] Indeed, as historians of colonial Latin America have long pointed out, while on paper the "two republics" of Spanish America appeared as separate spheres of colonial society, one Indian and the other non-Indian, in reality economic demands brought them together.[90] As a result, normative ideas about economic relationships and credit resulted from dialogue, interaction, and struggles among New Spain's subjects of diverse backgrounds.

Such an intricate mixture of peoples, economic demands, and personal interests is found in the trading disputes surrounding the largely Indigenous town of Tampamolón in the mid-eighteenth-century Huasteca.[91] This case captures a common set of relationships between small-scale agricultural producers and traders in New Spain's countryside.[92] It is also notable for its rich documentation of on-the-ground ideas about lending, fair trade, and just price at precisely the moment that the church hierarchy and other authorities began to adopt a more flexible attitude regarding credit practices and usury. Given that the eighteenth-century church began to relax its regulation of usury, detailed examinations of these issues are relatively hard to find in New Spain's late colonial archives. In this context, the Tampamolón dispute offers a clear example of how the vocabulary of just price and usury could be summoned to discuss economic regulation. At the same time, colonial subjects disagreed about these concepts more than they had in previous generations. In retrospect, then, this case unfolded in a colonial twilight in which the church still acted as the key market regulator, but its visibility as a moral lodestar began to fade as competing demands for economic flexibility eroded foundational ideas in church law and theology.[93]

The episode began when the priest in Tampamolón, Don Joseph Miguel Pereli, wrote to his superiors about some trading relationships he found suspect. Local merchants, the priest wrote, lured Indians into unfair contracts. In the late summer of a typical year, he related, the middlemen offered contracts for the future delivery of sugar, usually supplied in a conical and mostly unprocessed state referred to as *piloncillos*, at three pesos per load. They secured the contracts by immediately paying the local producers in cash for a promised delivery around harvest in the first months of the following year, roughly January to April. But upon receiving delivery of the sugar, the priest explained, the merchants promptly resold it at the current market price, which was usually in the range of six to eight pesos.[94]

The priest found these practices to be usurious and unjust. They were obviously sins. In his view they robbed Indigenous farmers of a good portion of the value of their product.[95] These traders also used their contracts to exploit the cyclical crises of credit faced by small-scale farmers. When Indian sugar producers found themselves strapped for cash between harvests and perhaps in need of funds to pay the king's tribute, the local middlemen capitalized on a yearly and very predictable moment of financial desperation. They then profited handsomely by speculating on future prices and providing a type of medium-term loan with effective interest rates in the range of 200 percent to 400 percent per year, wildly in excess of the 5 percent annual interest that was charged for most authorized forms of credit in New Spain. In financial terms, the priest reported practices that clearly violated colonial notions of economic fairness and restrictions against usury. In social terms, he described vulnerable Indian communities exploited by outsiders, a narrative that resonated with countless episodes of native mistreatment in the previous centuries and one that his superiors would have heard many times before. The archdiocese in Mexico City responded quickly to the allegations, ordering an end to such agreements and forbidding traders from contracting for future delivery at a price below the typical market rate.[96]

But subsequent documents that survived as part of the dossier soon complicated the relatively straightforward portrait offered by the priest of Tampamolón. The initial complaint, a quick description of events the priest dashed off to his superiors, evolved into a lengthy case file and legal dispute that lingered for years. The priest denounced the perpetrators of these trades in general terms only—as merchants, traders, and so on—yet as the case unfolded it became clear that some behind the alleged financial wrongdoing were themselves from native communities, most prominently an Indian *cacique*, or local leader and powerholder, from the village of Tancanhuitz. While this might be a surprise from our contemporary perspective, perhaps jostling our notions of egalitarian Indigenous communities, charges of exploitation leveled against native elites were common in New Spain. Indeed, the picture of the local economy and financial relationships that emerged in this case in the Huasteca is consistent with a more nuanced understanding of intravillage stratification uncovered by historians and historical anthropologists here and elsewhere in New Spain.[97]

More intriguing than the confirmation of communal hierarchies and economic inequality, which historians have long known about, was the language of individual initiative and risk taking that the cacique used to defend the contracts he executed with sugar producers. The cacique, Don Gregorio Mendoza, who by all accounts was a relatively small-scale reseller, was unimpressed by the priest's bold claims of usury and unfair trading in the region. By making contracts for future deliveries of sugar, Mendoza argued, he and other traders effectively absorbed a great deal of risk in the local economy, offering a guaranteed price to producers, while their own returns remained uncertain. And because the contract and delivery were spread over time, he explained, traders provided essential credit to bridge the gaps of cash between harvests. The priest who denounced the practice, the cacique continued, greatly exaggerated the consistency of harvest-time prices, which could in fact vary far outside the alleged six- to eight-peso range. It was not unheard of, wrote the cacique, for January prices to fall below the price paid in the August contracts of the previous year. As a result of traders' risk taking, he concluded, the profits he and others sometimes enjoyed were completely justified and could not be characterized as usurious. And the delivery contracts were not unfair or illegal but consensual economic agreements. The archbishop's order to cease the practice of writing futures contracts was itself unjust, he concluded, robbing the *traders* of their rights to enter freely into economic relationships.[98]

Mendoza offered, we might say, an argument of economic fairness based not on economic equality but on contractual obligation,
an idea most associated in the European tradition with Thomas
Hobbes, who argued that "injustice consisteth in the violation of that
covenant, and not in the inequality of distribution."⁹⁹ Mendoza also
couched his argument in a time-honored language of risk and a medieval notion of interesse, drawn from a long tradition of Catholic
usury theory.¹⁰⁰ In so doing he used the intellectual tools of tradition
and custom to make an argument that promoted a type of economic relationship that would prevail in the nineteenth and twentieth centuries. Rather than a modern product of seventeenth- and
eighteenth-century mathematics and probability, the cacique's understanding of risk derived from older economic norms applied to a
local economic context that demanded more credit and liquidity.

Some years later, a legal representative of the "community
and natives" of three nearby Indian pueblos, Coxcatlán, Axtla, and
Tamazunchale, wrote back to the archdiocese with a different perspective: that of producers, who also demanded a return of future-
delivery contracts. The prohibition against below-market futures
contracts had ruined the sugar trade in the region, they complained,
leaving native communities utterly decapitalized, since sugar was
their only marketable crop.¹⁰¹ According to their reading of events,
small producers used futures contracts to secure credit, goods, and
cash that were otherwise unavailable in the countryside. While consistent with the general position of the local traders and creditors,
such as that of Mendoza, the response of these villagers was a voice
from the other side of the transaction: individuals and families who
received cash and credit in return for a later repayment in sugar.

As Jonathan Amith and other scholars of colonial Spanish
America have noted in slightly different contexts, "Debt for the
debtor is credit for the creditor."¹⁰² In other words, we might interpret the position of the local sugar producers in one of two ways. A
more traditional reading would find their relationship to middlemen
akin to forced debtors or even debt peonage. From this perspective,
the producers had entered into credit transactions surrounded by
asymmetries of power and capital, leading to a yearly cycle of debt
and repayment under poor terms. The documents described financial
relationships in which some individuals were able to use a position of

relative economic power to supply credit to others whose economic circumstances offered them much less leverage.[103] The result was that merchant / creditors in the late colonial period assumed an increasingly powerful role as they effectively absorbed a large amount of the economic risk and reward of the agricultural properties they financed. In some ways, in that profits or losses could largely accrue to the creditors, they, not the formal property owners, became the indirect owners of these properties.

An alternate reading, one in step with the response of the representative of the pueblos of Coxcatlán, Axtla, and Tamazunchale, reverses the terms in the equation and suggests more agency on the part of those entering into debt. This reading emphasizes the ability of small-scale producers to wrest credit from a cash-starved economy. This conclusion is consistent with Jeremy Baskes's study of credit markets under the *repartimiento de mercancías* in colonial Oaxaca, an arrangement of forced production and monopolized trading. In this system, Indigenous producers received cash or goods from Spanish officials in return for later repayment in an agricultural product, especially, in the case of Oaxaca, the brilliant red cochineal dye. Baskes describes similar cases of priestly intervention against credit practices involving their parishioners. He reads these as sincere attempts by priests to defend their parishioners, yet notes that usurious rates were the only option for credit seekers. "The implicit interest rate of *repartimiento* transactions," Baskes writes, "always exceeded 5 percent. Usury perhaps, but nobody, not even the Church, was willing to lend funds to the Indians at the rate of 5 percent. If the Church's guidelines had truly dictated the terms of commerce, then peasants would have been denied access to credit."[104] Similarly, the story of exploited debtors offered by the priest of Tampamolón was reversed by the cacique of Tancanhuitz and its native sugar producers. Theirs was a narrative of (relatively) free trade that celebrated the essential role of credit in the regional economy and described how the production of an agricultural product acted as a spigot to tap credit markets.

The two narratives are so clearly at odds with each other. Which historical voices can one trust? Both the priest and his legal adversaries were correct. In other words, it probably makes the most sense to view these economic transactions from the perspective of debtors and creditors alike. This means we have to grapple with the messy reality that agency (of credit-seeking peasants) and vicious exploitation (by traders and middlemen) were not mutually exclusive. By all accounts, the credit that was available to peasants in the Huasteca was brutally expensive in real terms but nonetheless highly sought after given the economic demands faced by small-scale producers in this region. Indeed, Ludwig Wittgenstein's remark about the conceptual boundaries of one's world being defined by language—"The limits of my language means the limits of my world"—could be applied to the question of credit and time in late colonial New Spain. The sugar traders' and producers' discussion of economic rights and freedoms offered a version of Wittgenstein's maxim set in the context of financial instruments. For better and worse, the limits of their credit meant the limits of their (economic) worlds. It was also the limit of their temporal worlds, especially their futures, since credit shaped economic horizons as much as the prospect of a bumper crop or a blighted field.

In the middle of the eighteenth century the Roman Catholic Church began to pull back from its regulation of usury. This new stance was captured in the papal encyclical *Vix pervenit*, which defined usury as a simple loan at interest. Most other contracts, such as those discussed here, would now be free of the charge of usury, so long as church authorities determined that they were not direct loans. Over coming generations the church's transition continued, and by the nineteenth century the church was almost entirely uninterested in pursuing usury cases in Mexico or elsewhere. Alongside this new attitude, after Mexican independence in 1821, Mexican civil law began to trump church laws and teachings as the key regulator of economic markets. Simple loans at interest became the main form of credit.[105]

Yet, as we've seen, the emergence of a new credit environment can't be explained simply as a story of nineteenth-century modernization, the importation of liberalism, or the dismantling of colonialism. Economic actors at all levels, including the church, had transformed the market for credit much earlier. This shift occurred over the course of the colonial period and especially during the eighteenth century.

The late colonial world of credit was by no means a modern financial system. Most important, it still had substantial barriers to entry, particularly for those with limited economic resources, and no true banks. The appearance of a banking system in Mexico, and even then a rather anemic one, had to wait until well into the nineteenth century. As a result, the important role played by contemporary financial institutions as mediators between parties was largely absent. The lack of financial intermediaries in New Spain and early Mexico meant that the world of credit, even as practiced by larger institutions, such as the various arms of the church, continued to be based on personal networks, trust, and, above all, a direct relationship between creditor and debtor. It led to transactions that involved factors far beyond what we might think of as purely market relationships, a reality obvious in the case of Indigenous producers who faced limited credit options alongside the demands of royal tribute.[106] To the extent that new, more capitalist modes of production emerged over time in New Spain, they did so in an economic system in which the pursuit of interest, in both the medieval and more recent meanings of the term, was regulated by legal and moral concepts inherited from tradition. These concepts included the notion of a just or fair price, usury as a thief of time, and risk as a moral foundation for profit.

Similar forces shaped new ideas about religious community, individual and collective improvement, and salvation that flourished in eighteenth-century New Spain. There we also find new forms of individuality combined with appeals to community. There, too, a new emphasis on individual improvement and choice melded with practices that could reproduce traditional hierarchies and asymmetries of power.

To step into that historical problem requires a step behind the closed doors of New Spain's religious brotherhoods. In the most dynamic urban networks of the eighteenth century, innovations and futuremaking occurred through the most time-proven techniques. To many eighteenth-century observers, these practices seemed hazardous and fraught with pitfalls but also productive and powerful.

CHAPTER FIVE

Prayers

I N THE WANING YEARS of the eighteenth century groups of men gathered once a week to create a macabre setting in some of Mexico City's churches. In an oratory, or chapel, they spent the afternoon meticulously preparing for a meeting with other devotees. They covered the windows with thick drapes, blocking all light from the fading day. They lit candles that gave the room a faint glow. Soon their spiritual brothers entered this dim, quiet space, leaving the bustle of the city outside. As the door closed behind them they glimpsed familiar objects through the flicker of candlelight. At the front of the room an altar supported a simple, unadorned image of Mary. In front of the altar was a low bench, from which the leader of their group, the *padre de obediencia*, directed the evening's proceedings. The padre sat behind a table that held an assortment of practical and symbolic items: the group's bylaws, papers with the night's spiritual meditations, a watch, a handbell, a font of holy water, and a skeleton. The other brothers sat on low benches placed along the chapel walls. Another bench dominated the center of the room, reserved for those men who had been selected to receive a spiritual examination later in the evening.[1] Finally, at the foot of the altar rested two more skeletons and *manojos de disciplina*, whips and bundles of switches the brothers would soon use to lash their flesh in a collective act of mortification. Out of this mix of traditional tools and techniques the brothers sought to fashion new futures. They pursued a doubled future, in fact, one that focused attention on the penultimate reality of their worldly futures and the ultimate reality of their salvation in the hereafter.

The men attending the gatherings belonged to brotherhoods known as Santas Escuelas de Cristo, or Holy Schools of Christ.[2] The Holy Schools had a long presence in New Spain, with a handful of chapters in Mexico City beginning in the first decades of the eighteenth century. The groups then expanded dramatically over the next fifty years. By 1800 Mexico City had twelve Santas Escuelas; another two could be found in the city of Querétaro, and more than a dozen in other provincial cities and towns, including Puebla, Jalapa, San Miguel el Grande, and Guanajuato.[3] Beyond their institutional history, the groups' physical practices also had precedents in New Spain, where collective devotions and penitential mortification enjoyed a long, robust history. At first blush, however, they appear to be far out of step with a religious current then flowing through the cities of the viceroyalty. In the second half of the eighteenth century members of the church hierarchy began to encourage a more austere and reflective piety, "one that elevated the virtues of self-discipline and moderation and focused on a direct, personal relationship to God."[4] Above all, this reformed piety emphasized one's individual responsibility for achieving salvation, an assumption that undermined the spiritual utility of New Spain's many collective religious practices. Some of the Spanish elite enthusiastically adopted this new religious sensibility, its theological foundations, and the practices it demanded.[5] Precisely the same population—that is, ethnic Spaniards of substantial wealth or status—dominated the Santa Escuela movement. Alongside the enlightened pretensions of reformed piety, the Santas Escuelas and their rituals stand out as curious relics of a late medieval and baroque style of religious practice, a spiritual form that disagreed with New Spain's bishops and a Spanish crown supportive of religious reform. The escuelas offered a way of navigating the world that seems to be out of keeping with the century of the Enlightenment.

This chapter delves further into practices of futuremaking in New Spain by confronting this paradox. It draws out and resolves

the conundrum of the escuelas' growth during the apogee of reformed Catholicism by considering how cultural practices evolve.
To understand the spread of the Holy School movement, we need
to attune ourselves to the sense of historical time and futuremaking
found in the spiritual practices of eighteenth-century New Spain,
much of it quite similar to that encountered in other domains.
Adopting this temporal perspective prompts a series of questions:
How did the Holy School's form of collective devotion, which included rigorous mental prayer and ritualized pain, prove to be such
an appealing tool for individual and collective transformation at a
time of reform? In moments of great cultural change, how might
we understand the relationship between the past, present, and future? Put differently, what were the sinews that bound tradition
and innovation?

I raised some of these questions in previous chapters, and the
documents left by the Santas Escuelas help to answer them. Unlike
many devotional groups and religious associations in New Spain
and other parts of colonial Latin America, whose records tend to
focus on mundane questions of management rather than spiritual
perspectives or rituals, the escuelas left rich, detailed descriptions
of their activities. These documents demonstrate how the escuelas
employed traditional practices that many considered effective and
essential religious and social resources, including collective spirituality, the paternalist education of working people, and physical piety. Such long-established practices worked synergistically with the
shifting attention to the individual. In large part, the spiritual practitioners of the eighteenth-century present embraced the past, using the tools it provided in an attempt to build a better future. For
many, this held the prospect that their lives would materially improve in the near future. For some, it offered the possibility of
group and ethnic solidarity, moral rejuvenation, and even social
control. For all, it promised a more effective path toward salvation.
Beyond an ethnographic portrait of the future, the Holy School's
documents offer a way to resolve the historical puzzle of the
groups' expansion during this moment of enlightened Catholicism.
The textual practices of the Holy Schools are themselves a key to
understanding why innovation was not at odds with tradition in
this period but in fact required it.

Perhaps the most tempting way to interpret the Holy School movement is as an example of what scholars sometimes term an alternative, or hybrid, modernity, a moment when forward-looking ideas melded with older forms of practice and social organization. The appeal of the modernity paradigm is understandable, and it has become a standard frame for interpreting the colonial experience in Latin America and elsewhere.[6] It affords a tidy explanation for the popularity and growth of the escuelas, charting the development of a third way between a baroque, collective Catholicism of the past and an enlightened, individualized piety of the future. In this scheme, the arrow of historical causation would fly from future-oriented ideas (the reformed piety) to their future-oriented implications (especially a more vigorous focus on the individual) via an unlikely detour through the past-oriented practices of collective Catholicism (with all of its extravagant trappings). In the end, it would anoint the members of the Santas Escuelas and their backers as colonial moderns since their unique blending of religious thought and practice was prescient and somehow ahead of its time, the precocious moderns discussed earlier. As historical subjects they attract our attention because they have qualities that remind us of ourselves despite their other antique characteristics.

But we should be wary. Such an interpretive framework obscures more than it reveals, most importantly because it fails to capture how these historical actors understood the relationship between past, present, and future. In the introduction I described how Reinhart Koselleck, along with many other theorists of time experience, defined modernity as the moment when the present breaks decisively with the past. That is, as a moment when the past loses its relevance as a guide to the future, and historical actors develop a unique sense of self in relation to time. They understand themselves and their world to be truly different from the past.[7] The past might be known in a general sense, but it is also strange, unfamiliar, and of little use. It is history.

Yet the example of the escuela movement, along with the case studies throughout this book, suggest other modes of historical transformation. In these examples, the relationship between past, present, and future was quite different. Tradition was understood by eighteenth-century Mexicans to be an instrument, even a requirement, of change and innovation. Tradition meant more and different things to them than it does to us. Granted, it could be thought of as a kind of motionless object, an inert thing, a simple reference to previous times. But tradition was also understood as an implement or device, a resource for creating new things, similar to the inventive role of memory in the practice of confession or the way "time immemorial" could be used to justify innovative financial practices.[8]

We need to redirect the causal arrow in this history because the practices and ideas that allowed the escuelas to adapt to new contexts also ensured their long-term reproduction. The vector of change and futuremaking, in other words, moved outward from the same point that fostered stability and continuity, a historical dynamic sometimes overlooked in favor of conspicuous changes that punctuate the historical record. As David Sabean pointed out in his study of German peasant communities, "reproduction is also a process and as much subject to historical effort as any other process."[9] In many moments of cultural transformation as well as of reproduction and persistence the modernity paradigms do little to help us understand how these factors could relate to one another.

How, then, should we explain the relationship between tradition and innovation? In the case of the Holy Schools and the intensive documentation of their members' religious lives, we might first keep in mind Philippe Buc's reflections on the mediated nature of medieval ritual in Europe. "Studies of political ritual," Buc warns, "probably trust the letter of medieval documents more than method warrants, ... for challenges and manipulations happen in texts, and, in some political cultures at least, it may be ritual-in-text rather than ritual-in-performance that best legitimizes or delegitimizes."[10] Buc not only alerts us to the heavy textual mediation between the historian as observer and the actual medieval events, but also, more importantly, suggests that we consider the descriptions of those events to be rituals themselves: rituals in writing, not just documentation of their activities. Indeed, the relatively large, diverse body of documents left by the Santas Escuelas provides not just a historian's view of their activities—and, as Buc notes, we should be wary of possible discrepancies between the described and actual performance of those rituals—but also, qua documents, part of the explanation for the type of innovation that occurred in New Spain. The ties that linked old and new religious forms were texts (devotional manuals, petitions to church and civil authorities, official approvals, and so on) that authorized and placed boundaries around orthodox and traditional forms of piety, the rituals those texts described, and the array of practices surrounding the rituals.

But we need to modify Buc's phrase slightly in this case. While his "rituals-in-text" referred to the subtle changes in various accounts of medieval rituals, the Holy Schools engaged in rituals-*of*-text, rarely changing the descriptions of their devotions but marshaling and supplementing those textual resources with their own writings as they communicated with church and civil officials.[11] These were textual performances of tradition. In fact, it would have been almost unthinkable for the supporters of the Holy Schools to have modified the descriptions of their devotional activities, which would be one of Buc's rituals-in-text, since they trumpeted adherence to previous models as one of the movement's finest qualities. Instead, the Holy Schools' rituals-of-text demanded the faithful reproduction of bylaws and devotional manuals in almost unaltered form, a kind of textual genuflection to stability and order. This was one sense of tradition, and probably the meaning most familiar to us. But their rituals-of-text also required an elaborate process of petitioning and reporting to authorities. In these latter documents, which amounted to a paratext alongside the formal religious writings and statutes, the promoters of the Holy School movement used commentary to adapt the apparently stable practices of the group to current conditions. They attached fresh meanings to long-established activities and demonstrated the relevance of those practices with regard to contemporary challenges. They allowed individuals and groups to imagine and pursue new ways of being in the world while simultaneously preparing for the next world. This was the more expansive meaning of tradition—as tool and creative resource—and it can seem odd from our contemporary vantage now that the term has withered into a more limited constellation of meanings (set, fixed, conventional, orthodox, and so on). In turn, the traditions and rituals-of-text in the Santas Escuelas fostered feelings of spiritual efficacy and comfort that

*Figure 7. An image of Christ crucified found in a small guidebook used by religious sodalities in New Spain known as Santas Escuelas de Cristo, or Holy Schools of Christ. (*Cartilla breve de los rudimentos mas necesarios que debe observar el discípulo de Christo, Nuestro Señor y Maestro . . ., *x F1207.C191. Courtesy of the Bancroft Library, University of California, Berkeley.)*

proved adaptable to new contexts, both for their practitioners and for the authorities who supported them.

As in our world, hierarchies abounded in New Spain, and some colonial subjects had more opportunities to control and manipulate such textual resources than others. It is no coincidence that Spaniards led New Spain's escuela movement, in a society that was characterized by great social diversity and inequality. The Holy

Schools were almost exclusively male, and their membership was mostly ethnic Spaniards. Spanish members were both Creoles and immigrants from Spain itself, sometimes referred to as *peninsulares* in New Spain. Spanish laborers and artisans formed a large part of the escuelas' membership, although Spaniards of relatively high status, wealth, and occupational prestige controlled the positions of leadership.[12] Such ethnic exclusivity may have been an attempt to foster Spanish solidarity at a time when some Spaniards were concerned about the blurring of social boundaries.[13] In contrast, a smaller number of escuelas admitted non-Spanish members, as many of the groups began to espouse an ethos of worldly improvement alongside their spiritual mission. The leaders of these escuelas described their project as one of spiritual and moral uplift, in which non-Spaniards and working people in general would benefit from membership, but always under the careful watch and tutelage of the Spanish elite, who controlled the cultural assets and capital of these sodalities. These unique chapters developed under the umbrella of the same institute by deploying and adapting textual resources—both those of the movement itself (its history, statutes, and devotional tracts) and the paratexts written for each escuela.

The first clue to the significance of these textual resources is that the expansion of the Santas Escuelas in the cities and towns of New Spain occurred during the second half of the eighteenth century, at the high point of the so-called Bourbon Reforms. During this period the Bourbon monarchy that controlled the Spanish empire attempted to create a new relationship with its overseas possessions, with more political control exercised by the royal bureaucracy and peninsular Spaniards (rather than Spanish Creoles or other locals) and more resources flowing to the metropole in the form of trade, tribute, and taxation. It also sought to reduce or eliminate what it deemed to be waste or inefficiency, whether in the government or beyond. As part of this broader effort, the crown, eager to rationalize, streamline, and subordinate the Roman Catholic Church to its will, discouraged the founding of new religious institutions in its possessions, including New Spain. This policy supported both the political and the economic goals of the crown. Politically, the monarchy sought to strengthen the royal bureaucracy relative to the church, including both the church's local functionaries and its hierarchy. Economically, the crown wanted to limit the capital and productive resources under the control of religious institutions of all sorts, both those held by the church and those that operated independently. Economic theorists and advisers to the crown had argued that such arrangements impeded the free flow of capital and ultimately retarded the empire's productivity.[14]

The crown's reforms focused as well on particular devotions and celebrations it considered unproductive. On this front, the royal bureaucracy received the enthusiastic backing of the secular church hierarchy, especially a number of Spanish-born bishops and archbishops. These included Francisco Antonio de Lorenzana, the archbishop of Mexico from 1766 to 1772 and one of the leaders of the IV Provincial Council that debated and approved the *depósito irregular*. Lorenzana, other bishops, and church officials sought to rein in what they considered the excesses of popular piety in New Spain, which could range from extravagant funeral processions to elaborate celebrations in honor of a village patron saint to aggressive public flagellation. The bishops thought that many popular religious practices were misguided, dangerous, and unproductive, both spiritually and materially. Spiritually, the bishops were worried that the religion of the street and the village focused too much on externalities such as physicality, sensory experience, and the collective and not enough on the internal, including silent prayer, contemplation, and the individual. What's more, materially they wasted money and time that could be used for other, more productive purposes.[15]

For these reasons the reformist clergymen looked suspiciously at collective religion as practiced by New Spain's laity, which reached particularly high expression in the populous neighborhoods and crowded streets of cities. In their minds, not only were these externally oriented practices ineffective for devotees, but their public performance exposed others to the contagion of religious error. We should read such diagnoses with care, of course, since those promoting reform might have found it useful to label popular practices excessive, disorderly, or scandalous in service of a broader program of social control.[16] In any case, the interests of church and civil officials dovetailed in this moment of reform. For theological reasons the bishops wanted to limit and reform collective devotions because they deemed them spiritually misguided. For political and economic reasons the crown wanted to direct resources away from religious activities. In practical terms, the two pillars of the empire—the so-called *dos majestades* of crown and clergy—found a common enemy: traditional forms of group piety.[17]

It is against this historical and historiographical backdrop that the Santas Escuelas of the late eighteenth century appear so unusual. At the same time the crown and church began to attack many aspects of collective piety, especially religious sodalities, they left untouched the existing Santas Escuelas and enthusiastically endorsed the expansion of the institution in Mexico City and other urban areas. And while reformist bishops wrote eloquent, impassioned pastoral letters advocating a more individualized, interior, and less physical form of Catholic practice, they also approved new Santas Escuelas, groups that considered self-mortification an essential part of a collective quest for salvation.[18] More surprising still, wealthy and politically powerful Spaniards, that slice of New Spanish society that most embraced the new piety, formed the Santas Escuelas' leadership. On a number of levels, then, the escuelas seem to buck the historical trends in late colonial life.

But did they? The paradox of the reformist bishops' backing of the Santas Escuelas can be resolved by paying close attention to the groups' ritual practices and, in addition, to the texts that described those rituals. Intrinsically, the public and collective performance of ritual did not concern the church hierarchy. After all, the foundational practice of Catholicism, the Mass, was a shared, publicly accessible moment. Instead, they argued that much of New Spain's collective religion was tainted by the profane and misused by its practitioners. When committed in the street or plaza, religious abuses and excesses became public and might be absorbed by the rest of the faithful. On the other hand, a well-orchestrated procession or public devotion could offer enormous spiritual benefits, as these same bishops noted again and again.[19] Even mortification and pain might have a place at the table of religious renewal, the bishops held, so long as they could be closely regulated and their power could be directed toward unambiguous and legitimate goals.[20]

In this context, the Santas Escuelas' appeal, to both the authorities who approved them and the individuals who joined them, derived not only from their contemporary relevance but also from their mature roots. Santas Escuelas fused the piety advocated by reformers, including a reflective and interior sensibility that demanded greater individual propriety, with traditional practices, especially those that tapped the power of the Catholic liturgy and paraliturgical practices and that continued to form the bedrock of worship in New Spain.[21] By combining the established with the emerging, and the power of the collective with a focus on the individual, the Santas Escuelas were an ideal vehicle for a project of spiritual and social renewal at a time when civil and ecclesiastical reforms undermined and weakened other religious institutions.

By the second half of the eighteenth century, when the loose bundle of religious reforms reached their peak in the Spanish crown's American territories, Santas Escuelas had existed for a century in Spain itself. An Italian priest, Juan Bautista Ferruzo, and a group of prominent Spaniards formed the first Escuela de Cristo, as the establishment was called, in Madrid in 1653. Since 1646 the group had been practicing their devotional and spiritual exercises under the guidance of Ferruzo in the Hospital de los Italianos, which he managed. Ferruzo wrote the escuela's bylaws, which would later be redacted and expanded by Juan de Palafox y Mendoza, an important leader in New Spain's seventeenth-century church, upon his return to Spain as the bishop of Osma. In 1665 the revised statutes received papal approval in Alexander VII's brief *Ad pastoralis dignitatis fastigium*, beginning Rome's long-term support of the escuelas and their expansion throughout Spain.[22]

The Spanish escuelas' rituals and piety were copiously documented and enjoyed royal and papal approval, and they therefore constituted an institutional and textual foundation that fostered the groups' spread to New Spain during the eighteenth century. New Spain's escuelas used the bylaws of the Holy School founded in the Spanish city of Cádiz and reprinted them as needed throughout the eighteenth and early nineteenth centuries, a ritual-of-text required for the founding of new chapters. They also reprinted a number of devotional manuals used by the early Spanish escuelas. The initial establishments in New Spain were started before the crown and church had begun their most aggressive reforms of religious life. Devotees founded the first of Mexico City's Holy Schools in the Convento de La Merced in 1721 and another three in the city by

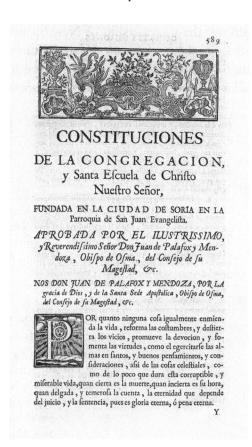

*Figure 8. Title page of the Holy School bylaws revised in the mid-seventeenth century by Juan de Palafox y Mendoza. (*Obras del ilustrissimo, excelentissimo, y venerable siervo de Dios, don Juan de Palafox y Mendoza . . . arzobispo electo de Megico, virrey, y capitan general de Nueva-España . . ., f F1207.P2.1762, v.6. *Courtesy of the Bancroft Library, University of California, Berkeley.)*

1740, along with one in San Miguel el Grande, in the Bajío region.[23] Between 1740 and 1810, however, priests and laymen established another eight in the capital and at least eighteen in other provincial cities and towns; this was the very period in which church and crown officials began to question the utility of some forms of collective devotion, and Spaniards, both Creoles and peninsulares, seem to have backed away from other religious sodalities.[24] In contrast, both the number and the membership of New Spain's escuelas increased substantially in the final decades of the eighteenth century.[25] By the beginning of Mexico's war of independence in 1810, more than thirty escuelas had received royal and church approval.

Table 2. Santas Escuelas in New Spain

City/Town	Escuela
Founded between 1720 and 1740	
Mexico City	Convent of La Merced
	Convent of San Francisco
	Convent of Espíritu Santo
	Convent of Santo Domingo
San Miguel el Grande	
Founded between 1740 and 1810	
Mexico City	Colegio de San Pedro
	Hospital Real de Indios
	Convent of San Agustín
	Parish of San Sebastián
	Hospital of Jesús Nazareno
	Parish of Santa Cruz y Soledad
	Parish of Santa Veracruz
	Parish of Santa María la Redonda
Querétaro	Hospicio de la Merced
	Convent of San Francisco
San Jerónimo de Coatepec	
Puebla	
Guanajuato	
Jalapa	
Veracruz	
Zacatecas	
León	
San Luis de la Paz	
Dolores	
Aguascalientes	
Irapuato	
Chamacuero	
Silao	
Toluca	
Sultepec	
Villa de Guadalupe	

Thus one cannot link the initial appearance of New Spain's escuelas to the period of reform, as these groups and their rituals were traditions (established, orthodox, fixed) by the eighteenth century. Instead, the previous history and printed resources of the escuelas help resolve the paradox of the church's support of them as they expanded in the second half of the century. To return to Buc's notion of ritual-in-text and the Holy Schools' rituals-of-text, authorities sanctioned not only the actual piety of the movement but also the way in which such piety was described and the very fact that it was described in text. When the Holy Schools and their champions advertised scrupulous adherence to preexisting rituals and faithfully reproduced devotional texts, they helped the groups to spread and, in addition, carved out a space for them to adapt to changing external conditions. This was the second meaning of tradition (protected space, resource, creative instrument). Tradition, in other words, provided the foundation for a moment of aggressive innovation, a model of adaptation in step with the financial and predictive futuremaking found in previous chapters.

What was that tradition? Why did it prove so adaptable in the dynamic eighteenth century of New Spain? The members of the Santas Escuelas practiced spiritual exercises based roughly on those developed by Saint Philip Neri (in Spanish, San Felipe Neri, 1515–95), the Oratorian movement he spawned in Italy, and its associated Brotherhood of the Little Oratory. The Oratorian movement emphasized collective reflection and discussion of spiritual questions and scripture, along with frequent confession and participation in the Mass. Ferruzo, an Oratorian, brought these practices to Madrid, where Spaniards adopted them enthusiastically. The connection between the Oratorian movement, which limited its members to secular priests, and the Santas Escuelas remained strong in Spain and New Spain. Like Ferruzo, the founding priests of the Santas Escuelas often had an Oratorian connection. Luis Felipe Neri de Alfaro, who established what would become New Spain's most important spiritual retreat house at Atotonilco along with Santas Escuelas throughout the Mexican Bajío, was originally a member of the Oratorian community in the nearby town of San Miguel el Grande. An important difference between the two groups, however, was that the escuelas reached out to nonclerics and sought to improve both their

spiritual and material lives. Alfaro, for one, ardently promoted the escuelas among the laymen of the Bajío and used the sanctuary at
Atotonilco to recruit potential members.[26] The church hierarchy and
crown praised the Holy Schools' attention to the broader community. "Experience teaches [us]," wrote one bishop's adviser, "that with
this most pious devotion—progeny of the towering presence of San
Felipe Neri—many laymen will refine their behavior, others will develop their spirituality, and all will occupy themselves with the holy
practices of prayer and reading during those most crucial hours in
the early evening."[27]

The statutes of the Santas Escuelas stipulated a membership
of no more than twenty-four priests and forty-eight laymen, or a
total of seventy-two brothers, a number that evoked the original
Disciples of Christ.[28] Capping the size of the group at seventy-two
was also meant to ensure that the relationships within the brotherhood remained intimate and united by spiritual practices. In so doing, the escuelas self-consciously distanced themselves from other
sodalities that they considered religious communities in name only,
groups whose worldly activities and investments could easily out-
shine the devotional commitments of their members. In contrast,
the members of Santas Escuelas dedicated themselves to a rigorous, individually tailored spiritual quest, but one that was supported by a community of fellow sojourners. The handbook of one
escuela declared, "The purpose of this Escuela is to aspire to and
take spiritual advantage of the will, precepts, and guidance of God:
each [member] walking toward perfection according to his own
position and obligations, reforming [his] life, [offering] penitence
and contrition for sins, purifying [his] conscience, praying, fre-
quenting the sacraments, [and performing] works of charity and
holiness, which are taught and practiced in the Escuela. With great
esteem for the eternal and contempt for the things of this world,
each [brother is] searching for the most secure and narrow path to
save himself, a path appropriate to his state in life. *Arcta via est,
quae ducit ad vitam: Intrate per angustam portam* [Narrow is the way
that leads to life: Enter through the narrow gate]."[29] The escuelas'
second bylaw ordered the brothers to treat one another with "love,
equality, and fraternal charity." "The Disciples of the Santa Escuela
de Christo are Brothers," the bylaw continued, "[and] this union

and charity [and] the nature of the exercises ... precludes a large membership."[30] Such intimacy, concurred officials in the bishopric of Michoacán, leads to a kind of self-reflection or "knowledge of oneself," but at the same time it "preserves those ties of mutual affection that should bond the faithful to one another."[31]

The statutes limited the escuelas to seventy-two members, but because of the popularity of the groups in the late eighteenth century, the number of brothers varied from approximately fifty to nearly two hundred.[32] Even when their memberships grew large, the escuelas maintained a strict program of spirituality that melded individual and collective piety. Each escuela met once a week to conduct its core practice, a set of spiritual exercises that consisted of prayer, sermons, and a version of public religious examination known informally as the *banquillo*. It also included collective self-mortification, or *disciplina*, the lashing of the flesh described in the groups' bylaws and other documents. The weekly meetings served as the "mystical workshop," as one member put it, where the escuelas forged their unique product of individual transformation through collective spiritual labor.[33] According to a brother in the escuela of Espíritu Santo in Mexico City, the Santas Escuelas could be easily distinguished from other religious sodalities. Whereas other devotional groups and sodalities engaged in the simple performance of religious rituals, the escuelas employed a set of techniques that imprinted Christian virtues on the minds of their members, reformed their comportment in the world, and ultimately spread virtuous behaviors throughout the rest of society.[34] In practice, this regimen meant not only that the escuelas asked their members to reflect on Christian maxims and to carry out good works in between weekly meetings, but also that they closely monitored the progress of individual members in fulfilling their duties, obligations, and practices. Theirs was a model of aggressive self-transformation consistent with the more intense form of confessional practice found in the eighteenth century.[35]

Contemporaries often praised the supposed equality of the escuelas, especially given the disparities of wealth and status within each group's membership. A chronicler of the Franciscan Order in New Spain, Diego Ossorio, celebrated the spirit of fraternity among the Santas Escuelas' burgeoning ranks, comparing them to the original Disciples on Pentecost, who were gathered in a moment of spiritual communion. The brothers of the Santas Escuelas, the friar preached, were also "disciples without difference, all equal without exception, as much the learned as the uneducated, as much the cleric as the layman, as much the rich man as the poor, all humble, all equal."[36] Such rhetoric masked the clear hierarchies within the groups as well as a marked paternalism and tutelage on the part of some escuela leaders toward their fellow brothers. Yet Ossorio's language spoke clearly to the ethos of individual improvement that pervaded the eighteenth-century escuela movement and to the time-proven techniques of communal spirituality that he and many others considered the most speedy and direct path to achieving spiritual and material progress.

On two points the Santas Escuelas' main practices seemed to clash with the tastes and sensibilities of the civil and church reformers. Reformers advocated a piety that exalted individual responsibility for spiritual health and questioned the effectiveness of external forms of worship, especially the physical senses, as a safe road for one's spiritual journey. The religious examination (banquillo), penitential scourging, and an activity known as the *exercicio de la muerte*, in contrast, emphasized a collective project of salvation and used physical piety to help achieve this goal. These practices, however, did not so much reject the individual and interior spirituality of the reformers as approach these goals through traditional methods. The physicality of the escuelas' piety was precisely a means to focus spiritual attention inward and, in a temporal sense, toward the future of worldly improvement and salvation, similar to the goals of confessional practices. One of the escuelas' most important devotional tracts, Francisco Espinosa y Rosal's *Despertador de la vida espiritual*, fashioned itself as a kind of spiritual awakening, as did many of the escuelas' preferred texts. Rosal's *Despertador* described physicality as a more efficient way to reach the divine. Since "the soul is bound to our physical bodies," it noted, "one can more easily grasp the material than the spiritual."[37] As a result, why wouldn't one use the body to reform the soul? Similarly, the devotees in the escuelas expected that collective practices would activate the spiritual and worldly potential of the individual, forming part of the "narrow path" to salvation referred to in another of the handbooks.[38] Such projects meshed with the re-formist goals of both the crown and church officials, since the Santas Escuelas sought to fashion nothing less than *hombres nuevos*, or new men, who would be more productive children of God and vassals of the crown.[39]

The escuelas of eighteenth-century New Spain thus enjoyed the full backing of church and civil reformers alike. Reformist authorities wanted a more rational, streamlined, and efficient Catholicism that they felt would improve the spiritual quest of New Spain's faithful as well as the economic productivity of the colony. Yet there was not a direct correlation between the arrival of this reformist spirit in New Spain and the emergence of the escuelas, because the institute had deep roots in Spain and New Spain and even reached back to the founding of the Oratorian movement in the sixteenth century. The reform currents did not create the eighteenth-century escuela movement, in other words, but energized it and repurposed it to new ends. A more accurate metaphor would be to think of these institutions, practices, and texts in an ongoing process of re-production and occasional renewal, much like the evolving financial instruments described in the previous chapter. The hombres nuevos whom authorities praised were not considered new or novel in our contemporary meaning of the words; they were individuals who had undergone a kind of spiritual rejuvenation, even a molting, working toward an improved, different future based in part on a return to an earlier, more pristine state.[40]

Consider the banquillo ritual, which the brothers deemed the foundational practice of the escuelas and the best tool to achieve spiritual renewal. The banquillo was a *confesión pública*, but a confession that was strictly limited to the obligations required by the escuela. It was meant to be a tightly controlled examination of conscience, not a rambling stream of thoughts, in much the same way the eighteenth-century priests described in chapter 2 wanted to control confession and the sacrament of penance. At the weekly meeting, the padre de obediencia ordered three brothers to approach the bench at the center of the oratory. The padre then selected one of the three to examine the other two. The examiner carefully questioned his fellow devotees to see whether they had completed the spiritual exercises and other responsibilities assigned

by the escuela in the previous week. The examined brothers also described their personal reaction to the week's spiritual meditation.
The banquillo was "the essential practice of the Santa Escuela,"
wrote one padre de obediencia. Without this activity, "our congregation would be no different from any other in which the faithful
complete spiritual exercises."[41] The brothers found the banquillo effective specifically because it forced the public confession of spiritual
failings. While we have no records of one of the actual interroga-
tions, most descriptions of the ritual described an intense experience
that evoked the strongest of emotions, from pride to embarrassment
to humiliation. They also suggest a kind of familiarity and intimacy
that made possible the project of renewal, which was an ongoing
process, a problem of persistence more than a one-time occurrence.[42] As another brother put it, "Because [the banquillo] humbles
the examined and the examiners, and suppresses our arrogance and
love of self—shaming us if we err in front of our brothers—it assails
man's animal instinct, but not his faculties of reason."[43]

At the end of the ritual the padre de obediencia gave each examined brother spiritual guidance and an act of penance. Once that
was completed, the members of the escuela reinforced the lessons
of the banquillo with a period of collective disciplina, snuffing all
the candles in the room and whipping themselves repeatedly while
chanting the Psalms, the Act of Contrition, and other prayers.[44]
Although it was a communal practice, the darkness turned the disciplina and prayer into acts that were more private than the rest of
the ceremony. In fact, much of what contemporaries found unique
and worthy of praise in the escuela movement was this productive
tension between not only the mental and the physical but also the
private and public and the individual and collective.

Like the banquillo confession, the exercicio de la muerte
formed part of the brothers' collective labor for individual salvation. Preparation for death and the afterlife consumed much of the
escuelas' energy. The bylaws warned the brothers of the impossi-
bility of predicting the moment of one's death and therefore the
importance of being prepared for one's inevitable and potentially
unexpected passing. The exercicio de la muerte was a method of
doing so. On a cyclical and ongoing basis, the exercicio divided the
brothers into three cohorts based on their seniority in the escuela.

Every four months—that is, once a year per member—the brothers of a cohort prepared methodically and completely for their
deaths. They performed a general confession, ensured that their
wills and testaments were in order, completed additional meditations on death and mortality, and offered prayers and indulgences
for their own souls and those of the fallen. The four-month exercise culminated with the celebration of a requiem Mass for their
dead brothers, a solemn nod to the past as they contemplated their
own fates.[45] Such attention to mortality was a classic feature of baroque piety. The founder of the escuelas in New Spain's Bajío region, Alfaro, famously slept in a coffin to keep his eventual fate
ever present, supposedly wearing out three of the *chalupas* in the
process.[46] The goal, as Alfaro and others understood it, was to focus intensely on the future, eternity, and the possibility of salvation
or damnation. This extreme orientation toward the future was
meant to guide one's thoughts and actions in the present.

Alongside their physical piety and their mental projection into
the future, the Santas Escuelas of New Spain engaged in practices
that highlighted their members' interior and individual religious
experiences. As a starting point, the escuelas physically distanced
themselves from the exuberant, sometimes raucous religious practices that took place in the streets and plazas of New Spain's cities.
They strictly forbade celebrations or any other public practices not
prescribed in their statutes. "At no time should the brothers perform celebrations outside, no matter what they are," one statute ordered, "because this Escuela is more interior and withdrawn, and
its principal practices are exercises of mortification and penitence."[47] By limiting the collective practices of the group to the interior space of the escuela, the groups sought to create an
insuperable border between their carefully controlled and heavily
supervised spiritual exercises and what they and the church hierarchy perceived to be the more anarchic religion of the street, where
the sacred and the profane mixed carelessly. Escuelas occasionally
took part in processions, and thus we know that there was some
slippage between their actual rituals and their rituals-of-text, but
church authorities and escuela leaders carefully orchestrated and
supervised such activities. In perhaps the only visual representations of an escuela taking part in a public event in New Spain, the

brothers processed without typical *penitente* garb.[48] Whereas most early modern penitential confraternities wore clothing and hoods that completely masked the members' individual identities, the brothers of the escuelas left their faces uncovered. Their self-presentation could be interpreted as part of the escuelas' emphasis on individual propriety and responsibility but also as part of their didactic mission in that it presented them to their communities as recognizable models of piety.[49]

Once enclosed within the walls of the escuelas, the brothers used specific forms of prayer to bring their spiritual energies further "inside." Thirty minutes of mental, or silent, prayer facilitated the inward journey. Mental prayer consisted of a meditation on specific religious lessons, a technique praised by reformist church leaders. During this period of silence the brothers reflected on a specific doctrine or virtue by silently reciting a *jaculatoria*, a short verse meant to imprint the spiritual lesson for the week through repetition, usually drawn from their small devotional texts.[50] Though these techniques were advocated by many of New Spain's church leaders in the late eighteenth century, the methods of *oración mental* required careful control and supervision. In previous generations church authorities had sometimes linked mental prayer with spiritual excesses. Most notably, silent prayer was implicated in the *alumbrado* heresy in sixteenth-century Spain, in which laypersons sought a direct, quiet relationship with God, and later in the case of Francisco Davi, a Jesuit in Mexico City accused by the Inquisition in the late seventeenth century of administering the Ignatian Spiritual Exercises to "all classes of people," whether women or the poor, without sufficient supervision and preparation.[51] Via the practice of silent prayer the Holy Schools offered a framework through which a broader swath of the population might take advantage of the power of meditation and the turn inward.

Such subdued and refined piety did not replace the physical mortification that followed later in the evening, but complemented it. The prayer that opened the weekly meetings reminded the brothers of the close connection between mental focus and physical suffering, which were both tools to improve their behavior and self-control. "Mental prayer is one of the absolutely essential exercises of this Escuela," it explained, "through which the [escuela]

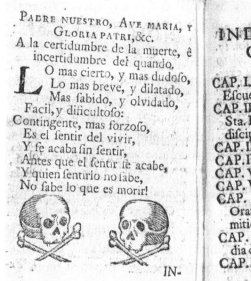

PADRE NUESTRO, AVE MARIA, Y
GLORIA PATRI,&c.
A la certidumbre de la muerte, è
incertidumbre del quando.

LO mas cierto, y mas dudoso,
Lo mas breve, y dilatado,
Mas sabido, y olvidado,
Facil, y dificultoso:
Contingente, mas forzoso,
Es el sentir del vivir,
Y se acaba sin sentir,
Antes que el sentir se acabe,
Y quien sentirlo no sabe,
No sabe lo que es morir!

IN-

INDICE DE LOS
CAPITULOS.

CAP. I. Del fin, è instituto de esta
Escuela.   fol. 1.
CAP. II. Del divino Maestro de esta
Sta. Escuela, y sus mas indignos
discipulos.   fol. 1.
CAP. III. Del Obediencia,   fol 3.
CAP. IV. De los Diputados. fol. 5.
CAP. V. Del Secretario   fol. 5.
CAP. VI. De los Nuncios.   fol. 7.
CAP. VII. De la disposicion del
Oratorio, y los que han de ser ad-
mitidos à èl.   fol. 8.
CAP. VIII. De los exercicios del
dia de la Escuela.   fol. 9.
CAP. IX. De los dias de Comunion
ge-

Figure 9. A jaculatoria, *or short prayer, on death and mortality. Holy School members were meant to recite such verses throughout the day. The goal was to keep as constant companions the ultimate futures: death and the afterlife.* (Constituciones de la Congregación, y Escuela de Christo, fundada debajo del patrocinio de la SS . . ., t F1207.C1908 x. *Courtesy of the Bancroft Library, University of California, Berkeley.*)

wishes to stamp the tender memory of the Passion and Death of its Divine Teacher on the souls of the Disciples."[52] A devotional manual from the period stated the matter bluntly. Quoting Saint Albert, it reminded its readers that "a simple meditation on the Passion is more important than to fast with bread and water every Friday for a year, to perform disciplina until [one's] blood spills, or to pray the Psalter every day."[53] In other words, the primary goal of self-mortification was spiritual education—the transformation of the self and soul—not the atonement of sins. The brothers of the escuelas thus considered the body and pain effective tools, but they were means to an end: they helped focus the mind on the abstract mysteries of the faith and in so doing reformed individual behavior.

In this respect the Holy Schools' disciplina differed from the mortification employed by early modern ascetics and mystics. Sixteenth-century Spanish mystics, such as John of the Cross and Teresa of Ávila, attempted to retreat deeply into the self to escape the mental distractions of the world. Self-inflicted pain, as they understood it, was useful because it could not be communicated to other living things. It muted the din of the external world and hence advanced one's inward journey. John of the Cross, for instance, held that "the soul must strip and void itself of all forms and kinds of knowledge . . . remaining naked and barren, as if these forms had never entered."[54] The utter and complete embodiedness of pain thus closed a mundane dialogue with one's fellow humans but opened a sacred, transcendent conversation with God. Ultimately, these mystics attempted nothing less than to destroy the worldly self.[55] In contrast, the escuelas valued ritual mortification and pain because they fostered worldly communication and therefore helped to build a community of practice and belief. For the escuelas, mortification and its resulting pain were not a retreat into the self but a way to generate empathy with Christ *and* their brethren.[56] It was a pedagogy of the body that drew upon an established religious tool, using it to create a worldly community and a future that included both spiritual and mundane concerns.[57]

Perhaps the most striking way the Santas Escuelas sought to achieve a more refined spiritual state through traditional practices was by publicly examining their members' spiritual activities. The leadership of each Santa Escuela named *celadores*, for example, who were required to report "whether they knew of any serious, or potentially serious, fault on the part of a brother."[58] Through the banquillo ritual and dedicated celadores, the brothers made their interior lives public, placing them within the purview of the collective. Semipublic rituals, which put individual faith under the scrutiny of a community and attempted to reform it collectively, reinforced the need for individual care of one's spiritual health.[59] They also undermined the groups' stated desire to keep the outside world at a distance. The confessions and monitoring by celadores threw open the doors of the escuelas and brought the exterior world into the brothers' interior spiritual practice. In this way the ritual foregrounded the melding of the public / private and

COMPENDIO DE LAS
obligàciones del Discípulo de
la Santa Escuela, segun la
Constitucion XIV.

Solo á Dios acudir en despertando,
Aplicar á su culto el mejor tiempo,
Zo dexar la Oracion por ningun modo,
Todos los dias oir Misa muy atento,
Acompañar á Dios Sacramentado,
En su presencia siempte con respetó,
Saber y repetir Jaculatoria,
Con la leccion espiritual desvelo,
Csar en cada noche del Exâmen,
En la muerte fixar el pensamiento,
La mas santa freqüente Comunicn,
Asistencia, piedad y buen exemplo.

Figure 10. The essential responsibilities of a Holy School member, organized mnemonically in a pocket-sized devotional manual. (Cartilla breve de los rudimentos mas necesarios que debe observar el discípulo de Christo, Nuestro Señor y Maestro . . ., x F1207.C191. *Courtesy of the Bancroft Library, University of California, Berkeley.*)

the collective / individual that so characterized the futuremaking of the escuelas.

In addition to these otherworldly benefits, the Santas Escuelas' practices complemented the crown's desire to improve the economic efficiency of the colonies. Betraying a Bourbon-era obsession with protecting productive capacity from religious waste, a number of civil officials and churchmen noted approvingly that the escuelas of New Spain deviated from their Spanish bylaws in order to accommodate the work schedules of the brethren, including those who toiled as manual laborers in Mexico City and elsewhere. Such a change was essential in the colonial cities, held one brother, because the ratio of working people to those who were "comfortably situated" was so much higher there than in Madrid.[60] Given that many of the brothers were laborers but most of the groups' leaders possessed wealth and status, Spanish officials also argued that the escuelas presented a unique opportunity to educate the masses of New Spain's cities.[61] These institutions would produce hombres nuevos—again, perhaps best translated as "rejuvenated" or "renewed men"—whose more productive spiritual lives would pay material dividends as well.[62] The late eighteenth-century Holy Schools of Mexico City pursued these goals wholeheartedly and replicated themselves by sending members to found new escuelas, including in working-class neighborhoods surrounding the city center.[63] Piety thus offered Spanish officials another way to transform plebeians into more productive subjects.[64] Given the church hierarchy's enthusiastic approval of the déposito irregular, mostly because of its importance to the economic health of New Spain, it is not surprising that many of these same bishops backed the escuela movement for its worldly and material benefits as well as its spiritual goals.

Authorities also believed that participation in the escuelas would spread the benefits of education and tutelage to the brothers' families. A legal adviser to the archbishop of Mexico reported that the crown supported the schools for simple and practical reasons: they promoted effective piety and reformed the customs and behavior of common people. As he put it, "We have seen many artisans and wretches improve their lives by taking advantage of such Holy Exercises ... and the day laborers who are [presently] employed can carve out some spare moments for the essential business of their salvation without affecting their jobs, at the same time learning the lessons of valuable texts with which they can educate their children and families."[65]

The escuelas promised to improve the welfare of "the entire civil and Christian republic."[66] Their rapid expansion led one padre de obediencia to argue that the groups offered an unparalleled means of exerting political control over Mexico City's masses. Because of the escuelas' unique form of popular education, he concluded, "the king has more than a thousand men from this infamous class of the plebe who are true Christians and loyal vassals."[67]

The Santas Escuelas of New Spain were therefore unusual institutions inasmuch as they enjoyed the support of both the Spanish crown and the church hierarchy, which were so often at odds in the late eighteenth century. While using established techniques of collective piety and mortification that were questioned by some enlightened sensibilities of the eighteenth century, the escuelas advanced the goals of both religious and civil reformers. In spiritual terms, they promoted a piety that was closely controlled by clergymen and carefully separated from popular religious practices. They also emphasized interior spirituality and greater self-regulation of one's conscience and religious life, which were both advocated by reformist prelates of the time. In material terms, they offered a unique form of education that was meant to transform the behavior and customs of their members. In so doing the escuelas aided the royal bureaucracy's ongoing attempts to squeeze additional resources and productivity out of the viceroyalty and its inhabitants. When they sought to expand existing Holy Schools or found new ones, petitioners channeled the language of efficiency, frugality, and moderation in another ritual-of-text clearly meant to appeal to the dispositions of authorities.[68]

Their petitions worked phenomenally well. The backing of civil and church officials fostered the spread of escuelas in the late eighteenth century and boosted their memberships. Although the groups' otherwise closely followed bylaws set a ceiling of 72 members, a number of Holy Schools in Mexico City sought and received approval to increase the size of their brotherhoods. By the 1790s the escuelas of the Colegio of San Pedro and the Hospital of Jesus Nazareno reported 166 and 179 members, respectively.[69] Other escuelas received permission to increase their size to 100, bringing the total number of brethren in Mexico City to well over 1,000 by the early 1790s.

But the support of the crown and the hierarchy alone does not explain the escuelas' increasing popularity. Officials stated their opinions only when preexisting groups sought a formal license or tried to expand their brotherhoods, or when a group of men wanted to found a new escuela. Current or prospective members initiated all such efforts and drew on the substantial textual resources, authorized practices, and reputation of the institute. The

Santas Escuelas left an unusually well marked documentary trail, especially compared with the records of other colonial sodalities. Many brotherhoods and informal devotional groups left few written records of their activities. Even the better-documented confraternities or archconfraternities, which sometimes recorded their financial transactions and internal organization in minute detail, were often frustratingly silent regarding their spiritual activities. In contrast, as we have seen, the escuelas assiduously documented their ritual practices and devotional routines. Their ability to do so depended in part on the financial resources of wealthy brothers, who paid for the publication of bylaws and guidebooks. But it also grew out of the spiritual goals of the escuela movement, which sought to reproduce an established spirituality among its members, both during the escuelas' weekly activities and in daily life. The publications produced by the escuelas reflected these goals, and many of the statutes and devotional manuals were tiny documents that could be placed in one's pocket and referred to throughout the day, again moving the practices of the escuelas outside the walls and more deeply into the individual lives of members and their families.[70] The publications helped replicate the schools' practices but also created textual and institutional resources that fostered the spread and reproduction of the Holy Schools themselves. Time and again, petitioners for new escuelas emphasized the chain of texts that would link their activities to previous escuelas, noting that their group would use an existing set of bylaws and would be modeled closely (*a imitación*) on another chapter.[71] Authorities responded positively to such language, celebrating the escuelas' textual legacy and its reproduction "without any alteration" since it demonstrated a respect for church authority and suggested that the institutions' piety would remain within the bounds of orthodoxy.

Related to these historical resources, the benefits escuelas offered their members also drove the brotherhoods' growth in the eighteenth century. Even though their leadership was dominated by powerful Spaniards, Spanish artisans and laborers were deliberately brought into the ranks of the movement. Consequently, the broad cross-section of Mexico City's Spanish population who joined the Santas Escuelas formed the most active network of Spanish piety in the eighteenth-century colonial city. The motivations that led

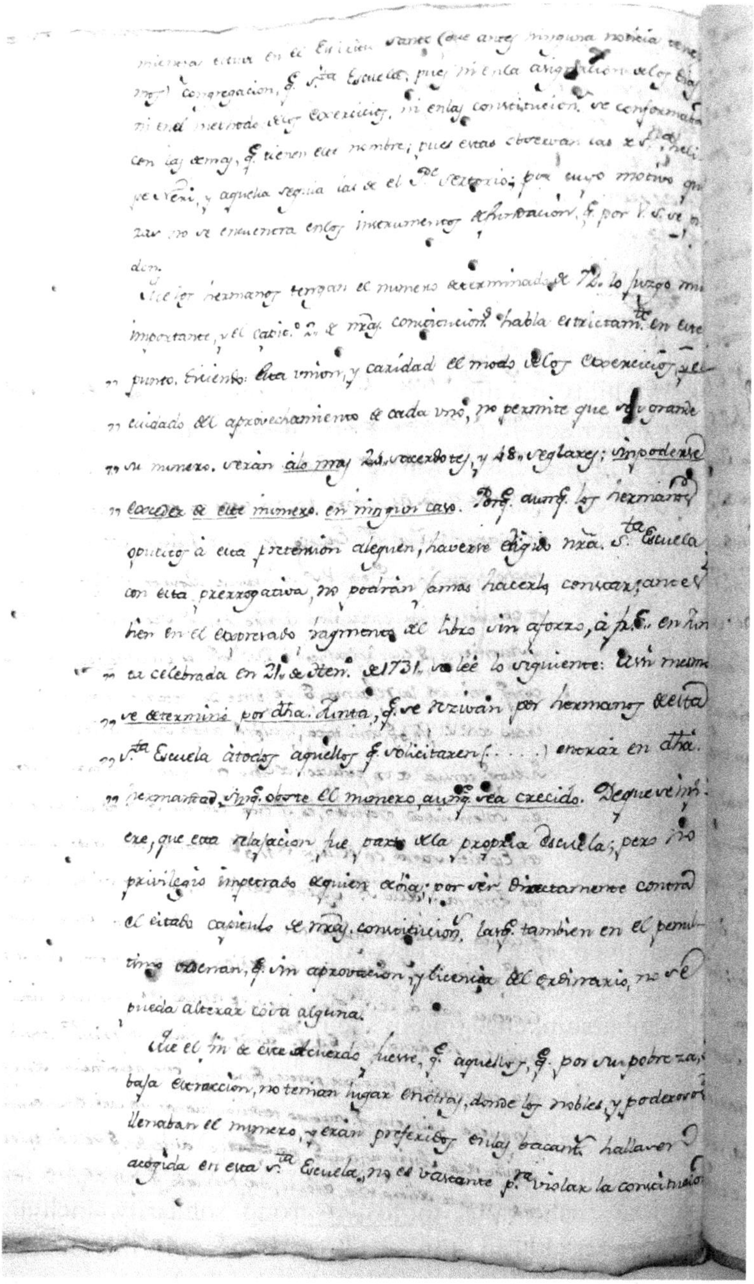

Figure 11. A communication from leaders of a Holy School in Mexico City to church authorities during an internal dispute over the size and social composition of the group. In this passage, one faction cites an older set of bylaws that stipulated a strict cap on the number of members, one of many rituals-of-text in the Holy School movement. (AGN, Indiferente Virreinal [Templos y Conventos], *caja 4520, exp. 16, fol. 15v, 1762–64.)*

higher-status Spaniards to join are somewhat easier to gauge, because theirs are the voices in the documentary record. On one level they considered the escuelas a most effective instrument for spiritual growth. The escuelas allowed them to pursue the goals of the reformed piety through long-established practices, including collective worship and disciplina. Because the escuelas were purely spiritual brotherhoods, with few or no economic commitments required of members, they created an officially sanctioned vehicle for religious sociability at a time when other religious collectives found themselves under severe pressure from the church and crown. On another level the escuelas provided an intimate way to reform popular behavior, one that complemented formal projects of social control initiated during the Bourbon era.[72]

The Holy Schools may also have reinforced their members' sense of self at a time when increased miscegenation and social mobility blurred the boundary between nonelite Spaniards and other colonial subjects in Spanish America.[73] Ethnic Spaniards made up the majority of escuela members, and some chapters were exclusively Spanish. In cases where escuelas allowed non-Spanish members, tensions arose among the brothers over the question of exclusivity. In 1765, for example, brothers in the Holy School at the Convent of Santo Domingo in Mexico City complained to the archbishop's office about an attempt by others in the congregation to increase its membership beyond the stipulated seventy-two. They produced and cited their statutes, which strictly limited the group's membership, engaging in their own ritual-of-text in an attempt to stop the plans for expansion and, by extension, exclude non-Spaniards. Their petition succeeded, as the archdiocese ordered strict adherence to the existing bylaws.[74] Such incidents resonated with others in late colonial Mexico City, where the laity used religious institutions to foster group solidarity, including along what we would call ethnic and racial lines.[75] In the few Holy Schools of mixed ethnicity, group leaders boasted of the material and moral benefits that would accrue to their laboring brethren. In both cases the writings of chapter officials and the structure of the Holy Schools themselves emphasized ethical development, paternalistic education, and social oversight. As one padre put it, when the education of the plebe is catalyzed by good Christian piety, such as that found in the Holy Schools, it not only eradicates vice but also creates subjects ready to obey both laws and superiors.[76] These very different attitudes toward group composition, including the question of non-Spanish members, were prime examples of the way in which eighteenth-century members adapted the Santas Escuelas movement to current conditions. In some cases this meant the brotherhoods served as a kind of bulwark against the perceived dangers of racial and ethnic mixing and the increasing blurriness of casta labels. In others it became a way to integrate some non-Spaniards into a Spanish-dominated association. Both possibilities seem to have included a substantial desire for social control. Innovative futuremaking, we should recall, was not necessarily in line with our own notions of fairness or social justice, but that is no reason to overlook forms of creative adaptation and refashioning of traditions.

In the end it is difficult to reconstruct completely the motivations of the Spanish elite in the escuela movement, let alone those of Spanish working people or the non-Spanish members mentioned in a few tantalizing documents. Even though our ability to reconstruct individual motivations is limited, we have a much better sense of the resources that members of the Holy Schools employed as they developed their movement. For some brothers such resources included the capital to publish the groups' devotional tracts or the ability to direct lengthy, time-consuming petitions to church and civil authorities. For others it could mean the literacy that allowed one to hold an office within the escuela or the personal connections that opened the doors of membership. Individuals of diverse social profiles manifestly employed the resources at their disposal to fashion their religious lives, but within the substantial limits of the time.

The growth of the Santas Escuelas and the varied reasons for their popularity suggest that a pragmatic, innovative religious culture emerged in eighteenth-century New Spain. But what sort of innovation? What path led toward the future? Contemporaries understood innovation to contain a substantial dose of imitation, mimesis, and patterning from tradition.[77] The brothers of the escuelas assimilated ideas associated with civil and religious reformers without breaking radically from the religious forms of the past. The result was a practice in which the collective and the individual were not in competition but in cooperation and in which interior spirituality complemented physical piety, the body, and pain as vehicles for spiritual and material improvement. Out of this context, the individual emerged as a more important subject of Catholic piety and practice in the late eighteenth century, as we saw so clearly in the case of the colonial confessional, but not at the expense of collective Catholicism.

Numerous changes in late colonial New Spain forced individuals to repurpose existing cultural competencies and practices. Keeping in mind that these competencies are rarely allocated equally or manipulated uniformly, we can begin to understand how religious practices such as those of New Spain's Santas Escuelas could be used to foster innovative forms of community *and* hierarchy. Studied in this way, the Holy Schools of New Spain do not emerge as an embarrassing hiccup of traditionalism on Latin America's path toward a more refined mode of spirituality. Yet neither can they be described as an early example of modernity or a "hybrid modernity" whose very significance as a historical case study is defined by its poor fit with earlier definitions of modern. If we were to do so, we would lose sight of how people actually engaged the future. Indeed, moving beyond the modernity paradigm offers a more complete and richer portrait of cultural life during this period. Focusing on the groups' reproduction—especially their rituals-of-text—helps us capture the apparently contradictory aspects of the Holy Schools, which from our perspective appear current and dated, forward-looking and reactionary.

In their moment, however, the brotherhoods provided an effective, adaptive response to changing religious and social conditions and developed spiritual and material goals for a carefully managed and improved future. They could do so because of access to resources (texts, devotions, orthodoxy) that fostered and patterned the groups' long-term reproduction. The strands of tradition and innovation in Mexican Catholicism formed a tight weave but also a supple whip that changed with the times. It is a mode of historical change that seems increasingly hard for us to imagine, bombarded as we are by the language of rapid change, instant obsolescence, and enhancement through novelty.

The turbulence and changes that characterized New Spain during the Holy School era would only increase in the coming years. As the colonial period came to an unexpected and violent close with Mexico's independence struggle in the early nineteenth century, the use of the past as a guide to the present and future remained prominent. In the political rhetoric of religious leaders, we find some of the most extreme examples of futuremaking through the language of tradition.

CHAPTER SIX

Promises

IN THE EARLY MORNING of September 16, 1810, Miguel Hidalgo y Costilla delivered his famous *grito*, a speech and call to action, to his parishioners in the town of Dolores. The priest spoke outside the richly adorned parish church, not far from the important mining town of Guanajuato. Both the church and the town were near the center of the vast colonial viceroyalty of New Spain. The grito and the movements it unleashed began more than a decade of conflict in New Spain that led eventually to the creation of the Mexican republic. Popularly remembered as the initial call to arms for Mexican independence, Miguel Hidalgo's grito in fact offered a much more ambiguous vision of political renewal within the framework of Spanish colonialism. The best approximations of the event suggest that the priest shouted something like, "Long Live Ferdinand VII! Long Live America! Long Live Religion! and Death to Bad Government!"[1] Hidalgo attacked Spanish governance (and some Spaniards in particular) at the same time he defended Catholicism and the restoration of the deposed Spanish king. He called for a renovation of the existing imperial relationship, but not for its end. Over the next ten years, to be sure, the main political dispute became whether or not New Spain should make a clear break with Spain. Nonetheless, the language of Hidalgo's initial grito betrayed the uncertainty of the era and foreshadowed a long-term struggle over the form of Mexico's political system. Should New Spain seek greater autonomy within a reconfigured Spanish empire, or should it become independent? If New Spain achieved independence, what form should it take: a Mexican monarchy, a liberal republic, or some hybrid form?

In the end Mexicans secured independence through a unique and relatively conservative compromise: a constitutional monarchy headed by an American-born Spaniard, or Creole, Agustín de Iturbide. Although the Mexican "empire," headed by Iturbide, and its "three guarantees" (independence, Roman Catholicism, and unity among Mexico's European and American residents) were meant to appeal to both defenders of the old order and independence-seeking insurgents, by no means did these end Mexico's core political divisions. Iturbide's empire imploded in relatively short order, and fundamental questions about the country's political future remained in dispute through much of the nineteenth century.

This complicated political narrative has been well studied by many historians. Rather than cover that ground again, I want to use this period of turmoil as a laboratory to examine forms of political futuremaking. What futures were possible to think in Mexico's independence era? Out of what materials were those futures brought into being? Answering these questions brings us chronologically to the end of the colonial period. In that the role of the past in the present and future would begin to shift in nineteenth-century Mexico, the chapter also stands as a coda to the shared forms of futuremaking of the colonial era.

Glancing back in time, one sees numerous precursors to this political turmoil. The cycle began with a political crisis that rocked the Spanish monarchy in 1808. The combination of the Napoleonic wars that swept Europe at the turn of the nineteenth century, French meddling in Spanish politics, and, eventually, an invasion of the Iberian peninsula by French troops led to the successive abdications of the Spanish throne, first by Charles IV, and then by his son, Ferdinand VII. On the now vacant throne Napoleon installed his brother, Joseph Bonaparte, as King José I. These events led to a wide variety of adjustments in the American colonies, from relatively localized jockeying for political power to autonomy movements with much grander aspirations.

Even earlier, the chronic fiscal instability and weakness of the Spanish empire vis-à-vis other European powers led to a series of imperial innovations in the second half of the eighteenth century, namely, the Bourbon reforms, which, among other goals, sought to reconfigure the relationship between the Spanish homeland and its American possessions. In contrast to the events of 1810, the Bourbon reforms did strengthen Spanish control over New Spain. We saw some evidence of this in the previous chapter, as many in the church hierarchy sought to limit popular religious expression they deemed excessive and wasteful. Their attempts to shape and limit religious celebrations and devotions took place alongside thoroughgoing changes to the viceroyalty's political system, fiscal management, and defense. From the perspective of the Spanish crown and its administrators, the efforts largely achieved their goals. Colonial administration was tightly controlled by Madrid. The empire maintained most of its American territory in the face of countless threats. Increased tax revenues propped up the Spanish treasury. Yet for many colonial subjects, the reform period, which reached a high point in the second half of the eighteenth century, created massive political, economic, and even cultural turmoil. The reforms meant that life, work, and worship were different, and often worse, in 1810 than they had been in 1750. In this longer context of the Bourbon era and its changes, the years 1810–21 in New Spain might be thought of as a particularly intense period in an age of tumult.

Uncertainty defined the era, and part of that uncertainty was emotional. Many of New Spain's subjects wondered how to navigate a rapidly changing present and an unpredictable future. Examples abound: Creoles fretted when they found their political power and local autonomy curtailed by Bourbon policies that promoted the appointment of *peninsulares* to government posts; wealthy Creoles and the church especially railed against a series of forced loans to the crown; Indian and casta subjects chafed under more aggressive taxation; and religious celebrants resented new limits on the amount and style of public worship. Beyond the Bourbon reforms, the revolutions in British North America, Haiti, and France were pivotal events for New Spain's Spanish elite, as these movements seemed to offer object lessons of dangerous political change. For working people, droughts and crop failures meant that a lifetime of just getting by could become a crisis of subsistence overnight; for all, periodic waves of epidemic illness confirmed the fragility of life. Indeed, although some historians have referred to the century from 1750 to 1850 as the "Age of Democratic Revolution," in New Spain and Mexico it would be no stretch to rename this period the Age of Anxiety.[2]

What did it mean to be anxious in this place and time? At a moment of collective crisis, how did anxiety relate to futuremaking? Focusing on sermons and similar texts from the era of Mexican independence, we can place the emotion of anxiety—which we might provisionally define as a concern or unease about events to come—under historical scrutiny. In response to escalating political crises, beginning with a series of imperial reforms in the late eighteenth century and culminating in the political crises of 1808 and 1810, Mexicans developed a complicated relationship with the future. As I have noted, for many, contemplating the future fostered intense feelings of apprehension and fear, a complex emotional response that we would call anxiety, angst, or unease. This was a logical product of a tumultuous moment.[3]

But as we've seen in previous chapters, New Spain's futuremaking was rarely focused solely on events to come, whether those imagined events inspired hope or fear. Rather, futuremaking occurred in a productive dialogue between the resources of the past and the demands of the present. Thus we need to historicize anxiety, to situate it in a particular time and place, and to interpret its relationship to the future by examining it in thought and action, much as I have done with regard to other forms of futuremaking. What practices and activities brought it into being? How did it function in ways similar to our contemporary concepts? In what ways was it different?

When New Spain's residents viewed the future of the independence era, they did so through a temporal lens of Christianity, whereby past, present, and future could be read, if imperfectly, through the interpretation of the Bible. As a result, the unpredictable future produced something quite different from the hopelessness of contemporary anxiety. Futuremaking of the Mexican independence era simultaneously generated fear *and* confidence because the hand of Providence ultimately shaped human history (and its future) and granted a measure of hope in times of great turmoil. Yet in the theology of early modern Catholicism, divine control also assumed a strong degree of choice or free will, what we would call autonomy and agency. Making use of this perspective, New Spain's preachers grappled with anxiety primarily as a collective phenomenon, something quite unlike our understanding of the emotion as afflicting individuals, and assumed that a shared response to current events could help advance the work of God on earth. Thus anxiety did not necessarily produce hopelessness or inertia, with severe dread overwhelming one's ability to act in the world; at times, it activated feelings of comfort, consolation, and even power that could, in turn, lead to political action.

Indeed, the emotional relationship to the future found in these sermons and exhortations cannot be reduced to any English cognate, including "anxiety." Preachers from the time rarely used the Spanish words *ansia* ("anxiety," "longing") or *ansiedad* ("anxiety"). Instead, they developed metaphors, analogies, and narratives meant to create in their audiences a dynamic orientation to the future, usually for political purposes. Their writings reveal some sources of uncertainty and angst in late colonial Mexico. In this sense they open a window into historical events and their emotional repercussions. But they also demonstrate how contemporaries related to the unfolding of time and history during political crisis as well as the important role sentiments played in that process.

A look at the historical usage of the terms that most closely approximated "anxiety" (*ansia* and *ansiedad*) helps to clarify this emotional labor. First, although its appearance dates to well before the eighteenth century, the term *ansiedad* was not employed with great frequency until the nineteenth century. At that point, it could be found most often in medical treatises, usually referring to physical ailments related to a type of fever or to circulatory or pulmonary disease.[4] Eighteenth-century dictionaries, however, noted some overlap between *ansiedad* and *ansia*. Both terms could refer to feelings of unease or disturbance, usually described as a type of physical suffering.[5] They also conveyed yearning or desire, thus making explicit an emotional link between the present and future that is a key feature of the modern understanding of anxiety. The 1770 edition of the *Diccionario de la lengua Castellana* captured all three meanings, defining *ansia* variously as "grief or fatigue that causes restlessness or violent movement in the body. Anguish or affliction of the soul. Longing, vehement desire." The sentiments found repeatedly in the religious talk of New Spain around the time of independence combined these facets of *ansia* and *ansiedad*, which for convenience I will place under the English label of anxiety. Politics, in our own times as much as in those of eighteenth- or nineteenth-century Mexico, is often a story of managed expectations and manipulated emotions, and emotions are embodied. Political struggles and their imagined futures are talked about, argued over, and thought through, but they are also experienced and felt.

Colonial preachers attempted to produce fear and apprehension in their audiences but managed such feelings by interpreting time, both historical and current time, through biblical precedents and Christian frameworks. In their sermons and writings, the emotions we call fear, uncertainty, and despair interacted in surprising ways with confidence, trust, and hope. The result of this mixture was a perspective on the future that offered the possibility for political guidance, control, and action in a time of great uncertainty.

Sermons are a useful entry point at which to begin this examination, in part because they were such an important source of news. By 1810 New Spain had only a modest print culture, and individuals of many social strata received information primarily through oral communication.[6] When coupled with the context in which a sermon was delivered, in the Mass or similar religious celebrations, this meant, as Carlos Herrejón has pointed out, that audiences for a sermon "were used to listening carefully, to retaining [its content] accurately and appreciating vocal projection and modulation—captive listeners, one might say, since there were few ways to occupy one's time outside the routines of work and family.... [T]he sermon was a privileged, regular, authorized and obligatory form of communication."[7] Sermons were thus one of the most important sources of information, especially about events occurring outside the community or region. The extant sermons from late colonial New Spain and early republican Mexico, which number in the hundreds, offer detailed commentary on the local and transatlantic political crises of the time.

There is a great irony in describing these documents as a useful index of news in a society dominated by oral communication, because the sermons available to us are all in written form. Typically, such sermons and other orations were published shortly after their delivery, and they represent only a tiny fraction of those actually preached during the period. To make it into this select group required not just money for typesetting and reproduction, but also the approval of church officials, which usually meant extensive front matter that would include various glosses and certifications that testified to the sermon's quality and orthodoxy. As a result, most of the sermons we have were given by prominent Spanish priests, who tended to project a conservative and royalist political perspective. Furthermore, those filling the pews for these types of sermons were typically other Spaniards, sometimes people of substantial wealth and status, rather than castas, Indians, or working people in general. Finally, although we have a general idea of the composition of audiences, our knowledge of how those audiences responded to the sermons' content is limited and fragmentary.[8]

The unique qualities of most printed sermons limit our ability to make broad generalizations about religious discourse or its reception, but this practical limitation turns out to be a methodological advantage in other respects. Because of their relative homogeneity—their orthodoxy and their often conservative, royalist, and Spanish perspective—these sources offer a relatively consistent sample in which to examine how the emotion of anxiety figured into symbolic language and political thought. To interpret the sources in a way that is appropriate to the period, one also needs to consider how the emotional lives of individuals related to collective sentiment. The authors of New Spain's sermons and its religious oration in general formed part of what Barbara Rosenwein calls "emotional communities," that is, "groups in which people adhere to the same norms of emotional expression and value—or devalue—the same or related emotions."[9] Emotional communities, according to Rosenwein, may be mapped onto various other sorts of communities we are familiar with, from families to localities to institutional affiliations. Like all collectivities, emotional communities may be overlapping, distinct, riven by internal factions, and so on and should be expected to change over time. Beyond such differences, however, emotional communities possess "systems of feeling," and the task of the re-searcher is to examine "what these communities (and the individuals within them) define and assess as valuable or harmful to them; the evaluations that they make about others' emotions; the nature of the affective bonds between people that they recognize; and the modes of emotional expression that they expect, encourage, tolerate, and deplore."[10]

To return to a point I raised earlier, it might therefore seem infeasible to examine the emotional communities surrounding Mexican religious oratory. Sermons seem to tell us a great deal about the emotions, values, and judgments of their authors but, in contrast, have apparently little to say about the emotional attitudes of the audience and broader community, let alone the "affective bonds" between members of those communities.

Here I want to pause to consider the peculiar relationship be-tween a sermon's author and his audience. All sermons appealed to a broad, potentially universal community, the church militant, also understood as the Mystical Body of Christ, a group that included both the preacher and his audience. Moreover, the core practice of the church, the Mass, was itself a ritualized performance of the church's collective labor in the world. This communal activity, of which the sermon formed a part, opened a rhetorical space where the distinction between author and audience was often ambiguous, even in moments when a preacher might chastise his flock for its collective sins or challenge it to reform. In practical terms, such overlapping meant that preachers moved in and out of the first and second person, from the individual to the collective, from I to you to we, from personal anxiety to collective anxiety and back to the personal again. As a result, the boundary between individual and collective sentiment could become quite blurry or even collapse.

Consider a sermon preached in Mexico City's grand cathedral by Archbishop Francisco Javier Lizana y Beaumont in 1808, just months after the Napoleonic invasion of Spain and the toppling of the Spanish king, Ferdinand VII.[11] Lizana y Beaumont equated Spain's plight to the Babylonian captivity of Israel. While the de-posed Ferdinand VII found himself in literal captivity in France, the Spanish people faced metaphorical captivity, their true leader usurped by foreign invaders and their interests in the hands of the French, whom another preacher called "the assassins from the north."[12]

One might rail against the crimes of the French, as many of Lizana y Beaumont's contemporaries did, but the archbishop placed most of the blame on Spaniards themselves. He opened his sermon with a dark quote from Ezekiel in which the prophet warned that God would "make a desolation. Because the land is full of bloody crimes and the city is full of violence."[13] Although Providence and thus the exact flow of worldly events is ultimately unknowable, Lizana reminded his flock, Ezekiel's prophecy communicated clearly that "God punishes us for our sins and if we don't stop them the punishments will continue and increase."[14] The sermon built up to a moment of individual and collective catharsis, ending in a collective prayer that called for God's mercy. "I speak to you," the archbishop concluded, "in the name of all my people: they all want to make peace with you, they all want mercy and for you to pardon their faults . . . they all clamor from the bottom of their hearts, saying 'Father of Mercies.'"[15]

Such rhetoric presents neither a clear view of the feelings of the orators / writers nor, as a form of discourse, can it be taken as the only evidence of the social reality of the time. Can we know with certainty, for example, that the archbishop believed Spain's Babylonian captivity was caused by Spanish sin and that he truly fretted over its consequences? If he did, can we be sure, in turn, that his audience felt the intense anxiety communicated in his sermon? Perhaps, but it is likely this language offers unassailable evidence of neither individual nor collective experience. Instead, I find these sermons useful for understanding the link between individual and collective sentiment. The sermons revealed (and created) some of the building blocks of future imaginaries. They fostered communication about the future, between individuals and between groups.[16] As in our time, the emotions of "us" and "we" grew out of the feelings of many individuals, their sentiments sometimes orchestrated by political rhetoric. This middle ground of emotional communication offers a glimpse of another common form of futuremaking in colonial New Spain.

The turbulence around the independence era affords an opportune moment for investigating such futuremaking. It was a time when uncertainty overflowed, political talk abounded, and most people focused their attention sharply on the future. But how should one analyze these foundations of political futuremaking? How might one conceptualize this process of communication?

As we have seen, the confession manuals discussed in chapter 2 both reflected and produced emotional sentiments related to sin and the future. Something similar took place in the genre of the sermon, and it is a relationship between text and thought that has been theorized in other contexts. The anxiety-laden rhetoric of Lizana y Beaumont and other clerics functioned along the lines of what William Reddy calls emotives. Emotives, Reddy proposes, "are emotional statements, gestures, and utterances that are influenced directly by and alter what they 'refer' to." "Emotives," he continues, "are themselves instruments for directly changing, building, hiding, [and] intensifying emotions."[17] Through the concept of emotives, in other words, Reddy points out that emotional communication partially represents the inner feelings of an individual, but always imperfectly, because the very act of emotional communication—its performance, as it were—helps both to call into being and to modify one's emotions. Reddy thus charts a third way between an extreme social constructionist position, in which language is taken to be a performance and literally creates the emotions to which it supposedly refers, and a more traditional form of social analysis, in which language is assumed to represent unequivocally the inner emotions of its speaker.[18] In Reddy's view it is insufficient to examine how politics might influence emotions. Instead, the relationship between parts must be reversed, along with their role in historical explanation. "Emotional control," he counters, "is the real site of the exercise of power: politics is just a process of determining who must repress as illegitimate, who must foreground as valuable, the feelings and desires that come up for them in given contexts and relationships."[19] One of New Spain's most aggressive royalist preachers, Fray Diego Miguel Bringas, might have agreed. "From its beginnings," the preacher argued, the insurrection was a "result of the passions incited against reason and justice."[20]

In this space, situated between individual agency and collective sentiment, sermons in the independence era articulated and helped activate a form of anxiety and futuremaking based in part on collective fear.[21] William Bouwsma, a historian of early modern Europe, has pointed out the natural tendency to convert anxiety into fear: in contrast to the diffuse unease of anxiety, "the object of fear is concrete and may be dealt with by some appropriate action," thus mitigating some of its emotional damage.[22] This observation is critical, as it helps explain why in New Spain the emotive of anxiety depended on specific references to local events and the crises occurring across the Atlantic. Even so, the conversion of anxiety into fear explains only part of the emotional meaning of anxiety during this period. Anxiety frequently coupled fear with some gesture toward confidence or certainty and, eventually, consolation.

But where did those gestures come from? Centuries earlier the Dominican missionary Vincent Ferrer (1350–1419), whose writings remained popular in eighteenth-century Spain and throughout Catholic Europe, suggested a similar solution to the problem of unchecked fear. Fear, he argued, could be best mitigated by *santo temor,* or the fear of God, itself a form of love, which converted "useless fear" (*vano temor*) into something beneficial that would strengthen the will. In a similar way New Spain's sermonists and their audiences gained purchase on an increasingly unsure future by mixing fear with confidence.[23] This was, in fact, the precise emotional mixture found in the almanacs and libros pronósticos, both in New Spain and in the broader literature from other parts of the Americas and Europe.[24] Like those practices of forecasting and other cases examined in the previous chapters, the emotions and rhetoric of the independence era drew on the traditions of colonial Catholicism, such as the ideas referenced by Bringas and Ferrer in the passages above. Out of this mix a form of political imagination and motivation developed that drew on the biblical past as a tool for adapting to the present and constructing new futures.

Consider the sermon preached by Francisco Javier Conde Pineda in Puebla on July 9, 1809, as part of a cycle of Masses meant to secure divine succor, given the ongoing calamities in Spain. Like many orators, he opened with a biblical reference, from Paul's letter to the Hebrews, which promised God's help in a people's time of great need.[25] He then discussed the emotional state he hoped the sermon would help his audience achieve. "I'm not trying to stir up your spirits, which are already so moved," the priest claimed, ". . . but I do want to lift them from the profound dismay and consternation that they've fallen into because of the unhappy news [from Spain]."[26] Conde Pineda's frank remarks speak to the duality of emotives, wherein emotional communication is both a product and a producer of individual or collective emotional states. Activating the latent emotional content in his audience, in this case the distress caused by the monarchical crisis in Spain, Conde Pineda described an ideal anxiety that also depended on his audience's predisposition to believe in a future defined by Providence. To reach this ideal anxiety required striking an Aristotelian mean between two potent emotions.[27] Confidence mixed with fear, he argued, offered the only effective response to the political uncertainty of the moment. He warned, "My sacred ministry prevents me from offering illusory prognostications. By itself, confidence in God isn't enough to free us from our ills, one must combine it with the fear of God [santo temor]. This gift from above [confidence] can't be severed from that virtue [the fear of God], nor that virtue from this gift—they are inseparable. Confidence alone will corrupt us, devolving into vain conceit, and fear alone would ruin us, plunging us into a terrible despair. . . . In two words: we approach the Lord with confidence and fear. With confidence, aware of His infinite power and goodness. With fear, aware of our utter weakness and malice."[28]

On this occasion, Conde Pineda made neither a major exhortation to his audience nor a specific call to action, in part because most subjects of New Spain could do very little to influence events on the far side of the Atlantic. The model of anxiety he employed and his framing of Spain and New Spain's current predicament in a biblical context, however, was the norm in sermons and other preaching. Finding a middle ground between despair and confidence provided a more useful orientation to the future: it offered his listeners a way of interpreting a chaotic, potentially threatening series of events over which they apparently had little control. On the other hand, Conde Pineda's sermon did not simply bring those emotional responses into being; it also acted on preexisting emotional registers shared by his audience. The independence-era sermonists did not develop these techniques, in other words, but drew upon a tradition of rhetoric and a shared way of reading the past and the future.

Other sermons preached in central New Spain during the first two years of the French intervention in Spain, prior to the outbreak of the Hidalgo rebellion in 1810, are equally revealing. The concerns of the preachers, particularly their observation of conditions in New Spain, are crucial. In 1808, Napoleon's brother, Joseph Bonaparte, assumed the Spanish throne following the forced abdications of Charles IV and Ferdinand VII. In the absence of a legitimate monarch, self-governing juntas (local councils) formed in a number of Spanish cities, including Seville, the site of the central junta. All ruled in the name of the deposed Ferdinand VII. Creole notables in a number of Spanish American cities, including Mexico City, argued for a coequal right to rule over American territory and agitated for the establishment of their own juntas. Although the details of their maneuverings are not relevant here, these political shocks in Spain and their reverberations in the Americas prompted an aggressive response from prominent clerics, whose orations addressed the potential rifts among New Spain's subjects, especially those between Creoles and peninsulares.

Many sermons emphasized the grave dangers faced by a society divided along what we would call ethnic and racial lines, divisions that nineteenth-century New Spaniards described in the language of casta, essence, and religion. In 1809 the senior canon of Mexico City's cathedral chapter, José Mariano Beristáin de Souza, called on all the subjects of New Spain to honor the (legitimate) Spanish monarch and Spain itself as they did their father and mother. Preaching to a group of fellow priests, Beristáin, a Creole but one who had strong familial and personal ties to Spain, reminded his audience that New Spain, like Andalusia and Castile, formed part of the Spanish monarchy. Although they were separated by great distances, he explained, "all are provinces of Spain." "You are Mexicans," he told the priests in the audience, "but you don't stop being Spaniards."[29] As Beristáin described it, the categories of Mexican (in this context meaning Spanish American, or Creole) and Spaniard were nested, complementary, and closely linked. The strength of that relationship, moreover, depended on the common bonds of Catholicism. "We form a body," he added, "a building, a spiritual and political house, even though we are separated by our [physical] bodies. We are united and bound by an alliance, a bond, a mixture and pitch so much stronger.... Oh! Religion on one side, reason and justice on the other, and all around love and blood, essence [*naturaleza*] and gratitude."[30]

It is not surprising that Beristáin understood Catholicism to bridge political, social, and ethnic divisions in New Spain. For him and other clerics, one's Catholicism preceded and trumped other categories of belonging. To take but one example: in 1820, after a decade of insurgency and as new categories of political belonging began to emerge, a prominent cleric could still proclaim with confidence, "We are Christians before we are citizens."[31] Yet Beristáin and other preachers appealed to a shared sense of self not only through Catholic affiliation but also through interpretive practice and traditions in Catholicism. We might think of these as resources for collective futuremaking, which drew upon shared understandings of time and the idea of the mystical / social body as foundations for political life.[32]

Preachers of the era gave present relationships and political predicaments a temporal depth through biblical references and then projected them into a partially interpreted future. Stated differently, futures could be conceived of only through the foundations of the past. Vicente Navarro manipulated temporality, or the experience of time, in this way when he preached in Madrid in 1808 following the Napoleonic invasion.[33] The Mass and sermon celebrated a recent victory by Spanish troops, although the outcome of the larger conflict remained very much in doubt. In this moment of crisis, Navarro offered his audience a glimpse into the future. "Spain," he promised, "need not fear its utter destruction."[34] At first glance, Navarro noted, the calamities faced by Spain and its monarch seemed incomprehensible and thus apparently offered no emotional guidance. Through biblical interpretation, however, the present could be understood. "The finger of God, of this great God," Navarro proclaimed, "who with a mere glance can cut through centuries past and future, wanted to show us some two thousand years in advance the tragic scenes that we've just experienced in our Spain."[35] Just as the Israelites faced God's wrath on numerous occasions, so too did Spain suffer at the moment, consoled only by the biblical precedent of a favored people's delivery from ruin.

Like many of his fellow preachers, Navarro leaned heavily on a form of scriptural exegesis called typology, in which biblical events were interpreted as prefigurations of later occurrences.[36] In theological readings confined to the Bible itself, Christians had long used typology to demonstrate how the life of Christ and, in general, the events in the New Testament fulfilled the prophecies of the Old Testament. In this framework, the Old Testament included a vast store of types, or foreshadowings, that were eventually realized in the events of the New Testament, the antitypes of what came before.[37] Beginning at least with Saint Augustine (354–430), however, Christian scholars employed biblical typology to explain and give meaning to the broader sweep of human history. Many ancient and medieval biblical interpreters described typology as a kind of memory work or even a form of invention. In the traditional meaning of the concept, discussed in the context of confession, invention as creative act and inventory as mental resources formed part of one rich process of *inventio*. In other forms of futuremaking examined throughout the book, innovation and invention drew upon traditions to create possible futures. Early biblical interpreters did something similar, using metaphors drawn from architecture and construction to describe their work. Scripture was a framework on which to build and discover new meanings. Their sacred text provided a foundation but not a completed building.[38]

In the writings of the Calabrian abbot Joaquim de Fiore (1135–1202), whose millennial vision of history was accepted by many of the early Franciscan missionaries to the New World, typological reasoning took on an important new direction. As practiced by Fiore, typology afforded a general outline of human history but could also be used to interpret the meaning of contemporary events and even to peer into the future.[39] Few later writers matched Fiore's elaborate chronologies and frameworks, but the less extreme applications of his method became commonplace and accepted, practical tools clerics could use to make sense of the present and future as well as a technique employed over succeeding generations throughout New Spain.

Manuel de la Bárcena employed this method in the city of Valladolid (now Morelia) in western New Spain as he grappled with the same events as Navarro. When citizens gathered at the cathedral to swear an oath of loyalty to the deposed Ferdinand, de la Bárcena primed them by glossing the biblical coronation of King Solomon. Noting the Israelites' joy at the sight of their new king, the preacher asked, "But, oh Catholics, is this history or rather prophecy?"[40] One could only conclude the latter, as de la Bárcena had noted a parallel euphoria among the Spanish people when Ferdinand VII had assumed the throne earlier in the year. Their joy was short-lived, however, and Spaniards soon found themselves swamped with "cruel anxieties" following Napoleon's removal of Ferdinand VII to Bayonne.[41] Thus, although recent events in Spain proved to be the antitype or fulfillment of Old Testament prophecy and therefore suggested a future that would be tightly controlled by Providence, such a vision of the future did not stop the emergence of a collective unease over what was to come, but neither did it lead to political inertia.[42] Indeed, as we will see, de la Bárcena would use the rest of his sermon to manipulate the qualities of anxiety as he called on his audience to commit themselves to Ferdinand VII.

In New Spain the crisis in the monarchy sparked a debate about local autonomy. To what extent should juntas like the one in Mexico City enjoy political control relative to those governing in Spain itself? At the same time de la Bárcena was preaching, such discussions reached a fever pitch. Word of the rapid turn of events in Spain arrived in Mexico City in the summer of 1808, most notably information about the abdication of Ferdinand VII and the formation of juntas in a number of Spanish cities. In the ensuing months two factions developed among the Spanish elite of Mexico City. One group, dominated by Creoles and associated with the city's Ayuntamiento, pressed the peninsular viceroy, José de Iturrigaray, to recognize their right to create a junta in Mexico City. The other, comprising mostly peninsulares and tied to the viceregal high court, or Audiencia, resisted any such moves toward increased local autonomy. To address the growing political uncertainty and the emerging rifts between the city's power holders, Iturrigaray called for a series of four advisory meetings in the capital. Held between August 9 and September 9, the meetings brought together many of the key social and political bodies in the city, including not only the Ayuntamiento and Audiencia but also guilds, church representatives, and the leaders of Mexico City's semiautonomous Indian districts (*parcialidades*). At stake was the political relationship between New Spain and the Spanish juntas governing in the name of Ferdinand VII. Much to the distaste of the peninsulares involved in these discussions, Iturrigaray appeared to side with those Creoles who agitated for increased local control. The viceroy justified his move on pragmatic grounds. "Spain is now in a state of anarchy. There are supreme juntas everywhere," he explained, "and we should not obey any of them."[43]

Preaching at the time of these contentious meetings, de la Bárcena offered a more abstract argument that also warned his audience of the dangers it faced in this moment of uncertainty. Freely mixing metaphors, he described New Spain's political environment as a smoldering volcano, ready to blow, or even a Pandora's box, which, once opened, "will cover our homeland with troubles." Here was a bleak vision of the future, a future seemingly impossible to control. The preacher recited a litany of potential disasters to produce fear—an essential component of anxiety—and thus motivate a population unsure about the future. But what might head off de la Bárcena's gloomy predictions? Only the stability offered by a legitimate monarch could keep a lid on Pandora's box.[44] A monarchy, de la Bárcena argued, is the best form of government because it is the most simple and stable. Although Spain still possessed a monarchy, on its throne sat a foreign usurper unworthy of the position. In contrast, the preacher added, Ferdinand's credentials separated him from any pretender: he lauded "El Deseado" (the Desired One) for his impeccable lineage, fine education, and outstanding virtue. "In sum," de la Bárcena concluded, "observation, reason, the march of time, human history, the advantages of monarchical rule, the ills that it avoids, all demonstrate our satisfaction to have a King: *vivat Rex.*"[45] His pithy statement of royal legitimacy was reassuring and refined the raw fear developed earlier in the sermon. Yet, although de la Bárcena offered his audience the return of Ferdinand VII as a long-term goal, for the time being he pleaded with God to "send us an angel to deliver us from such bitter uncertainties."[46]

In turn, he urged his audience to recognize the familial and religious bonds that linked Spaniards, whether Creole or peninsular, in a transatlantic union. "We Spaniards that live in America believe that a common fatherland gave us our religion and our distinguished background. . . . [A]nd we see in our countrymen a father, a husband, a kinsman, a friend. For one to offend another would be to wound the very core of our hearts, so strike any thoughts you might hold that undermine our unity ... open your eyes to the truth and hear the call of our common interest."[47] Early the next year Beristáin made a remarkably similar appeal for a pan-Hispanic identity: "We're children of the same parents, branches of the same tree, and thus brothers whose interests should be the same."[48] He also warned of the dangers that accompanied reckless political change— a transformation without connection to tradition—because Spanish rule in Mexico offered a three-hundred-year precedent of good governance: "Be damned by God and his angels, and cursed by us, anyone that dare delude us with new forms of government and foolish hopes that they'll bring better fortune."[49]

This is not to say that such references indicate any sort of radical innovation in the way preachers used Catholicism for collective identification. On the contrary, scholars have documented numerous examples of preachers and political pamphleteers who appealed to the religious foundations of Spanishness well before the crisis of 1808 and consciously deemphasized American or European distinctions.[50] Such works demonstrate a common lexicon with which most preachers and their Creole or peninsular audiences would have been familiar. But during this period of increasing political turbulence in New Spain, especially following the toppling of Ferdinand VII in 1808 and the Hidalgo rebellion in 1810, such symbolic references intensified. An almost obsessive concern with Creole and peninsular unity remained a central feature of royalist writings after the Hidalgo rebellion, as did familial metaphors used to describe the qualities of that bond.[51]

After the grito, clerics continued to use biblical analogies and typology as a way to orient their audiences toward a potential end to the independence era's political turmoil. The sermon preached by Pedro José de Mendizábal in Querétaro in late 1810 is a good example of this trend and also of the role of anxiety during an utterly pivotal moment in the independence era.[52] The sermon came on the third day of a novena cycle of Masses following the arrival in the city of a revered image of Mary, Nuestra Señora del Pueblito, at San Francisco church. Devotees shepherded the image from its shrine in a nearby Indian village to Querétaro, near the epicenter of the two-week-old Hidalgo insurrection.[53] The Mass cycle was meant to secure divine assistance against the insurrection, which was quickly turning into a wide-scale rebellion. Not surprisingly, the rapid expansion of the Hidalgo movement had amplified the latent anxiety among many Spaniards. The insurrection brought to a head the unresolved political relationship between New Spain and Spain that was at the center of the Creole-peninsular rift in 1808; furthermore, it created visceral fears of popular rebellion in a society where wealth and marginality were crosscut by ethnic and racial distinctions. In 1810 Spaniards were a small minority of New Spain's population, roughly 18 percent, or 1,108,000 out of a total population of approximately 6,122,000. The majority of the viceroyalty's population was Indigenous, either identified or self-identified as Indian, often with unique overlapping ethnic identifications, such as Zapotec, Otomí, Mazahua, and Mixe. Combined, the total Indigenous population was in the range of 3,676,000, or roughly 60 percent of New Spain's total population. Persons of mixed Indian, European, and African descent, collectively referred to as castas, made up another 1,338,000, or 22 percent. Finally, as noted earlier, the Spanish population itself was further divided between Creoles and peninsulares, the latter being just a small segment of the total Spanish population. Although this was the demographic reality prior to the insurrection, it became especially threatening to Spaniards after 1810, given the overwhelming presence of non-Spaniards in the ranks of the insurgency.[54]

Almost immediately New Spain's ethnic divisions influenced the course of the insurrection and its later interpretation by royalists. On September 28, 1810, just two days prior to Mendizábal's sermon, Hidalgo's forces faced their first major engagement with royalist forces in the mining city of Guanajuato. The commander of the forces at Guanajuato prepared for a siege by bringing his troops and many civilians into the city's fortified granary, the *alhóndiga de granaditas*. Hidalgo's forces quickly stormed the granary, however, and subsequently slaughtered most of those seeking refuge, indiscriminately killing Creoles and peninsulares. As Querétaro and other important cities in the Bajío were a relatively short journey from Guanajuato, news of the massacre quickly reached them.

After the massacre at Guanajuato the primary source of anxiety for many ethnic Spaniards became concrete, local events rather than abstract, transatlantic debates. In his sermon at Querétaro, Mendizábal began by reminding his audience of Jesus's admonition to the Pharisees: "Render therefore to Caesar the things that are Caesar's, and to God the things that are God's."[55] He and his listeners held a similar responsibility to respect both temporal and divine authority, the preacher argued, but it was a responsibility that could be much more simply fulfilled: they must take up arms against the "vile priest" of Dolores "and his wicked henchmen."[56] To satisfy both Ferdinand and God, Mendizábal preached, one needed to recognize that Providence, the hand of God, was inextricably bound up with worldly affairs and civil authority. Accomplishing God's long-term plan, in concrete terms, demanded an aggressive response against the insurgency. Two weeks later a preacher in Puebla made much the same case, noting, "There is no legitimate authority save that which is God ordained, while all things that come from God are well ordered."[57] This conservative response, a call to defend the established order, was couched in the language of Providence. It assumed a flow of time and events that the faithful could influence only partially, like the middle ground of future telling available in natural astrology. Thus the preachers attempted to channel fear into political action by offering a reading of the future that mitigated the uncertainty of current events. They sought not to suppress anxiety but to manage it, combining fear and hope, incertitude and reassurance.

As in Querétaro, royalist preachers in the months and years that followed kindled their audiences' anxiety by referencing the supposed barbarity and savagery of insurgents. In many such sermons the storming of the alhóndiga in Guanajuato served as a potent symbol of the dangers of the insurgency, and the ethnic element to the popular rebellion lurked just beneath the surface of the preachers' rhetoric. In a sermon preached in Mexico City to the viceroy and other important officials, a peninsular cleric imagined the horrors that would have occurred if Hidalgo's forces had entered Mexico City and repeated the carnage of Guanajuato: "Oh, poor Mexico! You would have already seen your streets and squares awash in the innocent blood of your children, and you would have

seen these tender bits of your soul torn to shreds by the barbarous
fury of [Hidalgo's] bloody hordes."[58]

The sentiments expressed in royalists' sermons were a precursor
and perhaps even origin points for a strident form of Mexican conservatism that, along with liberalism, would become one of the poles
of national politics in the nineteenth century. These voices expressed an intense desire to maintain (and, later, to revive) the past
as a source of stability and order and in many cases to sustain preexisting social, economic, and racial hierarchies. Yet even within this
staunchly conservative vision and the somewhat ambiguous relationship between biblical typology and predestination, these tools could
be used to foster political action and adaptation, such as the vigorous calls for ethnic unity in the aftermath of the Hidalgo uprising.

At other points on the political spectrum and at other moments during the independence era those same techniques were
put to work to imagine new political futures, to innovate in the colonial sense. The early insurgency was famously led by a pair of
priests: the Creole Hidalgo and, following his defeat and execution
in 1811, a mestizo, José María Morelos y Pavón. While we know
that numerous sermons were preached among the insurgent forces,
hardly any survive, either in manuscript or printed form. Yet the
few that were recorded in one form or another offer intriguing
glimpses of the way in which insurgent preachers drew upon many
of the same methods as their royalist counterparts to support a
much different vision of the political future.

The early insurgency was anti-Spanish (meaning antipeninsu-
lar) without being antiroyalist. That is, the initial insurgent political
plans were conceived of as a renewal or, at most, a reconfiguration
of the relationship between the king and his subjects, alongside the
emancipation of New Spain from unjust governance and Spanish
tutelage. Even so, the early movement was framed as a defense of
religion and tradition and, in a sense, a defense of the idea of Spain;
it was described as a bulwark to save Catholicism from a Spain now
overrun by a godless France.[59] Hidalgo's grito, though its actual
wording remains uncertain, captured this sentiment: "Long Live
Ferdinand VII! Long Live America! Long Live Religion! and
Death to Bad Government!" Over the next decade the goals of the
insurgency shifted toward outright independence. Yet throughout

this period insurgent preachers drew biblical connections, as did the royalists, to explain their project and to praise their leaders. Sometimes these were allusions to the New Testament, as in 1812, when a creole priest and doctor of theology, Francisco de Velasco, celebrated the birth of the martyred Hidalgo, comparing this Miguel to the Archangel Michael and his battle with Lucifer. More often Hidalgo and other insurgent leaders were aligned with heroic Old Testament figures, especially Moses or the Maccabees, leaders of the great Jewish revolt in the second century BCE.[60] The goals of these sermons were similar to those of the royalists: to rally their listeners behind a political cause and to respond to the anxiety of present turmoil. Their preferred rhetorical strategy was to give temporal depth to current events by placing them in a biblical framework. In turn, this meant the tremendous changes of the present could be interpreted as fulfillment or renewal rather than rupture or novelty. When taken to the extreme, Hidalgo, Morelos, and those who later celebrated them positioned their movements as the apotheosis of the emerging nation, as a renewal and return to a Christian utopia that was more Catholic and traditional than what was offered by royalists.[61]

As we have seen, royalist preachers repeatedly described the intense doubt and fear that gripped the transatlantic community of Spaniards following the events of 1808 and 1810. As de la Bárcena put it, Spaniards found themselves wracked by "cruel anxieties, torn between fear and hope."[62] Insurgent leaders faced much the same dilemma, as they were forced to motivate their ranks over a decade of bloody conflict, military stalemate, and shifting goals. Preachers encountered and described a collective and pervasive sense of anxiety that, left unchecked, could lead to the dithering or inertia reported by de la Bárcena and others.

   We've noted how such feelings of anxiety are related to the future and also how they develop from the interaction of the future with other states of time. Thus whether one considers the incessant bombardment of the immediate future—the relentless stream of future nows—or the more measured drifting of what lies further ahead, the flow of time and our perception of its speed shape how we experience the emotion.[63] Do we find the political future overwhelming

and paralyzing? Or does it become a source of energy and empower-
ment? Timeless questions, to be sure.

To mitigate the unease circulating among their flocks, New
Spain's preachers offered a solution to the temporal crisis presented
by a precarious future. As we have seen, throughout this period
preachers used a shared set of tools as they described uncertainty and
its relationship to time. Most important, they explained past, present,
and future through biblical analogy and precedent. After the events
of 1808 and especially 1810, however, the future seemed to approach
at a breathtaking and, for some, horrific pace. This was most notable
in the attitudes and sermons of royalist preachers. A perceived accel-
eration of time, prompted in part by the ways in which sermonists
described the future, increased anxiety in New Spain. In turn,
preachers converted a diffuse worry or disquiet into concrete fears
about the dangers of political change and mass rebellion.

Preachers then extended to their audiences a method with
which an individual could rehabilitate the negative aspects of fear.
Conde Pineda stated the matter clearly when he noted that confidence *mixed* with fear bestowed upon listeners an ideal inner state
in which to approach God and the future. The emotional pathway
staked out by Conde Pineda and others historicized current experiences, placing them in the march of time. This was a common interpretive move. More surprisingly, however, these preachers also
"futurized" the emotions of their audiences. They explained contemporary events through a deep history of biblical typology and
then tamed the precariousness of the future with the reassurance
of Providence. This was a method that drew on shared notions of
historicity—what counted as a possible and therefore usable past—
but a relationship to the past very different from our notions of
history. From this usable past potential futures emerged. It was an
instrument of manipulating time that worked well because audiences knew it well.

Is this a technique of futuremaking that leads only to conservative outcomes? The strong role of Providence in this rhetoric suggested a form of predestination and thus a limited ability to alter
the future. In July 1810, just weeks before the beginning of the
Hidalgo insurrection, José María de Alcalá, a canon in Mexico
City's cathedral chapter, described a Providence so potent that

"without his sovereign will, neither a bird falls on the earth nor a speck moves through the air."[64] But as we've seen repeatedly throughout this book Providence did not mean predestination. To reach a providential future required work in the present, in this case a collective effort of politics to shore up potential cleavages among New Spain's population. This was the position of royalist preachers, whose strident voices dominate the historical record. But similar techniques were used by insurgents to imagine and bring into being different futures.[65] Both royalists and insurgents worked within the paradox of free will and its relationship to divine intervention, those Catholic dogmas that were widely understood in New Spain and that animated many conversations about futuremaking.

Because confidence in a divine plan and confusion about its course were taken to be complementary states, much of the political work of the Mexican independence era began as emotional labor. Through the cultivation of anxiety, with its productive mix of fear and confidence, preachers and their audiences groped toward an uncertain future.

In hindsight, the independence-era sermons were preached at the beginning of a long twilight of colonial forms of futuremaking. As that form of time experience faded in the nineteenth century, the future would remain unclear, or at least contested, for generations. In part, this was owing to the changing role of the past in the Mexican present. In nineteenth-century Mexico, visions of the future took new directions. One was akin to the modernist vision of history, fueled by an aggressive nineteenth-century liberalism, that saw the past as a burden offering little guidance for interpreting the future. The second was a sort of mourning for the past that drove many conservatives, a romantic longing for an impossible return to an earlier state. The two visions were at odds with one another, and they took decades to harden into their most extreme forms, but in both cases temporal ruptures trumped renewal.[66]

CHAPTER SEVEN

Epilogue, as Prologue
Futures and Their Pasts

IN THE LATTER PART of the twentieth century, historians began to discover, and in some cases rediscover, a perplexing set of documents created in New Spain. Referred to as *títulos primordiales*, or primordial titles, the sources described the founding of Indigenous communities in the aftermath of the Spanish conquest in the sixteenth century. They narrated remarkable events, sometimes in images, sometimes in text, often in breathtaking combinations of both.

They also disturbed the history we thought we knew. They offered accounts of the deep origins and transformations of Indigenous communities whose chronologies and sense of self seemed to undermine many of the standard interpretations of the colonial period. We learned of native towns and their elders receiving the conquistador Hernán Cortés and other Spanish leaders with great warmth; we learned of Indigenous authorities eagerly accepting the arrival of Christianity yet fighting tenaciously for the defense of communal lands; we encountered key events and dates at odds with those found in Spanish-language sources; we saw images and symbols of European origin knitted intricately with those from the Mesoamerican tradition.

174

A primordial title written in Nahuatl in the town of Soyatzingo captured some of these wonders:

> Alas, Oh lord God, we honored the moon and the stars, the property of God the ruler of the universe. Oh my dear children, you must entirely understand that Cortés don Luis de Velasco Marqués [sic] brought us the true faith. Let no one flee when he arrives. He brought the true belief in the precious honored body of our lord Jesus Christ, so that we would become Christians. We need to make a house of God where we can attend mass and learn the four ways of knowing our lord Jesus Christ (in our own words or language?), so that there we can confess and prepare ourselves to receive the precious honored body of God, and so we can be baptized there, and when we die we will be buried there. Thus Cortés don Luis de Velasco Marqués ordered us. My dear children, ask yourselves what saint shall we serve.[1]

Many of the surviving examples were written in Nahuatl, but similar documents came to light in other Indigenous languages, including Maya, Purépecha, Matlatzinca, Zapotec, and Mixtec. Scholars had known about some of these records for years, in a few instances as far back as the nineteenth century. But as more turned up, historians increasingly began to scrutinize them as a category of documents that shared features, even conventions.

The provenance of the documents raised the most immediate questions. Where did they come from? When were they written? Who wrote them? Were these really documents from the sixteenth century, even from the immediate aftermath of the conquest?

Over time it became clear that in most cases these were not early colonial documents at all but much later creations. Indigenous intellectuals and town leaders produced most of them in the late seventeenth and eighteenth centuries, in some cases two hundred years or more after the events they were supposed to describe.[2] The Soyatzingo title described events from the early to mid-1500s, in the immediate aftermath of the conquest, but was probably written in the late 1600s. What's more, the dating of

events narrated in the texts did not always match up with those referenced in other sources. At times the titles conflated the names of
the persons they described, as in the passage above, in which the
author combined into a single person the conquistador Hernán
Cortés with a later viceroy, Don Luís de Velasco.

This deeper understanding of the origins and history of the
documents raised additional questions. What should we make of
texts that were written in a style and voice that purported to be
from an earlier period? How should we explain their historical inaccuracies?

The study of the genre and related documents started a lively,
productive conversation and offered answers to these questions.
Other historians, myself included, happily mined the work of these
scholars to use the documents as historical marvels, as examples of
the unique and creative responses of native communities to the
conquest and its long-term aftermath. Otherwise, discussions of
the titles remained confined to the conversations of ethnohistorians and other specialists.[3]

Why bring up the primordial titles in the conclusion to a book
that is not primarily about the region's ethnohistory?

According to traditional interpretations of these documents,
their contents can be read in one of two ways. On one hand, they
can be interpreted as forgeries that self-consciously adopted an ar-
chaic style and voice to achieve some goal. They were tricks, in
other words, meant to achieve some short-term goal (the defense
of land, the preservation of community privileges) through the art
of deception. Their function dominates our interpretation of their
meaning. On the other, they can be read as evidence of historical
memories, often distorted by the passage of time but lending
themselves to being gleaned for historical evidence of actual
sixteenth-century events. In their imperfect representation of the
past, the títulos then become evidence of the tattered historical
memories of Indigenous communities later in the colonial period.
If we are able to strip away their patina of inaccuracies, we might
find a layer of the authentic past.

As a number of studies have shown, however, it might make
more sense for us to think of them as *both* invention and memory.[4]
This interpretation takes as its starting point the perspectives, as

best they can be understood, of the people who created these documents. What did they take the titles to mean? What resources did they draw upon when creating them? What did they hope to achieve by bringing them into the world? What world did they bring into being when they read them, gave them to Spanish officials, or held them in secret?

In some ways answering these questions would mean simply following the traditional historical imperative of avoiding anachronism, being sensitive to the logic of our sources, and using period or "actor-centered" categories of analysis. On the other hand, as Greg Anderson has recently pointed out, most of us historians have received the admonition to avoid anachronism, yet even when we heed that call the result can be unsatisfying. Our work often takes the form of belittling cultural history, an emic anthropological account and supposedly a view from inside but one that remains patronizing. In other words, we might make sure to offer working definitions of our key historical terms, avoid using terms that were not present at the time in question, and carefully present the various ways of thinking and being in the world of our historical subjects; but in the end we do the heavy historical lifting, the real interpretive work, using our own ontological categories and commitments, our own understanding of what is real in the world and what matters.[5] The result is that we've exoticized the worldviews of our historical subjects, placing them in a kind of diorama of historical explanation, where they stare at us, silently, inertly, and where we historians do the speaking and acting. We are docents in the museum of history.

These historical reflexes, baked deeply into our ways of understanding the past, make it difficult to answer the questions raised above. In our minds we tend to hold invention and memory as separate things. After all, what metaphors and images do we have available to process memory and invention as the same thing? Yet it seems plausible that some of the primordial titles were just that. Neither forgery nor garbled memory, they recorded historical moments when the past as recall and the past as resource were one. To us this might seem like an exotic, even monstrous species with the head of one animal on the body of another. To the people who created them, such moments would not seem exotic or strange at all.

Figure 12. An image from the Mapa de Cuauhtlantzinco, *a collection of paintings and text in Nahuatl and Spanish in the genre of primordial titles. The* Mapa *emphasizes the role of local Indigenous elite in the quick acceptance and spread of Christianity. Here, the native leader Tepoztecatzin, shown in full warrior dress, leads Spanish troops toward other Indigenous men who have not yet accepted Christianity. Their pre-Christian status seems to be represented by metaphorical slumber. (Wood,* Transcending Conquest, *chapter 4.* Mapa de Cuauhtlantzinco, *Manuscripts Collections, the Latin American Library at Tulane University. Courtesy of the Latin American Library at Tulane University.)*

Tradition could be used to create things, to adapt to the present, and to prepare for the future.[6]

In this way the títulos resonate strongly with other colonial documents of futuremaking and the shared ways of relating to time surveyed throughout this book. The Indigenous authors of the primordial titles engaged in a radical act of situating themselves in time: they marshaled the resources of the past, the resources of memory, and the resources of tradition to achieve goals in the present and craft diverse futures. Sometimes they presented their assembled resources as a narrative of the sixteenth-century present (the language of "behold these events"), at other times in the form of history or chronicle (the language of "recall these times"). James Lockhart described the sense of time in these documents as an absence, atemporal, timeless, even mythic. That makes sense if we use our own definition of time as a standard, where timefulness requires past, present, and future to be linked in an unending and regular succession and where a modernist notion of history acts as a gatekeeper for those things from the past that can be introduced into the present as evidence, resources, or historical reality (what specialists would call the historicity of the past).[7] It also makes sense if we limit our analysis to the texts themselves, in a formal reading of their contents that is separated from their context. But the titles were never disconnected from the world and people around them. They were used and understood differently from myths. They were deeply embedded in the events and moments when they were created, and they demonstrate a sense of time experience on the part of their authors that was far from mythic or timeless. Lockhart himself makes this clear in an elegant explanation of the historical inconsistencies in the Soyatzingo title and, by extension, those of the genre as a whole. References to the sixteenth-century past, say, the arrival of Christianity or the name of key Spanish officials, had taken on a canonical status by the time the titles were created. Dipping into this canon, this past, became a way to legitimate the text, to anoint it with authority that would appeal to multiple audiences, both within the community and outside of it.[8]

Stepping back into the disparate forms of futuremaking of the previous chapters, we have seen that the past also turned out to be quite abundant and available for creating new futures. It was a prolific past, a past that was alive. Yet it has been harder for us to see these forms of innovation through the prism of history, refracted as they are through documents that are heavy with the language of orthodoxy, custom, repetition, time immemorial, and tradition. Indeed, we should be forgiven, at least partially, for our failure to see colonial futures, because so often they were deeply enmeshed in forms of reproduction and persistence.[9] But we moderns are not without some responsibility. We are socialized into a vision of the world that frames traditions as raw materials for the status quo. Viewed negatively, they are sources of stagnation. Seen in a positive light, they might offer a way to conserve the past and engender social cohesion but rarely much more than that. As a result, we have also overlooked the culture of colonial futuremaking because we don't readily associate tradition, let alone religious thought, with change and innovation.[10]

Yet this way of relating to time, as we have seen in various examples throughout this book, was commonplace in colonial New Spain. It was an everyday, ordinary, repeated practice. It peppered the records of colonial institutions, economic transactions, the genre of the weekly sermon, and the vast range of sources that documented activities we would call religious or spiritual. These sources occasionally recorded extraordinary circumstances, such as the violence and uncertainty of the independence era, but more often they recorded the everyday, as when lenders and traders discussed their business or laypersons sought approval for a spiritual gathering.

Futuremaking through tradition was commonplace and also a common place, in the ancient and medieval sense of the term. That is to say, colonial subjects used tradition, the past, time immemorial, and related terms as standard references that others quickly understood: as formulas, devices, and tools that could be used to legitimate action in the present. We have seen examples of how these common places fostered hierarchy, social control, economic marginalization, and other persistent forms of inequality that are well documented in the history of New Spain and colonial Latin America. But we have also encountered their role in adaptation, change, and innovation and in forging creative responses to present predicaments.

These threads of tradition and innovation cannot be separated. Even if they could, we shouldn't try. Doing so would only distort the time and people we hope to understand. But neither should we celebrate colonial futuremaking as something to be revived, like fragments of DNA that we've found in a bit of amber.

But if this relationship to change and innovation is not for reviving, it is worth remembering. For one thing, it offers a distinctive way of framing the turmoil of Latin America's nineteenth-century postcolonial history. We can begin to examine the postcolonial period for loss as well as legacy and for the evolving sense of future-making among nineteenth- and twentieth-century Latin Americans. This relationship also provides a different perspective on the past in a methodological sense. It suggests another way of doing history, another way of reading the past that might prove fruitful in the study of New Spain and beyond. This approach would give futuremaking a place alongside pastmaking, anticipating alongside remembering. But in the end the lost common place of colonial futures can offer something more modest, something the past as history should always do: an example of being in the world that might challenge, confirm, and enrich our own forms of futuremaking.

Notes

Chapter One. Introduction

1. For the case of Latin America, a good introduction is found in Adelman, *Colonial Legacies*.
2. O'Hara, *A Flock Divided*.
3. On these points, see the suggestive commentary of Adelman, *Colonial Legacies*, Preface and Introduction; Cañizares-Esguerra, *Puritan Conquistadors*, chapter 6.
4. Quoted in Valdés-Ugalde, "Janus and the Northern Colossus."
5. Fukuyama, *Falling Behind*.
6. Haber, *How Latin America Fell Behind*. As Breen and Cañizares-Esguerra have noted, a similar mode of explanation has crept into histories written about the Atlantic World; "Hybrid Atlantics."
7. O'Gorman discusses these theoretical and historiographical problems in *México, el trauma de su historia*; see also Lomnitz, *Deep Mexico, Silent Mexico*, especially chapter 4.
8. Florescano, *Memory, Myth, and Time in Mexico*, 228.
9. This holds true not only for the attempts of earlier generations of Latin American intellectuals to pinpoint the deep roots of national identities but also for more recent academic interventions in Latin America and the United States. For the former, see Paz, *El laberinto de la soledad*; Bonfil Batalla, *México profundo*; Freyre, *Casa-grande & Senzala*; Mariátegui, *Siete ensayos*.
10. See his *Futures Past*.
11. This book is deeply influenced by Reinhart Koselleck's use of time as a category of historical analysis. Koselleck argues that most "historical time," or the changing human experience of time in a given society, exists alongside of and overlaps with other ways of temporal thinking. Nonetheless, it is difficult to reconcile this theoretical model with his notion of modernity

as "the total otherness of the past." Quoted in Zammito, "Koselleck's Philosophy of Historical Time(s)," 133, which provides a detailed assessment of Koselleck's work.

12. On this point, see the remarks of Cooper in chapter 5 of *Colonialism in Question*.

13. On the tendency of postcolonial scholars to overemphasize the distinction between modern and premodern, see Molina, "Spirituality and Colonial Governmentality," 134.

14. Gurminder Bhambra offers some of this criticism in "Historical Sociology, Modernity, and the Postcolonial Critique." Also useful in this context is Dipesh Chakrabarty's reminder that we need to decouple institutional change (modernization) from the experience of and desire to be modern (modernity), two processes with potentially distinct periodizations that are frequently conflated under the label of modernity. "The Muddle of Modernity," 671. Björn Wittrock's concept of "promissory notes of modernity" and their "new assumptions about human beings, their rights and agency" is a theoretical opening for reconsidering the role of culture in the creation of an institutional modernity. Even in this suggestive formulation, which remains rooted in the notion of an epistemic rupture in eighteenth-century Europe, one gets the impression that such ideas developed with little direct relationship to mundane cultural codes or practices. Nor is it clear how one would be able to untangle the modern and antimodern cultural underpinnings of modernity. "Modernity, One, None, or Many?" 37.

15. Following the work of the sociologist Ann Swidler and other practice theorists, I assume that culture provides a repertoire or toolkit that historical actors can draw upon to solve various kinds of problems. In this model, cultural analysis examines persistent "strategies of action," that is, behaviors and practices that take advantage of existing "cultural competencies." Swidler, "Culture in Action." See also Biernacki, *Fabrication of Labor*; Ortner, *Anthropology and Social Theory*; Sewell, "A Theory of Structure."

16. Tavárez, *Invisible War*. Some recent interventions on the topic for New Spain include Christensen, *Nahua and Maya Catholicisms*; O'Hara, *A Flock Divided*; Pardo, *Origins of Mexican Catholicism*, which, alongside other recent scholarship, complement classic studies such as Burkhart, *Slippery Earth*. For good examples from other areas of Spanish presence, see Rafael, *Contracting Colonialism*; Harrison, *Sin and Confession in Colonial Peru*; Mills, *Idolatry and Its Enemies*.

17. Taylor, *Magistrates of the Sacred*. Gruzinski, "La 'segunda aculturación'"; Pescador, *De bautizados a fieles difuntos*; Mazín Gómez, *Entre dos majestades*; Voekel, *Alone Before God*; Brading, "Tridentine Catholicism and Enlightened Despotism."

18. Among a large literature, important and representative works include Connaughton, *Ideología y sociedad en Guadalajara*; Brading, *Church and*

State in Bourbon Mexico; Herrejón Peredo, *Del sermón al discurso cívico;* Melvin, *Building Colonial Cities of God;* Nesvig, *Ideology and Inquisition;* Schwaller, *Church and Clergy in Sixteenth-Century Mexico.*

19. For some rich examples, see Bricker, *The Indian Christ, The Indian King.*
20. Though drawing on different fields of study, see the approach of Bianca Premo, who creatively blends the methods and research questions of ethnohistory, legal history, and the history of ideas in "Custom Today."
21. Brubaker and Cooper, "Beyond 'Identity.'"
22. Some recent scholarship on colonial Latin America has rejected this framework. For notable examples, see Tutino, *Making a New World;* Molina, *To Overcome Oneself;* Schwartz, *All Can Be Saved;* Cañizares-Esguerra, *How to Write the History of the New World* and *Nature, Empire, and Nation;* Silverblatt, *Modern Inquisitions.*
23. Adelman, *Colonial Legacies,* Preface.
24. The careless use of such binaries, as Marcello Carmagnani has noted, can easily oversimplify both the process of historical change and the agency of historical actors. *The Other West,* 5. On the tradition / modernity pairing, see also the remarks of Tenorio-Trillo in *Historia y celebración.*
25. For a discussion of anticipation and prospection from the perspective of psychology and cognitive science, see Seligman et al., *Homo Prospectus.*

Chapter Two. Confessions

1. See the suggestive discussion of these and related issues in Pardo, *Origins of Mexican Catholicism,* 9 and passim.
2. For a discussion of Nahua rituals of forgiveness, see ibid., chaps. 3–4; Burkhart, *Slippery Earth;* Gruzinski, "Confesión, alianza, y sexualidad entre los indios de la Nueva España."
3. Augustine, *Confessions,* book 2, chapter 4.
4. Cervantes, *The Devil in the New World,* 108–13. There is some evidence of the Augustinian vision waning in the eighteenth century. Taylor, *Magistrates of the Sacred,* 19.
5. Lucas, *Astrology and Numerology in Medieval and Early Modern Catalonia,* 13.
6. The theological and philosophical currents and their transmission to New Spain are mapped in Kuri Camacho, *El barroco jesuita novohispano.*
7. Burkhart, *Slippery Earth,* 30.
8. On the widespread fear of death and judgment in New Spain, see von Wobeser, "Certezas, incertidumbres y expectativas en torno a la salvación del alma."
9. Religious leaders would continue to lean on these explanations through the end of the colonial period. For relevant examples, see the discussion of sermons during Mexico's independence era in chapter 6. A similar case occurred in Venezuela in 1812, when an earthquake hammered the city

of Caracas, then in the midst of its own independence struggles, and the archbishop blamed the quake on the collective sinning of Venezuelans past and present. Rodríguez, "1812: El terremoto que interrumpió una revolución." See also, Walker, *Shaky Colonialism*, who describes how religious figures made similar links between notions of social sin and the city of Lima's many earthquakes throughout the colonial era (27).

10. Burkhart, *Slippery Earth*, 28.

11. Or, in Pardo's words, "As the missionary literature of the times makes apparent, Nahua culture became the unavoidable frame of reference within which Christianity had to be explained." *Origins of Mexican Catholicism*, 12.

12. Burkhart, *Slippery Earth*, 28.

13. Ibid., 29.

14. "The *tlatlacolli* concept," Burkhart concludes, "provided some common ground between Christian and Nahua belief. *Tlatlacolli* is sin, but not in the full extent of the Christian usage, and it has some meanings alien to Christianity; the concepts overlap, but are not synonyms." Ibid., 31.

15. Orthodox understanding of sin interacted in myriad ways with local conceptions of transgression, whether conceived of as moral failing or some other form of error. For examples, see Corcuera de Mancera, *Del amor al temor*; Burkhart, *Slippery Earth*; Tavárez, *Invisible War*; Harrison, *Sin and Confession*.

16. Native peoples were generally not subject to the Inquisition, given their theological status as "neophytes." They might be pulled into particular Inquisitorial investigations, however, and were often subject to other forms of church oversight and discipline. These included investigations conducted by bishops that in practice could be quite similar to the Inquisition, if sometimes less formal and legalistic. Tavárez, "Legally Indian"; Greenleaf, "The Inquisition and the Indians of New Spain." These jurisdictional matters stemmed from the decision of church authorities that Indians should not be held to the same standards as "mature" Christians. This distinction would become deeply problematic and sometimes ironic later in the colonial period. While the designation of native peoples as spiritual neophytes persisted in much theological and legal reasoning and carried real institutional and material implications, by the eighteenth century the label could apply to individuals and communities that had been evangelized in the sixteenth century and thus had been part of a Mesoamerican Catholic tradition for generations, in some cases for two hundred years or more.

17. Pardo discusses how medieval theologians understood the relationship between the sacraments, the life cycle, and spiritual perfection. *Origins of Mexican Catholicism*, 12–15.

18. Myers, *Poor, Sinning Folk*, 8.

19. But penitents also needed to confess their sins completely and perform the penance or restitution imposed by the priest. Francisco de Vitoria,

the famed sixteenth-century theologian and jurist, stated the requirements succinctly in his own *confesionario:* "El pecado mortal se perdona
por quatro cosas. i. Por contrición del alma. ii. Por confessión de la boca.
iii. Por satissfación de la obra. iiii. Por propósito de emienda";
Confesionario util y provechoso.

20. Tentler, *Sin and Confession on the Eve of the Reformation,* chapter 1 and
p. 52 ("inner forum"). For additional background on penance in Catholic
Europe leading up to the sixteenth century, see Myers, *Poor, Sinning
Folk;* O'Banion, *The Sacrament of Penance and Religious Life in Golden Age
Spain;* Borobio, "The Tridentine Model of Confession in Its Historical
Context."

21. On evasion of the sacrament in late colonial villages and towns, see
Taylor, *Magistrates of the Sacred,* 241–43.

22. See, for instance, Bartolomé de Alva's, *Confessionario mayor y menor en lengua mexicana,* a bilingual Nahuatl–Spanish manual, or Augustín de
Quintana, *Confessonario en lengua mixe* (Mixe–Spanish); Juan Bautista,
Advertencias para los confessores de los naturales, fs. 38r–51r. Other *confesionarios* omitted any material other than the most basic questions to aid in
the process of confession, perhaps to keep the texts inexpensive and por-
table. A good example is Marcos de Saavedra, *Confessonario breve, activo y
passivo, en lengua mexicana.*

23. Bartolomé de Alva, *A Guide to Confession Large and Small in the Mexican
Language, 1634,* 70–72.

24. Matt. 22:37–38, Revised Standard Version (RSV).

25. "Has dudado algo de lo que nos manda creer la Santa Madre Iglesia, y la
Fe?" Manuel Pérez, *Farol indiano y guía de curas de indios,* 176.

26. Saavedra, *Confessonario breve,* s/f.

27. Quintana, *Confessonario en lengua mixe,* 5–6 (both quotes); *Advertencias
para los nuevos confesores,* Archivo Histórico de la Provincia de San Alberto
de los Carmelitas Descalzos, carpeta 1669, fs. 6–8; Alva, *A Guide to
Confession,* 66, 70; Bartholome García, *Manual para administrar los santos
sacramentos de penitencia, eucharistia, extrema-unción y matrimonio.*

28. On the concept of affective residue, see Baumeister, Vohs, DeWall, and
Zhang, "How emotion shapes behavior."

29. Foucault, *The History of Sexuality,* especially 18–21. Tentler offers a more
detailed study that supports similar conclusions. See his *Sin and
Confession.* On this process in New Spain, key studies include Gruzinski,
"Individualization and Acculturation," "Confesión, alianza, y sexualidad
entre los indios de la Nueva España," and "La 'conquista de los cuerpos,'"; Molina, *To Overcome Oneself;* Klor de Alva, "Sin and Confession
among the Colonial Nahuas."

30. Quintana, *Confessonario en lengua mixe,* s/f. ["enseñar moral"] ["conque se
puede preguntar todo, lo que se quisiere *mutatis mutandis*"]; Molina notes
similar qualities in the writings of Ignatius and his Spiritual Exercises,

"which charts a bare outline of what was to be a highly individuated experience." *To Overcome Oneself,* 35.

31. Exodus 20:13 (RSV).

32. Saavedra, *Confessonario breve,* s/f. "No es menester preguntar todo lo que está aqui, sino solamente lo que fuere necesario, según la calidad de las personas, y su confesión." Gruzinski, "Confesión, alianza, y sexualidad," 204.

33. Quintana, *Confessonario en lengua mixe,* 1.

34. *Advertencias para los nuevos confesores;* Pardo, *Origins of Mexican Catholicism,* 81. This attention to the material implications of sin, and its description using the language of risk, is quite different from many of the earlier confessionals. The *Advertencias* was never published, existing only in manuscript form, and was written in an informal, almost conversational style. I find this source to be suggestive evidence that by the eighteenth century colonial subjects used sin and other religious concepts in a variety of calculations of risk, danger, and probability where the spiritual and material overlapped to a substantial degree.

35. The work of Foucault and some of the studies carried out in that vein of inquiry (cited above) are the most obvious examples.

36. Alva, *A Guide to Confession,* 106; *Advertencias para los nuevos confesores,* fs. 6, 21, 61–62, 69–70.

37. This emotional relationship to the future is strikingly similar to what we find in political sermons from the time of Mexican independence (see chapter 6).

38. On these points, see the interesting discussion in *Advertencias para los nuevos confesores,* fs. 76–78; also, Molina, *To Overcome Oneself,* 115–16.

39. Carruthers, *Craft of Thought,* 4.

40. Ibid., 12 (quote), see also 2–5, 9–15. Michelle Molina makes the connection between Carruthers's discussion of *memoria* and the active confessional subject. She examines what might be the paradigmatic example of this process, the Jesuit practices of general confession and the Spiritual Exercises, and emphasizes how these techniques must be understood as physical, embodied practices, not simply mental exercises. *To Overcome Oneself,* 33–35, 45–47, 199–200. Recent work in the natural and social sciences suggests similar processes at work in human memory. Seligman et al., *Homo Prospectus,* 14.

41. On these points, see also Carruthers's discussion of *intentio,* which referred to an appropriate and productive "attitude" or "inclination" toward the things to be remembered. In Augustine's terms, it is described as a "movement of the mind toward" some goal, a phrase notable for its combined spatial and temporal qualities. Though Carruthers discusses this theory in relation to specific practices of memory work in the medieval monastic setting, the connections to auricular confession are clear, in part given the importance of appropriate emotional states (contrition, in-

tention) for a successful conclusion of the sacrament. *Craft of Thought*, 14–16 (quote 16); Molina, *To Overcome Oneself*, 34.

42. Consider the interesting ways in which this model resonates with new insights into financial accounting, where anticipation and assumptions about the future turn out to be requirements for financial reporting. "The argument is that there is a difference between events-as-reportable / recordable / wittnesable [*sic*] and events-as-actuality not merely because of the incompleteness or constructivist character of descriptions of the past, but because some events—essential for such descriptions—are imaginary in the sense that they are anticipated. Anticipations of the future make possible a report of the past. For financial reports of the past not everything necessary is, or has been, present." McSweeney, "Looking Forward to the Past," 770.

43. On active memory, see Seligman et al., *Homo Prospectus*, 14–15.

44. Pardo, *Origins of Mexican Catholicism*, chaps. 3–4, especially 80.

45. *Advertencias para los nuevos confesores*, f. 4.

46. For example, ibid., fs. 36. For an insightful discussion, see Ramírez, "Mendacious Texts." For similar points in the Spanish context, see O'Banion, *The Sacrament of Penance*, 6–10.

47. For an intriguing example, see Aho, *Confession and Bookkeeping*, which argues that double-entry bookkeeping arose primarily as a rhetorical technique in response to the awareness of sin and moral indebtedness on the part of medieval merchants.

48. Quintana, *Confessonario en lengua mixe*, 54; Beeler, *The Ventureño Confesionario of José Señán, O.F.M.*, 48–51; García, *Manual para administrar los santos sacramentos*, "Sexto mandamiento." See also the exhaustive translation of *pecado* and related terms in an anonymous late-colonial Zapotec–Spanish dictionary, *Vocabulario castellano-zapoteco*. Gruzinski discusses Quintana in "Confesión, alianza, y sexualidad," 202–4.

49. On the rise of a more individualistic piety, see especially Voekel, *Alone Before God*; Larkin, *The Very Nature of God*.

50. Foucault, *The History of Sexuality*, 20.

51. This observation was made by Gruzinski, "Confesión, alianza y sexualidad": "Once again the Mexican countryside became a kind of testing ground for measures, strategies and techniques that would then be applied in Western Europe," 173. See also the insightful discussion in Molina, *To Overcome Oneself*, 16–18, 45. I am deeply indebted to both in my thinking about these issues. The key examples in Nahuatl are Alonso de Molina, *Confessionario mayor en lengua mexicana y castellana*; Alva, *Guide to Confession Large and Small*; see also the Tarascan / Purépecha guide of Ángel Serra, *Manual de administrar los santos sacramentos a los españoles, y naturales de esta provincia* (Michoacán); also the later examples of Quintana, Señán, García, and others.

Chapter Three. Stars

1. This account draws mainly on the fine study by Crewe, "Brave New Spain." A number of longer treatments of Lombardo's life are available, including Meza González, *El laberinto de la mentira*; González Obregón, *D. Guillén de Lampart, la Inquisición, y la independencia en el siglo XVII*; and Ronan, *The Irish Zorro*.

2. A sampling of *libros pronósticos*, including Inquisitorial criticism, emendations, and approvals, can be found in Quintana, *La astrología en la Nueva España en el siglo XVII*. An overview of the literature in New Spain, focusing especially on the licensing process, is available in Trabulse, *Los orígenes de la ciencia moderna en México (1630–1680)*. See also his *El círculo roto*, passim but especially chapter 2; Peraza-Rugeley, "Los almanaques de Carlos de Sigüenza y Góngora"; Corona, *Lunarios*; Tena Villeda, "Gabriel López Bonilla, un astrónomo-astrólogo en el siglo XVII mexicano."

3. Jiménez Rueda, *Herejías y supersticiones en la Nueva España*, 222–24.

4. AGN, *Inquisición*, vol. 335, exp. 94, "Denuncia presentada por Fray Juan Menéndez, Mercedario, de que en su convento se practica mucho la astrología judiciaria," 1622; AGN, *Inquisición*, vol. 298, exp. 13, "Proceso contra Leonardo Bernabé por quiromántico," 1613; AGN, *Inquisición*, vol. 335, exp. 102, "Denuncia contra una negra llamada Cecilia, porque anuncia las llegadas de las naos adivinando con exactitud las mas veces," 1621; AGN, *Inquisición*, vol. 1205, exp. 19, fs. 1–103, "El Sr. Inquisidor fiscal de este Santo Oficio contra Pedro Vidal o Vidales de Ledezma, de oficio curandero y barbero, por curandero supersticioso, quiromántico planetario con sabor de astrología judiciaria," 1704.

5. On this issue in fifteenth- and sixteenth-century Europe, see Westman, *The Copernican Question*, 63–64.

6. For examples, see the long *proceso* of Gaspar de Rivero Vasconcelos, astrologer and student of canon law, which includes a list of those deposed in Rivero's trial but also a list of the individuals implicated by the accused in the course of his testimony. AGN, *Inquisición*, vol. 435, exp. 248, "Proceso contra Gaspar de Rivero Vasconcelos, mulato libre, estudiante canonista descendiente de Portugueses, natural de Tanger, por astrólogo judiciario, calumnidor del Santo Oficio y sus ministros," 1650, fs. 476r–77r and passim. Also, AGN, *Inquisición*, vol. 1205, exp. 19, fs. 1–103, 1713, "El Sr. Inquisidor fiscal de este Santo Oficio contra Pedro Vidal o Vidales de Ledezma, de oficio curandero y barbero, por curandero supersticioso, quiromántico planetario con sabor de astrología judiciaria" or AGN, *Inquisición*, vol. 329, exp. 9, fs. 335–86, "Proceso contra Hipólita Mora por decir que es zahorí y ve el porvenir," 1620.

7. Crewe, "Brave New Spain," 54 (n. 2).

8. For example, Leonard, *Baroque Times in Old Mexico*; Trabulse, *El círculo roto*.

9. The following list by no means exhausts the literature, but some notable works that are particularly relevant to this chapter include Curry, *Prophecy and Power*; Curry, ed., *Astrology, Science and Society*; Grafton, *Cardano's Cosmos*; Grafton and Newman, eds., *Secrets of Nature*; Cañizares-Esguerra, "New World, New Stars." A magisterial book that ranges far beyond astrology but is an indispensable guide to the relationship between astrological science and other branches of knowledge is Westman, *The Copernican Question*. Additional background can be found in Tester, *A History of Western Astrology*; Geneva, *Astrology and the Seventeenth Century Mind*; Ackerman Smoller, *History, Prophecy, and the Stars*.

10. Grafton, *Cardano's Cosmos*, 10. On the intellectual credibility of early modern astrology, see also the remarks of Cañizares-Esguerra, "New World, New Stars," 35–36.

11. AGN, *Inquisición*, vol. 356, exp. 141, "Testificación contra Lucas de Figueroa, por pronosticar y tener libros de astrología," 1626; AGN, *Inquisición*, vol. 436, exp. 23, fs. 99–103, "Testificación contra Jerónimo, astrólogo," 1650; AGN, *Inquisición*, vol. 1205, exp. 19, fs. 1–103, "El Sr. Inquisidor fiscal de este Santo Oficio contra Pedro Vidal o Vidales de Ledezma, de oficio curandero y barbero, por curandero supersticioso, quiromántico planetario con sabor de astrología judiciaria," 1713; AGN, *Inquisición*, vol. 753, "Antonio Rodríguez, contra un hombre que no sabe como se llama, por leer en las rayas de las manos," 1713; AGN, *Inquisición*, vol. 435, exp. 248, "Proceso contra Gaspar de Rivero Vasconcelos, mulato libre, estudiante canonista descendiente de Portugueses, natural de Tánger, por astrólogo judiciario, calumnidor del Santo Oficio y sus ministros," 1650. This sort of interaction across lines of caste and other social markers is well documented for seventeenth-century witchcraft cases in Lewis, *Hall of Mirrors*.

12. Trabulse, *La ciencia perdida*, 26.

13. Kuhn, *The Structure of Scientific Revolutions*.

14. Curry, *Prophecy and Power*, 4; Westman, *The Copernican Question*, 30, 34–40.

15. See the remarks of Thomas, *Religion and the Decline of Magic*, 667–68.

16. On the marginalization of knowledge emerging from Spanish America, see Cañizares-Esguerra, *How to Write the History of the New World*, and "New World, New Stars"; Breen and Cañizares-Esguerra, "Hybrid Atlantics."

17. Allen, *Star-Crossed Renaissance*, 150.

18. Ibid., 151.

19. Ibid., 152.

20. Curry, *Prophecy and Power*, 4; Trabulse, *La ciencia perdida*, 51–52.

21. An overview of the distinction between natural and judicial astrology can be found in Curry, *Prophecy and Power*, 8–15.

22. For introductions to the topic, see Foster, *Hippocrates' Latin American Legacy*, chapter 1; Earle, *The Body of the Conquistador*, chapter 1; see also Cañizares-Esguerra, "New World, New Stars."

23. Earle, *Body of the Conquistador,* 37.
24. Allen, *Star-Crossed Renaissance,* 148. See also Westman, *The Copernican Question,* 91.
25. Gruzinski, *What Time Is It There?* 94. For a short introduction to Martínez's life, see Hoberman, "Enrico Martínez: Printer and Engineer."
26. Curry, *Prophecy and Power,* 8–9. For a discussion of how early modern astrologers drew and interpreted genitures, see Grafton, *Cardano's Cosmos,* 24–31.
27. Grafton, *Cardano's Cosmos,* 10–11.
28. *Summa theologiae,* 1.115.4, trans. Fathers of the English Dominican Province, cited in Lucas, *Astrology and Numerology in Medieval and Early Modern Catalonia,* 12. The larger discussion draws on pages 7–13. For a clear discussion of this theological and intellectual conundrum, see Flint, "The Transmission of Astrology in the Early Middle Ages," 1–2.
29. Curry, *Prophecy and Power,* 10.
30. Cited and discussed in Peterson, "Heavenly Influences," 25–26; Trabulse, *Los orígenes de la ciencia moderna,* 83–84, 134–36.
31. Gruzinski, *What Time Is It There?* 97.
32. Hoberman, "Enrico Martínez," 339.
33. The term is Hoberman's, "Enrico Martínez," 339. On the Inquisitorial view of heresy as contagion, see Nesvig, *Ideology and Inquisition,* especially chaps. 2, 9; Nesvig, "'Heretical Plagues' and Censorship Cordons."
34. AGN, *Inquisición,* vol. 1205, exp. 19, fs. 1–103, "El Sr. Inquisidor fiscal de este Santo Oficio contra Pedro Vidal o Vidales de Ledezma, de oficio curandero y barbero, por curandero supersticioso, quiromántico planetario con sabor de astrología judiciaria," 1713.
35. Hoberman, "Enrico Martínez," 340. In 1620 Gaspar de Mier denounced Martínez to the Inquisition for divination, though apparently his case was never tried. Martínez had allegedly determined that three local women caused a recent illness suffered by Mier. Peterson, "Heavenly Influences," 198–99.
36. Sigüenza y Góngora, *Pronóstico para 1678,* in Quintana, *La astrología en la Nueva España,* 157.
37. Joseph Mariano de Medina, *Heliotropio crítico racional prognóstico computado a el meridiano de la Puebla de los Ángeles para el año 1752* (Puebla: Viuda de Miguel de Ortega), in Trabulse, ed., *Historia de la ciencia en México: Estudios y textos, Siglo XVII,* 2:167.
38. Ibid.
39. Ibid.
40. Sigüenza y Góngora, *Pronóstico para 1678,* in Quintana, *La astrología en la Nueva España,* 163.
41. AGN, *Inquisición,* vol. 670, exp. 27, f. 272v, 1672.
42. Such wariness about astrological knowledge finding its way into the hands of the simple, ignorant, or poorly educated was consistent with the

censors' belief in a hierarchy of knowledge, a concept drawn from Aquinas. As it related to heresy, Aquinas held that those without a thorough education (the vast majority of the laity) should be held to a lower standard of doctrinal knowledge and should be forbidden from writing about precepts of the faith. Nesvig, *Ideology and Inquisition*, 51–54.

43. Hannah Marcus explores some of these themes in "Banned Books." "Ultimately," writes Marcus, "censorship of medical books in the sixteenth and seventeenth centuries was a form of promulgation that established a community with recognized expertise and a discourse on utility that became a lasting feature of scientific culture" (3). See also Nesvig, *Ideology and Inquisition*.

44. Jiménez Rueda, *Herejías y supersticiones*, 214–15.

45. Peña, "Quiromancia y adivinación en la Nueva España," 62–63, and "De varios infortunios en un tratado de quiromancia novohispano."

46. On this point, see the discussion in Reith, "Uncertain Times."

47. Quintana, *La astrología en la Nueva España*, 147. See also the discussions in Trabulse, *Ciencia y religión*, 62–65.

48. Quintana, *La astrología en la Nueva España*, 145.

49. AGN, *Inquisición*, vol. 670, f. 250, 1647, "La experiencia ha mostrado los inconvenientes. . . ." See also the discussion in Peraza-Rugeley, "Los almanaques de Carlos de Sigüenza y Góngora," 29, 109.

50. On this issue, see the comments of Alberro, *Inquisición y sociedad en México, 1571–1700*, 183–84.

51. AGN, *Inquisición*, vol. 435, exp. 160, "Denuncia contra el Br. Juan de los Reyes, por adivinar por las rayas de las manos," 1650; AGN, *Inquisición*, vol. 435, exp. 179, "Denuncia contra Francisco de la Banda, difunto, por decir el futuro por las rayas de las manos," 1650; AGN, *Inquisición*, vol. 435, exp. 161, fs. 301–5, "Denuncia contra Martín Cristóbal, difunto, por decir futuros contingentes por las rayas de las manos," 1650; AGN, *Inquisición*, vol. 435, exp. 163, "Denuncia contra un fulano Rendón (difunto) por decir futuros contingentes por las rayas de las manos," 1650.

52. AGN, *Inquisición*, vol. 435, exp. 233, "Denuncia contra Francisco de Grajales, por pronosticar por las rayas de las manos," 1650; AGN, *Inquisición*, vol. 435, exp. 247, "Testificación contra José Díaz Pimienta, por brujerías herbolarias, aprendió en Argel, prognosticaba," 1650.

53. Among many examples, see AGN, *Inquisición*, vol. 1205, exp. 19, fs. 1–103, 1713 (astrology/chiromancy); AGN, *Inquisición*, vol. 858, fs. 541–42, 1732 (astrology/chiromancy); AGN, *Inquisición*, vol. 478, exp. 43, fs. 309–26, 1613 (astrology/chiromancy); AGN, *Inquisición*, vol. 435, exp. 179, 1650 (chiromancy/peyote); AGN, *Inquisición*, vol. 322, exp. 5, 1619 (metopomancy—reading the lines in the forehead/chiromancy); AGN, *Inquisición*, vol. 308, exp. 51, 1615 (metopomancy/chiromancy). On the practical and intellectual links between astrology and other forms of divination and magic, see Thomas, *Religion and the Decline of Magic*, 631–36. I

borrow the term "unsanctioned domain" from Lewis, *Hall of Mirrors*, who uses it to refer to ritual and healing practices involving witchcraft, where traditional power and caste hierarchies were reversed, "in ways that privileged Indians and Indianness, while subordinating Spaniards and Spanishness, and reorienting blacks, mullatoes, and mestizos, who could now attach themselves to Indians in an effort to undermine Spaniards" (6).

54. In the early eighteenth century a French healer was allegedly circulating around the northern town of Saltillo and offering palm readings. When asked by a prospective client whether his predictions of the future were similar to what the Gypsies did in Spain, he responded that he learned the art from a Jesuit who was one of the most "wise and learned" mathematicians in France. The reading ensued. AGN, *Inquisición*, vol. 858, fs. 541–42, "Denuncia que hace D. Baltasar Francisco Mosquera y Valerio, vecino y almacenero en esta ciudad de México, contra un cirujano or curandero francés, llamado Pedro de Feez ... que conocía y alcanzaba muchas cosas por las rayas de las manos," 1732, f. 541r. The man who denounced him, Don Baltasar Francisco Mosquera y Valerio, meticulously cataloged the chiromancer's predictions, noting those that came true and those that were false (541v), as did many other denouncers of astrology and divination.

55. AGN, *Inquisición*, vol. 322, exp. 5, "Testificación contra Melchor de los Reyes, porque adivina las rayas de la frente," 1619; AGN, *Inquisición*, vol. 329, exp. 9, fs. 335–86, "Proceso contra Hipólita Mora por decir que es zahorí y ve el porvenir," 1620; AGN, *Inquisición*, vol. 335, exp. 72, "Información contra María Castillo, por zahorí," 1622; AGN, *Inquisición*, vol. 486, exp. 22, fs. 98–105, "Testificación contra Francisco Hidalgo, por zahorí," 1621; AGN, *Inquisición*, vol. 376, exp. 1, "Testificaciones contra Juan de Cárdenas y su hijo por zahorí y Diego Rangel por el mismo delito," 1632; AGN, *Inquisición*, vol. 1051, no exp., fs. 201–2, "Denuncia que hace María Jacinta Torres, mulata libre casada con Juan Antonio, contra una hija suya llamada María Antonia de cuatro años de edad, por decirse es zahorina," 1713.

56. AGN, *Inquisición*, vol. 952, exp. 3, fs. 19–21, "El Sr. Inquisidor Fiscal del Santo Officio contra Juana ... por supersticiosa que decía el porvenir leyendo en las rayas de las manos," 1705.

57. AGN, *Inquisición*, vol. 329, exp. 9, fs. 335–86, "Proceso contra Hipólita Mora por decir que es zahorí y ve el porvenir," 1620; AGN, *Inquisición*, vol. 335, exp. 72, "Información contra María Castillo, por zahorí," 1622; AGN, *Inquisición*, vol. 376, exp. 1, "Testificaciones contra Juan de Cárdenas y su hijo por zahorí y Diego Rangel por el mismo delito," 1632. See also the case in early seventeenth-century Taxco of a *tlachiztli* (from the Nahuatl *tlachia*, "to see"), a term that described a diviner who operated in ways similar to a *zahorí* and was sometimes used as a synonym. The alleged diviner, a mulato named Cristóbal Hontiveros, fashioned

himself a witch hunter, oddly enough, and said that he went after individuals, including other *zahoríes*, who had bewitched notable Indians in the region. He claimed that multiple civil and church officials (and even God) had authorized his activities. The case and term are carefully reconstructed in Schwaller, "The Importance of Mestizos and Mulatos as Bilingual Intermediaries in Sixteenth-Century New Spain," 722, 735.

58. See, for example, the insightful discussion in Villa Flores, "Talking Through the Chest." On divinatory powers as gifts from God, see also Thomas, *Religion and the Decline of Magic*, 266–67.

59. Quintana, *La astrología en la Nueva España*; Corona, *Lunarios*; Peraza-Rugeley, "Los almanaques de Carlos de Sigüenza y Góngora."

60. For a good discussion of this view and its remarkable persistence in seventeenth-century Europe, see Geneva, *Astrology and the Seventeenth-Century Mind*, 84–97.

61. Trabulse, *Los orígenes de la ciencia moderna*, 129–30, and Leonard, *Baroque Times in Old Mexico*, 204–9.

62. Leonard, *Baroque Times in Old Mexico*, 198.

63. Ibid., 209.

64. In a recent study that examines Sigüenza's role as the curator of an emergent "local archive," Anna More notes the limitations of studying him as simply a forerunner of Enlightenment rationality. She prefers instead to consider his work "as part of the 'high Baroque' in Spanish America: a coalescence of style, epistemology, and politics that combined hermeticism and scientific critique." *Baroque Sovereignty*, 26, 260–61 (quote on 261).

65. Cited in Trabulse, *Ciencia y religión*, 64.

66. Trabulse, *Los orígenes de la ciencia moderna*, 129–33; *Ciencia y religión*, 62–65.

67. Trabulse, *Círculo roto*, 25–40.

68. Trabulse, *La ciencia perdida*, 13; *Círculo roto*, 28–38. In 1622 a fellow Mercedarian alleged that Rodríguez and others in his convent practiced judicial astrology and drew up horoscopes, allegedly at the request of their vicar general. The denouncer, Fray Juan Menéndez, pegged Rodríguez as the ringleader of the astrologers. There is no record of the Inquisition pursuing the case. AGN, *Inquisición*, vol. 335, exp. 94, "Denuncia presentada por Fray Juan Menéndez, Mercedario, de que en su convento se practica mucho la astrología judiciaria," 1622.

69. Cañizares-Esguerra, "New World, New Stars," 52–53.

70. This is the position of Trabulse, who in his many works has offered a nuanced version of the development of critical epistemology in New Spain. For a strong statement along these lines, see *Los orígenes de la ciencia moderna*, 131.

71. This general narrative of Pérez de Soto is drawn primarily from Leonard, *Baroque Times in Old Mexico*, 85–98, but also from Jiménez

Rueda, *Herejías y supersticiones en la Nueva España*, 217–20; Castanien, "The Mexican Inquisition Censors a Private Library, 1655"; Trabulse, *Los orígenes de la ciencia moderna en México*, 85–90, 136–57.

72. Castanien, "The Mexican Inquisition"; Leonard, *Baroque Times*, 92–98; Trabulse, *Los orígenes de la ciencia moderna*, 136–53.

73. Peterson, "Heavenly Influences," 198 (n. 76).

74. Jiménez Rueda, *Herejías y supersticiones en la Nueva España*, 215, 223–24. Peña, "Quiromancia y adivinación en la Nueva España," 61.

75. For the eighteenth century, see the many licenses for publication in Quintana, *La astrología en la Nueva España*, and others in the AGN's *Inquisición ramo*, such as AGN, *Inquisición*, vol. 1332, exp. 27, fs. 140, 143–58, 1732, "D. José Bernardo de Hogal, vecino de esta ciudad, impresor y mercader de libros en ella, a nombre del Dr. D. José de Escobar, catedrático de matemáticas, presenta el pronóstico de temporales, para el año de 1733," or AGN, *Inquisición*, vol. 1332, exp. 24, fs. 131–32, 1794–95, "D. Mariano José de Zúñiga y Ontiveros, matemático de esta capital, presenta los pronósticos de temporales y calendario." A strong demand for almanacs that offered some forms of prognostication continued well into the nineteenth century in Mexico. After the abolition of the Inquisition in the early nineteenth century, almanacs and other ephemera began to include more material that made loose references to the divinatory arts and the occult, all of which would have been suppressed by the Inquisition and would have resulted in severe punishment during the colonial era. On this nineteenth-century literature, see Wright-Rios, *Searching for Madre Matiana*. This curiosity cannot be assigned to some kind of backwardness or superstition unique to nineteenth-century Mexico, as such interests were widespread in the United States and Great Britain, those avatars of nineteenth-century modernization and modernity. Historians estimate that the most popular almanac in England, *Moore's Almanack*, or the *Vox Stellarum* (The Voice of the Stars), which was first published in 1699, grew from a print run of 25,000 per year in 1738 to reach an astonishing 560,000 copies per year in 1839. One scholar estimates that fully a third of the English population read the *Vox Stellarum* and similar works by the middle of the eighteenth century. Fara, "Marginalized Practices," 497–99; Curry, *Prophecy and Power*, 56, 102. The British North American colonies also held substantial markets for almanacs. See Butler, "Magic, Astrology, and the Early American Religious Heritage."

76. In 1789 the parish priest of Tzinacantepec described a *lunario* that contained judicial content circulating in the countryside surrounding Toluca. There is no record of the Inquisition investigating the report. AGN, *Inquisición*, vol. 1258, no exp., f. 6r, "El Br. D. Raphael Antonio Sánchez cura de Tzinacantepec por carta de 23 de abril me presentó el adjunto papel . . .," 1789.

77. AGN, *Inquisición*, vol. 751, exp. 28, fs. 427–41, "Declaración y exhibición de un cuaderno de Juan Antonio González," 1711.

78. AGN, *Inquisición*, vol. 1049, exp. 17, fs. 264–67, "Denuncia que hace Patricia Josefa, vecina de la ciudad de Querétaro, contra una mujer llamada Dolores, que vive en la Calle del Guachi. Por zahorina," 1795.

79. "Que quien vence sin contrario, / no puede decir que vence." The Inquisitors denied the request to publish. AGN, *Inquisición*, vol. 926, exp. 36, fs. 370–78, "Se manda detener en este Santo Officio el 'Pronóstico del Caballero Aventurero,'" 1795, f. 374v.

80. Thomas, *Religion and the Decline of Magic*, 641–68. Though he notes that "the ultimate origins of this faith in unaided human capacity remain mysterious," 663.

81. Butler, "Magic, Astrology, and the Early American Religious Heritage, 1600–1760," 339–45.

82. On this point, see the interesting remarks of Coronado, *A World Not to Come*, 10.

83. Geneva, *Astrology and the Seventeenth-Century Mind*, 9; Westman, *The Copernican Question*, 63–64.

84. Trabulse, *Los orígenes de la ciencia moderna*, 129.

85. AGN, *Inquisición*, vol. 926, exp. 36, fs. 370–78, "Se manda detener en este Santo Officio el 'Pronóstico del Caballero Aventurero,'" 1795, f. 376–77v.

86. Trabulse, *Los orígenes de la ciencia moderna*, 131. See also Charles Ronan's discussion of the "Christian Enlightenment" in New Spain, an intellectual stance which valued new knowledge that could be harmonized with Catholic traditions. Ronan, *Francisco Javier Clavigero, S.J. (1731–1787)*, 48.

87. Peterson, "Heavenly Influences," 25–26.

88. AGN, *Inquisición*, vol. 356, exp. 141, "Testificación contra Lucas de Figueroa, por pronosticar y tener libros de astrología," 1626, f. 308r.

89. AGN, *Inquisición*, vol. 298, exp. 13, "Proceso contra Leonardo Bernabé por quiromántico," 1613, f. 233r. See also AGN, *Inquisición*, vol. 376, exp. 1, "Testificaciones contra Juan de Cárdenas y su hijo por zahorí y Diego Rangel por el mismo delito," 1632; AGN, *Inquisición*, vol. 322, exp. 5, "Testificación contra Melchor de los Reyes, porque adivina las rayas de la frente," 1619, 14v–15v.

90. AGN, *Inquisición*, vol. 858, fs. 541–42, "Denuncia que hace D. Baltasar Francisco Mosquera y Valerio, vecino y almacenero en esta ciudad de México, contra un cirujano or curandero francés, llamado Pedro de Feez … que conocía y alcanzaba muchas cosas por las rayas de las manos," 1732 (referring to events in 1715–16), f. 542r.

91. AGN, *Inquisición*, vol. 478, exp. 43, fs. 309–26, "Testificación contra Fray Pedro Martín, Dominico, por astrólogo y quiromántico," 1613; AGN, *Inquisición*, vol. 435, exp. 248, "Proceso contra Gaspar de Rivero Vasconcelos, mulato libre, estudiante canonista descendiente de Portugueses, natural de Tánger, por astrólogo judiciario, calumnidor del

Santo Oficio y sus ministros," 1650, fs. 485r–86r; AGN, *Indiferente Virreinal (Inquisición)*, caja 946, exp. 12, "Relativo al proceso . . . contra Antonio Bazán español por decir que podía ver las enfermedades viendo las rayas de las manos," 1640 f. 4r.

92. AGN, *Inquisición*, vol. 858, fs. 541–42, "Denuncia que hace D. Baltasar Francisco Mosquera y Valerio, vecino y almacenero en esta ciudad de México, contra un cirujano or curandero francés, llamado Pedro de Feez . . . que conocía y alcanzaba muchas cosas por las rayas de las manos," 1732, f. 541v.

93. AGN, *Inquisición*, vol. 356, exp. 76, "Testificación contra Ana Bohorques, por adivinar por las rayas de las manos," 1626, f. 112r; AGN, *Inquisición*, vol. 486, exp. 22, fs. 98–105, "Testificación contra Francisco Hidalgo, por zahorí," 1621, f. 100v; AGN, *Inquisición*, vol. 335, exp. 102, "Denuncia contra una negra llamada Cecilia, porque anuncia las llegadas de las naos adivinando con exactitud las mas veces," 1621; AGN, *Inquisición*, vol. 328, exp. 49, fs. 343–48, "Testificación contra Sebastián Hernández, por alzar figura quiromántica y otras hechicerías," 1620, f. 344r.

94. AGN, *Inquisición*, vol. 436, exp. 23, fs. 99–103, "Testificación contra Jerónimo, astrólogo," 1650, f. 103r; AGN, *Inquisición*, vol. 435, exp. 161, fs. 301–5, "Denuncia contra Martín Cristóbal, difunto, por decir futuros contingentes por las rayas de las manos," 1650, f. 303r; AGN, *Inquisición*, vol. 1205, exp. 19, fs. 1–103, "El Sr. Inquisidor fiscal de este Santo Oficio contra Pedro Vidal o Vidales de Ledezma, de oficio curandero y barbero, por curandero supersticioso, quiromántico planetario con sabor de astrología judiciaria," 1713.

Chapter Four. Money

1. On the relationship between money and spirituality in New Spain, see the interesting remarks of Asunción Lavrin. Money became "spiritualized," Lavrin argues, as it made possible activities in the world that served otherworldly ends. Just as, conversely, colonial subjects sometimes tracked and described spiritual activities with the techniques and vocabulary of accounting. "Cofradías novohispanas," 64. See also Burns, *Colonial Habits*; Larkin, *The Very Nature of God*; Voekel, *Alone Before God*; Ramos, *Death and Conversion in the Andes*; Eire, *From Madrid to Purgatory*.

2. Le Goff, *Your Money or Your Life*, 71.

3. Cited in Kamen, *Empire*, 289 (quote), 135 (Dominican, Mexico).

4. In most regions of Spanish America, however, slavery and other forms of coerced labor persisted throughout the colonial period, including state-led labor drafts that the crown imposed on native communities. In some areas and activities slavery remained the dominant labor form. This was often the case in tropical regions dominated by plantation agriculture.

For a good overview, see Klein and Vinson, *African Slavery in Latin America and the Caribbean*.

5. See, for example, John Tutino's study of the economy and social relations in New Spain's Bajío region, *Making a New World*.

6. Cited in Kamen, *Empire*, 88.

7. MacLachlan and Rodríguez O., *The Forging of the Cosmic Race*, 168–79. For a contemporary description, produced by an eyewitness to the boom years in Peru, see Acosta, *Natural and Moral History of the Indies*, book IV, chapters 9–13.

8. Stein and Stein, *Silver, Trade, and War*, 23–24; Elliot, *Spain and Its World*, 19. Even higher figures are suggested by Frank, *ReOrient*, 143.

9. Vaggi and Groenewegen, *A Concise History of Economic Thought*, 16. See also Marichal, "The Spanish American Silver Peso," 26.

10. Tomás de Mercado, *Tratos y contratos de mercaderes* (Salamanca, 1569), in Grice-Hutchinson, *The School of Salamanca*, 96.

11. On the accumulation of reserves as a goal of mercantilist policy, see Vaggi and Groenewegen, *Concise History of Economic Thought*, 16. Bakewell, *A History of Latin America*, 199.

12. There is a large literature on this topic, but a good summary is found in Stein and Stein, *Silver, Trade, and War*, 19–26.

13. Spanish creditors supplied just 15 percent of the twenty-nine million ducats' worth of loans taken out during the rule of Charles V from 1516 to 1556. Braudel, *The Wheels of Commerce*, 393–94; Kamen, *Empire*, 51–52, 89.

14. Pomeranz, *The Great Divergence*, 159.

15. Ibid., 160.

16. Ibid., 160, 271.

17. Ibid., 159–62, 269–74; Mann, *1493*, 126; Graeber, *Debt*, 309–13; Frank, *ReOrient*, especially chapter 3 (for the estimate of American silver to China, see 142–49).

18. Stein and Stein, *Silver, Trade, and War*, 278, n. 34.

19. Elliot, *Spain and Its World*, 226–27; Graeber, *Debt*, 309, 339; Lynch, *Spain, 1516–1598*, 176–77.

20. Sokol, "Unequal Words," 460.

21. Kagan, *Urban Images of the Hispanic World, 1493–1780*, 101–5. Scott, "A Geography of Mineral Wealth."

22. Acosta, *Natural and Moral History*, 173–74; Mann, *1493*, 139–40; Kagan, *Urban Images*, 101.

23. Acosta, *Natural and Moral History*, 175.

24. Ibid., 178.

25. Quoted in Kamen, *Empire*, 286.

26. Joly Barthélemy, *Voyage en Espagne, 1603–1604*, ed. L. Barrau Dihigo (1909), 17, quoted in Braudel, *Wheels of Commerce*, 171. On increasing income inequality and declining real wages in sixteenth-century Spain, see Lynch, *Spain, 1516–1598*, 182–83.

27. Cited in Lynch, *Spain, 1516–1598*, 178.

28. Vilches, *New World Gold*, 186–88.

29. In Grice-Hutchinson, *The School of Salamanca*, 94.

30. Vilches, *New World Gold*, 36, 139 (Mendoza quote), 150.

31. Flynn, "A New Perspective of the Spanish Price Revolution: The Monetary Approach to the Balance of Payments," 400, cited in Graeber, *Debt*, 339. On the use of *juros* as a source of crown revenue in the Americas, which were themselves an extremely complex but creative form of debt finance, see Andrien, "The Sale of *Juros* and the Politics of Reform in the Viceroyalty of Peru, 1608–1695."

32. Vilches, *New World Gold*, 30–31; Graeber, *Debt*, 339.

33. Vilches, *New World Gold*, 185–88, 207.

34. Lomnitz, "Time of Crisis."

35. Gómez Camacho, "Crédito y usura," 66.

36. Noonan, *The Scholastic Analysis of Usury*, 193.

37. The real-world effects of credit and debt are widely debated, as is the question of their social justice. For poles on the spectrum, see Ferguson, *The Ascent of Money*, and Graeber, *Debt*.

38. Le Goff, *Your Money or Your Life*, chapter 3.

39. Cited in Le Goff, *Your Money or Your Life*, 30.

40. Thomas Aquinas, *Summa Theologica*, cited and translated in Kerridge, *Usury, Interest, and the Reformation*, 81–82.

41. Ibid., 15.

42. Ibid., Introduction.

43. Ibid., 1, 5–15.

44. Cited in ibid., 5.

45. On this point, see the remarks of Noonan, *Scholastic Analysis of Usury*, 195.

46. Ibid., 155.

47. Von Wobeser, "Mecanismos crediticios en la Nueva España," 4–8, 11; Noonan, *Scholastic Analysis of Usury*, 155–64; Bauer, "The Church in the Economy of Spanish America."

48. Noonan, *Scholastic Analysis of Usury*, 110. Though, in the theological terms of art, the conditions that created *interesse* were extrinsic to money.

49. Bauer, "The Church in the Economy of Spanish America," 725.

50. My general discussion on usury and *interesse* relies on Noonan, *Scholastic Analysis of Usury*, 106–32, 155–59, and, for the later debate, 249–68; Graeber, *Debt*, 290, 322–23; Bauer, "The Church in the Economy of Spanish America," 725.

51. Martínez López-Cano, *El crédito a largo plazo en el siglo XVI*, 188; von Wobeser, "Mecanismos crediticios," 5–6.

52. Civil legislation ordered a decrease in the rates associated with *censos* from 10 percent to 7.14 percent in a 1563 decree and then again to 5 percent in 1608, which applied retroactively to all existing contracts.

The less liquid *censo perpetuo* carried a lower rate of interest in the sixteenth century, perhaps half that of the redeemable *censo al quitar* or *censo redimible*. Berthe, "Contribución a la historia del crédito," 26; von Wobeser, "Mecanismos crediticios," 11.

53. Von Wobeser, "Mecanismos crediticios," 4–10, 14–15; Martínez López-Cano, *El crédito a largo plazo en el siglo XVI*, 184–91; Berthe, "Contribución a la historia del crédito," 26–29.

54. Schwaller, "La iglesia y el crédito comercial en la Nueva España en el siglo XVI," 82; Hoberman, *Mexico's Merchant Elite*, 59–61; Cummins, "The Church and Business Practices in Late Sixteenth Century Mexico"; von Wobeser, "La postura de la Iglesia católica frente a la usura."

55. Hoberman, *Mexico's Merchant Elite*, 56–58 (quote on 58).

56. Ibid., 61–62 (quote on 61).

57. Martínez López-Cano, "Aproximación al crédito eclesiástico en el siglo XVI en la Ciudad de México"; Hoberman, *Mexico's Merchant Elite*, 60–62.

58. Hoberman, "El crédito colonial y el sector minero en el siglo XVII, 66; Cummins, "The Church and Business Practices in Late Sixteenth Century Mexico," 429. Minted coin remained in short supply even in the late colonial period, especially in the countryside. On this point, among others, see Claude Morin, who also notes that the shortage of currency tended to exacerbate asymmetries of economic and social power that characterized so much of New Spain's "market" activity. *Michoacán en la Nueva España del siglo XVIII*, 178–84, 201–2.

59. Von Wobeser, "Mecanismos crediticios en la Nueva España," 1–5; Schwaller, "La iglesia y el crédito comercial en la Nueva España," 82; Hoberman, "El crédito colonial," 66; Cope, *Limits of Racial Domination*, 109–10.

60. Martínez López-Cano, *El crédito a largo plazo en el siglo XVI*, 51.

61. Cope, *Limits of Racial Domination*, 114.

62. Martínez López-Cano, *El crédito a largo plazo en el siglo XVI*, 41, 189.

63. Sokol, "Unequal Words"; Marshall, "When Money Talks," 181.

64. For a detailed study of convents in colonial Peru that also commanded large portfolios of property and debt, see Burns, *Colonial Habits*.

65. Sor Juana Inés de la Cruz, *Poems*, 58–59.

66. Sor Juana Inés de la Cruz, *Selected Works*.

67. Enrigue, "Sor Juana, contadora," 19, 21.

68. Sokol, "Unequal Words," 460.

69. Brading, *The First America*, chapter 15.

70. Von Wobeser, *El crédito eclesiástico en la Nueva España (siglo XVIII)*, 45, n. 26.

71. In contrast, the *censo* usually required some form of real property as collateral. See, for example, Burns, *Colonial Habits*, 65.

72. For contemporary discussions that probed both sides of the argument, see "Dictamen theológico-canónico-moral sobre el contrato de depósito

irregular," 1767, Sutro Library; Don Nuño Nuñez de Villavicencio, *Dictamen sobre la usura en la Nueva España,* 1767.

73. *Censos* could be redeemable or irredeemable, but in practice even redeemable contracts were rarely closed out by borrowers in the early colonial period. The low conversion rate reflected cash shortages and low levels of liquidity (both to some extent products of the types of credit available), the church's preference for irredeemable or "perpetual" loans in the sixteenth century, but also a different set of future expectations and time horizons built into the *censos.* Von Wobeser, *El crédito eclesiástico,* 39–43.

74. Because the *depósito* was tied to a person and not to property, it also reduced the amount of liens against real estate, a common feature of long-term *censos* and a phenomenon in New Spain's property markets that many contemporaries criticized.

75. The preceding discussion is drawn from von Wobeser, *El crédito eclesiástico,* 39–50, and "Los créditos de las instituciones eclesiásticas de la ciudad de México en el siglo XVIII."

76. "Dictamen theológico-canónico-moral sobre el contrato de depósito irregular," 1767, Sutro Library. The phrasing also carried legal overtones since customary law informed judicial and administrative decisions. For an excellent introduction to some of the relevant concepts and scholarship, see Premo, "Custom Today," 355–63.

77. Martínez López-Cano, "La usura a la luz de los Concilios Provinciales Mexicanos," 306; Zahino Peñafort, ed., *El Cardenal Lorenzana y el IV Concilio Provincial Mexicano,* 385–98.

78. Rivadeneira, *Disertación primera, sobre los depósitos irregulares,* 825.

79. Ibid.; Martínez López-Cano, "La usura a la luz de los Concilios Provinciales Mexicanos."

80. IV Concilio Provincial, Libro 5, Título 5, Parágrafo 2, "De las usuras," in Zahino Peñafort, ed., *El Cardenal Lorenzana,* 264.

81. IV Concilio Provincial, Sesión LXIII, en el orden XXVII, "De disciplina," in Zahino Peñafort, ed., *El Cardenal Lorenzana,* 387.

82. Martínez López-Cano, "La usura a la luz de los Concilios Provinciales Mexicanos," 308, 312.

83. Luque Alcaide, "Debates doctrinales," 66.

84. IV Concilio Provincial, Sesión LXII, en el orden XXVI, "De disciplina," in Zahino Peñafort, ed., *El Cardenal Lorenzana,* 385.

85. Concilio Provincial, Sesión LXII, en el orden XXVI, "De disciplina," in Zahino Peñafort, ed., *El Cardenal Lorenzana,* 386. For a discussion of risk as a perspective on the future, see Reith, "Uncertain Times."

86. Escobar Ohmstede, "El comercio en las Huastecas."

87. Escobar Ohmstede and Fagoaga Hernández, "Indígenas y comercio en las Huastecas," 340, n. 18.

88. For some of the regional context, see Escobar Ohmstede, *De la costa a la sierra;* Ducey, *A Nation of Villages.*

89. Gerhard, *A Guide to the Historical Geography of New Spain*, 357.

90. Escobar Ohmstede, "La población en el siglo XVIII y principios del siglo XIX," 290.

91. AGN, *Criminal*, vol. 622, exp. 11, fs. 241–370, "Autos de oficio de la jurisdicción eclesiástica contra algunos vezinos deel pueblo de Tampamolón por usureros," 1757–58.

92. For notable studies that have examined these issues, see, among others, Baskes, *Indians, Merchants, and Markets;* Dehouve, "El crédito de repartimiento por los alcaldes mayores" and "El pueblo de indios y el mercado"; Amith, *Möbius Strip.*

93. For a discussion of these issues in the context of late colonial grain provisioning, see Amith, *Möbius Strip*, 507–9.

94. AGN, *Criminal*, v. 622, exp. 11, f. 242r. Emilio Kourí describes a similar trade in *piloncillo* sugar involving Totonac Indians in the Tecolutla river basin to the south of the Huasteca; *A Pueblo Divided*, 64.

95. Historians have found many examples of similar trade and credit practices in other parts of New Spain. See, among others, Morin, *Michoacán en la Nueva España del siglo XVIII*, 185; Dehouve, "El crédito de repartimiento" and "El sistema de crédito al día en los pueblos indígenas durante el siglo XVIII."

96. AGN, *Criminal*, vol. 622, exp. 11, f. 245r.

97. On the Huasteca and nearby regions, see Escobar Ohmstede, *De la costa a la sierra* and "El comercio en las Huastecas"; Ducey, *A Nation of Villages;* Kourí, *A Pueblo Divided.* For examples from other regions, see Fisher, "Worlds in Flux, Identities in Motion"; Amith, *Möbius Strip;* Van Young, "Conflict and Solidarity in Indian Village Life."

98. AGN, *Criminal*, v. 622, exp. 11, ff. 250r–55r.

99. Cited in von Wobeser, "La postura de la Iglesia católica frente a la usura," 139.

100. Noonan, *Scholastic Analysis of Usury*, 110; Amith, *Möbius Strip*, 509.

101. AGN, *Criminal*, vol. 622, exp. 11, ff. 354r–56r. Throughout the region *piloncillos* served as a unit of exchange. On this point, see Ducey, *A Nation of Villages*, 18. Escobar Ohmstede and Fagoaga Hernández, "Indígenas y comercio en las Huastecas," 400.

102. Amith, *Möbius Strip*, 357.

103. For a detailed examination of these issues in the region in question, see Escobar Ohmstede and Fagoaga Hernández, "Indígenas y comercio en las Huastecas." In late colonial New Spain such power asymmetries were not limited to native or small-scale producers and their creditors. Margaret Chowning finds similar sorts of credit arrangements, sometimes under the label of so-called *habilitación* contracts, between prominent Spanish merchants and large-scale agriculturalists in the archbishopric of Michoacán (west central New Spain). *Habilitación* contracts typically arranged for a merchant to provide agricultural finance

and then to receive repayment in the form of monopoly access to the product of the property in question, often at fixed and prearranged prices. Chowning notes that these agreements, which in some ways mimicked a kind of futures contract for commodities, could sometimes work in favor of agricultural producers, for example, when the market price fell below the contracted price at the time of delivery. Generally they seem to have favored merchants, however, who used their positions as creditors to secure agricultural products at below-market prices. *Wealth and Power in Provincial Mexico*, 49–50. See also Kourí, *A Pueblo Divided*, 98, 198.

104. Baskes, *Indians, Merchants, and Markets*, 88.

105. Von Wobeser, "La postura de la Iglesia católica frente a la usura," 140–43.

106. Claude Morin provides solid evidence of these practices in the late colonial economy, noting, for example, nonstandard forms of payment in the mining sector that undermined real wages for laborers or the tendency of merchants to build credit relationships with a relatively small circle of associates who might have come from the same region or were part of an extended kinship network. See his *Michoacán en la Nueva España del siglo XVIII*, 201–2, 297–99. See also the discussion of late colonial cotton trade in Amith, *Möbius Strip*, 370–71.

Chapter Five. Prayers

1. AGN, *Cofradías y Archicofradías*, vol. 10, exp. 8, fols. 245v–46r, 1792. See also the published bylaws of the Holy Schools, such as *Constituciones de la congregación y Santa Escuela de Christo: Fundada baxo del patrocinio de la Santísima Virgen María Nra. Sra. y del glorioso San Felipe Neri* (Mexico City, 1789); *Constituciones de la Santa Escuela de Christo Señor Nuestro: Fundada bajo la protección de la Virgen María, Nuestra Señora y de los gloriosos S. Juan Nepomuceno y S. Felipe Neri en el Hospital de Nuestra Señora de la Concepción y Jesus Nazareno de esta ciudad* (Mexico City, 1774).

2. Scholars of early modern Italian sodalities translate *scuola* simply as "confraternity." New Spain's *escuelas*, while also a type of confraternity, emphasized their didactic mission to such a degree that the English cognate "school" seems a fitting translation.

3. On the Santas Escuelas of Mexico City, see AGN, *Cultos Religiosos*, vol. 1, exp. 1–3, fols. 1–277, 1783–1803; AGN, *Bienes Nacionales*, vol. 884, exp. 2, fols. 1–10v, 1756; AGI, *Mexico*, 2650, 1801; for Querétaro, see AGN, *Cofradías y Archicofradías*, vol. 10, exp. 8, 1792; ibid., exp. 7, fols. 220r–23v, 1790–91; for towns in the Mexican Bajío, see Hernández, *La soledad del silencio*, 50–51.

4. Voekel, *Alone Before God*, 1.

5. Ibid.; Larkin, *The Very Nature of God*; see also Larkin, "The Splendor of Worship" and "Confraternities and Community."

6. The literature on the topic is vast. For variations on the "multiple," "alternative," or "hybrid" modernity theme, see some of the contributions to the recent *AHR* Roundtable "Historians and the Question of 'Modernity,'" *American Historical Review* 116, no. 3 (June 2011): 631–751.

7. Koselleck, *Futures Past* and *The Practice of Conceptual History*.

8. Carruthers, *The Craft of Thought*, 2–15.

9. Sabean, *Power in the Blood*, 30.

10. Buc, *The Dangers of Ritual*, 8. See also Buc, "Ritual and Interpretation."

11. This bundle of texts and rituals is along the lines of what William Sewell has referred to as resources, which are "*read* like texts, to recover the cultural schemas that they instantiate . . . [and] can be used by actors to generate power"; "A Theory of Structure," 13. In Sewell's terminology, "schemas" refer to the informal and sometimes unconscious rules and assumptions that guide action in the world. I have found his framework to be a useful hermeneutic, in part because his notion of resources is capacious enough for the diverse range of texts, practices, and traditions of the escuelas, but also because it captures the simultaneous constraint and agency of historical actors who drew upon such resources.

12. On the social composition of the groups, see AGN, *Cultos Religiosos*, vol. 1, fols. 147r–49v (Espíritu Santo); fols. 158v–59r (Hospital Real); fol. 246v (Santa Cruz y Soledad); fol. 260r (San Pedro); fol. 234r (Santa Domingo); fol. 207v (Santa María la Redonda). In the Mexico City reports, three Santas Escuelas (Jesús Nazareno, Santa María la Redonda, and Santo Domingo) reported being open to individuals of all calidades—a term that translates roughly as "caste" but could also encompass social or ethnic identity—and the reports noted that most escuelas admitted Spaniards exclusively. For an earlier reference to a dispute over non-Spanish members in Mexico City's Espíritu Santo congregation, see AGN, *Indiferente Virreinal (Templos y Conventos)*, caja 4520, exp. 16, 1762–64, "Juicio ordinario seguido por el Juez Provisor y Vicario General del Arzobispado de México para que la Santa Escuela de Cristo en el convento de Sto. Domingo en la ciudad de México se apegue a sus constituciones." A passing reference to an Indian sacristan attending devotions at one of Querétaro's escuelas is made in AGN, *Inquisición*, vol. 1321, exp. 1, fols. 1–36, 1791. For a more detailed treatment of this individual's unusual religious life, which included participation in a group whose members pretended to be Franciscan friars, see O'Hara, "The Orthodox Underworld of Colonial Mexico."

13. This is the period when the genre of *casta* paintings reached its peak in New Spain. Because the paintings usually show a series of inter-*casta* couples and their offspring, most scholars consider them to be evidence of an increasing racial anxiety on the part of some of the Spanish elite in the region. This unease developed in part from a demographic boom in the *casta* population and the limitations of *casta* labels as a form of social differentiation or control.

14. Brading, *The First America;* Herr, *The Eighteenth-Century Revolution in Spain;* Llombart, *Campomanes, economista y político de Carlos III.* For the best study of how these and other reformist ideas influenced local religious life, see Taylor, *Magistrates of the Sacred.*

15. O'Hara, *A Flock Divided,* 65. On the spread of this piety among the elite of New Spain, see Voekel, *Alone Before God;* Brading, "Tridentine Catholicism and Enlightened Despotism in Bourbon Mexico." Brian Larkin also discusses the emergence of enlightened Catholicism in New Spain but notes the persistence of a traditional, image- and liturgy-centered religious practice among many of the capital's Spanish residents. See Larkin, "Baroque and Reformed Catholicism," "The Splendor of Worship," and "Liturgy, Devotion, and Religious Reform in Eighteenth-Century Mexico City."

16. On this question, see O'Hara, *A Flock Divided,* especially chapter 5; Viqueira Albán, *¿Relajados o reprimidos? Diversiones públicas y vida social.* For a striking case that demonstrates the many layers of motivation beneath an episode of supposed religious impropriety, see Gill, "Scandala."

17. In 1794 this would lead Archbishop Núñez de Haro to call for the suppression of 450 associations in the archdiocese, including more than 40 in Mexico City. Larkin, "Confraternities and Community," 199. AGN, *Cofradías y Archicofradías,* vol. 18, exp. 5–6, fols. 262–68. For the best general works on Spanish confraternities in Mexico City, see Bazarte Martínez, *Las cofradías de españoles en la ciudad de México (1526–1860);* García Ayluardo, "Confraternity, Cult, and Crown in Colonial Mexico City, 1700–1810." For additional case studies of New Spain's religious associations, see, among others, Chance and Taylor, "Cofradías and Cargos"; Larkin, "Confraternities and Community"; Lavrin, "La congregación de San Pedro" and "Mundos en contraste"; Martínez López-Cano, von Wobeser, and Guillermo Muñoz Correa, eds., *Cofradías, capellanías y obras pías en la América colonial.*

18. For examples of the reform sentiment in the prelates' writings, see Archivo Parroquial de la Santa Veracruz (APSV) (Mexico City), *Edictos / Cartas Pastorales / Circulares (1669–1954),* Archbishop Núñez de Haro y Peralta, "Sobre el via crucis …," January 24, 1799; Archivo Histórico del Arzobispado de México (AHAM), caja 123, exp. 6, 1785, "Carta pastoral del arzobispo Alonso Núñez de Haro y Peralta sobre la oración famosa de cuarenta horas llamada vulgar y abusivamente jubileo."

19. APSV, *Edictos / Cartas Pastorales / Circulares (1669–1954),* Archbishop Núñez de Haro y Peralta, "Sobre el via crucis …," January 24, 1799. See also the archbishop's sermon *De la Asunción de Nuestra Señora, titular de la Santa Iglesia Metropolitana de México.* Indeed, while suppressing many other *cofradías,* he and other eighteenth-century prelates supported the spread of the Blessed Sacrament confraternity, which would be closely supervised by parish priests and fit the profile of a more moderate and

frugal institution. On this point, see Belanger, "Secularization and the Laity in Colonial Mexico."

20. On the compatibility of the reformed piety with collective practices, see Chowning, "Convent Reform, Catholic Reform, and Bourbon Reform" and *Rebellious Nuns*. Chowning points out that some of the prelates most associated with the reformed piety also advocated a return to the *vida común*, or communal life, in New Spain's convents; "Convent Reform, Catholic Reform, and Bourbon Reform," 30. Larkin also describes the reformed turn toward interiority as a "shift in emphasis" rather than a complete rejection of physicality and exteriority; *The Very Nature of God*, 126.

21. Larkin's study of wills left by Spaniards in Mexico City demonstrates that "liturgical gestures," which were practices that ranged from the invocation of symbolically potent numbers to self-flagellation and which were meant to invoke "mystical unions" between the divine and the devotee, remained steady over the long eighteenth century and actually increased during the high point of religious reform in the 1770s. Larkin, "Liturgy, Devotion, and Religious Reform," 517.

22. Sánchez Castañer, "José María Blanco White y Alberto Lista en las Escuelas de Cristo Hispalenses"; Viguri Arribas, *Trescientos veinticinco años de historia*; Labarga García, "Mons. García Lahiguera y la revitalización de la Santa Escuela de Cristo." Clement IX's 1669 brief *Sacrosancti Apostolatus Officium* confirmed the earlier approval by Alexander VII. Prior to becoming pontiff, Clement IX had been a member of Madrid's *escuela* while he served as papal nuncio to the Spanish court. Viguri Arribas, *Trescientos veinticinco años de historia*, 42.

23. The founding of the first Holy Schools in Mexico City occurred at roughly the same time that two *casas de ejercicio*, or retreat houses, were founded for individuals to pursue the Jesuit Spiritual Exercises: at Puebla, built 1725 / opened 1727 and at Mexico City, built late 1740s / opened 1751. While the Ignatian techniques had been practiced in New Spain since the late sixteenth century, they expanded in the late seventeenth and early eighteenth centuries. The Spiritual Exercises shared some important qualities with the Holy Schools, such as the careful oversight of devotees (given the powerful but potentially dangerous practices involved), individual spiritual practices in a group setting, and the combined goal of worldly and otherworldly self-improvement. Molina, *To Overcome Oneself*, 133–35, 140.

24. In 1737, for example, approximately 25 percent of Spanish testators in Mexico City stated membership in a confraternity. By 1813 the number had declined to 5 percent. Larkin, "Confraternities and Community," 201.

25. AGN, *Cultos Religiosos*, vol. 1, fol. 116v (Espíritu Santo); fols. 151r–53v (Jesus Nazareno); fol. 251r (Santa Veracruz); fol. 259v (San Pedro); AGN, *Indiferente Virreinal (Templos y Conventos)*, caja 4520, exp. 16 (Santo

Domingo); AGN, *Indiferente Virreinal (Cultos Religiosos)*, caja 4281, exp. 15 (Querétaro, Convent of San Francisco).

26. Hernández, *La soledad del silencio;* Sánchez Castañer, "José María Blanco White y Alberto Lista en las Escuelas de Cristo Hispalenses"; Viguri Arribas, *Trescientos veinticinco años de historia;* Labarga García, "Mons. García Lahiguera y la revitalización de la Santa Escuela de Cristo"; Ávila Blancas, "El venerable Padre Luis Felipe Neri de Alfaro." The Brotherhood of the Little Oratory also included both clerics and laymen.

27. AGN, *Indiferente Virreinal (Colegios)*, caja 2105, exp. 6, 1765, "Licencia otorgada por el arzobispo don Manuel Joseph Rubio y Salinas para fundar la Santa Escuela de Cristo en el convento de la ciudad de Toluca."

28. With one exception the Santas Escuelas of Mexico City and Querétaro reported no female members. In 1798 Miguel Méndez, the parish priest of Mexico City's Santa Cruz y Soledad parish and the leader of its Holy School, reported that the group admitted two women, Doña Gertrudis Padilla and Doña Petra Villalva, because of the substantial financial assistance they had given the escuela. The priest expected additional support from Padilla, including the large sum of two thousand pesos to refurbish and rebuild the group's oratory. Therefore, the priest wrote, "we find ourselves obligated to reward such pious dedication, promptly making her a participant in all the sacrifices, penitential acts, masses for the dead, prayers, and other pious works practiced in said *escuela.*" AGN, *Cultos Religiosos*, vol. 1, exp. 1, fols. 41r–v.

29. *Constituciones de la congregación y Santa Escuela de Christo.* Drawing on lines from the sermon on the mount in Matt. 7:13–14, "Enter by the narrow gate; for the gate is wide and the way is easy, that leads to destruction, and those who enter by it are many. For the gate is narrow and the way is hard, that leads to life, and those who find it are few."

30. AGN, *Cofradías y Archicofradías*, vol. 10, exp. 7, fols. 242r–v, 1790–91.

31. AGN, *Clero Regular y Secular,* vol. 120, exp. 3, fols. 54–103, "El Pbro. del Obispado de Michoacán, Bachiller Don José Miguel Lejarsa, sobre licencia para construir una escuela en la congregación de Irapuato."

32. On the number of brothers in Mexico City's escuelas in the 1790s and episcopal approval of expansion beyond the seventy-two stipulated in their by-laws, see the reports in AGN, *Cultos Religiosos*, vol. 1, exp. 1–3, fols. 1–277.

33. AGN, *Indiferente Virreinal (Arzobispos y Obispos)*, caja 3442, exp. 6, 1796, "Expediente promovido por el licenciado Don Blas Ochoa Abadiano, abogado de la real audiencia sobre la aprobación de normas que regirán la Santa Escuela de Cristo de la Iglesia del Espíritu Santo."

34. AGN, *Cultos Religiosos*, vol. 1, Padre Luciano Joseph de Medina, fol. 88r, August 3, 1796.

35. Ibid., fols. 98r–v, August 3, 1796; *Constituciones de la congregación y Santa Escuela de Christo*, Capítulo 14, "De los exercicios fuera de la Santa Escuela."

36. *Estabilidad y firmeza de la Santa Escuela de Christo Sr. Nro: Fundada con autoridad apostólica y ordinaria en el Convento de N.S.P. Sr. San Francisco de México* (Mexico City, 1756?).

37. *Estabilidad y firmeza de la Santa Escuela de Christo Sr. Nro: Fundada con autoridad apostólica y ordinaria en el Convento de N.S.P. Sr. San Francisco de México* (Mexico City, 1756?).

38. *Constituciones de la congregación y Santa Escuela de Christo.* In and of itself, the collective religiosity of the escuelas should not be cast as radically traditional. Rather, what distinguished the escuelas from the reformed piety but also from other collective practices, including associations supported by the church hierarchy, such as the Confraternity of the Blessed Sacrament, was the interdependence of individual salvation and collective labor. This was a porous vision of the self and its relationship to the collective, to use Larkin's phrase, and a distinguishing feature of an earlier, baroque piety. Larkin, *The Very Nature of God*, 96.

39. AGN, *Cultos Religiosos*, vol. 1, fol. 210r, Juan Nicolás Abad, Padre Obediencia of the Santa Escuela of Espíritu Santo (Mexico City), August 26, 1799. In some respects, as noted earlier, their activities resembled the Jesuit Spiritual Exercises. This was certainly true of the escuelas' internal, self-regulated accounting of one's spiritual health. Molina analyzes the Jesuits' program of spiritual renewal in *To Overcome Oneself.*

40. On this point, see Girard, "Innovation and Repetition," a rich essay that has shaped my thinking on the development of the escuelas, most importantly by pointing out the false dichotomy between pure innovation and imitation. In contrast, Girard suggests, innovation "is often so continuous with imitation that its presence can be discovered only after the fact, through a process of abstraction" (14).

41. AGN, *Cultos Religiosos*, vol. 1, exp. 1, fol. 80r, May 4, 1796, Juan Nicolás Abad, Padre Obediencia of the Santa Escuela of Espíritu Santo (Mexico City).

42. Such emotional responses, including the affective bonds between individuals, are often implicated in conversion and other moments of intensive spiritual change as well as in the labor of maintaining conversion over time. For a suggestive case, see Molina, "Father of My Soul."

43. AGN, *Cultos Religiosos*, vol. 1, fols. 101v–2r, August 3, 1796, Padre Luciano Joseph de Medina. Some members found the banquillo so onerous that they sought to modify its practice or eliminate it altogether. On this point, see ibid., fols. 207v–8r, August 26, 1799; and Bazarte Martínez and Cruz Rangel, "Las Santas Escuelas de Cristo en la segunda mitad siglo XVIII." Some confraternities in fourteenth- and fifteenth-century Bologna also required a semipublic confession of a member's failure to uphold group bylaws. The Oratorians performed a similar ritual and carefully distinguished it from the actual sacrament of penance. For Bologna, see Terpstra, *Lay Confraternities and Civic Religion in Renaissance*

Bologna, 39, 136. On the Oratorian practice, see *Constituciones de la Congregación del Oratorio de Roma: Fundada por el glorioso patriarca San Felipe Neri, con la bula de su confirmación, por las que se goviernan todas las congregaciones del Oratorio* (Mexico City, 1780).

44. AGN, *Cofradías y Archicofradías*, vol. 10, exp. 8, fols. 248r–50r, 1792.

45. *Constituciones de la congregación y Santa Escuela de Christo*, Capítulo 11. The *exercicio de la muerte* developed out of the late medieval European tradition of a "good death," advocated most forcefully in the *Ars moriendi*. For a case study of a Jesuit-led congregation that sought to prepare ethnic Nahuas for death, see Schroeder, "Jesuits, Nahuas, and the Good Death Society."

46. A similar ethos of collective spiritual improvement guided sixteenth-century Italian confraternities, in which "mutual guidance, support, and admonition disciplined a moral life animated by love of God and neighbors. In joining a confraternity, members swore to give and receive this discipline." Terpstra, *Lay Confraternities and Civic Religion in Renaissance Bologna*, 134. For a discussion of death imagery in eighteenth-century New Spain, see Lomnitz, *Death and the Idea of Mexico*, chapter 6. Richard C. Trexler provides a pithy introduction to the *imitatio Christi*, the effort to mimic and honor the life of Christ, particularly as it relates to representations of the Passion in early modern Europe and New Spain. See Trexler, *Reliving Golgotha*. For the Alfaro reference, see Chowning, *Rebellious Nuns*, 24; Díaz de Gamarra y Dávolos, *El sacerdote fiel, y según el corazón de Dios* (Mexico City, 1776).

47. AGN, *Cofradías y Archicofradías*, vol. 10, exp. 8, fol. 264r, 1792.

48. Santiago Silva, *Atotonilco: Alfaro y Pocasangre*, 399.

49. For an insightful study that discusses the multiple and sometimes contradictory meanings of the hooded veil, see Schneider, "Mortification on Parade." Like the Santas Escuelas, the penitents studied by Schneider considered themselves a "spiritual elite" and contrasted their activities to the excesses of popular devotion and popular culture in general, forming part of a broader attempt by official culture "to tame or transform the Rabelaisian city" (125–26). Some of these groups combined a rigorous spiritual program with a commitment to social action and control. On this point, see also Schneider, *Public Life in Toulouse, 1463–1789*, especially chapters 6, 7.

50. AGN, *Cofradías y Archicofradías*, vol. 10, exp. 8, bylaw 8, 1792. For examples of the *jaculatorias*, see *Oraciones jaculatorias que practican los discípulos de Christo Señor Nuestro en su Santa Escuela: Fundada con autoridad ordinaria y arreglada a las constituciones pontificias en una de las iglesias de N.S.P. Sr. S. Francisco de la ciudad de Querétaro* (Mexico City, 1789).

51. Molina, *To Overcome Oneself*, 142–49 (quote on 143).

52. *Constituciones de la congregación y Santa Escuela de Christo*.

53. Francisco Borja Ochoa de la Rea, *Septenario y exercicio a mayor culto de la milagrosa imagen del Santo Christo que se venera en la parroquia de la Sta*

Vera-cruz, de esta ciudad de México, con el título del Señor de los Siete Velos (Mexico, 1788). For fifteenth-century Bolognese confraternities, Terpstra argues that "flagellation was less an act of individual expiation than a collective act of remembering Christ's passion," *Lay Confraternities and Civic Religion in Renaissance Bologna*, 62.

54. Quoted in Flynn, "The Spiritual Uses of Pain in Spanish Mysticism," 270.

55. Ibid., 269–70. For an example from New Spain, see Gunnarsdóttir, *Mexican Karismata*, especially chapter 5, where Gunnarsdóttir describes how Francisca de los Ángeles used physical piety to develop a "mystical union" with the divine. See also Muriel, *Las indias caciques de Corpus Christi;* Jaffary, *False Mystics;* Haliczer, *Between Exaltation and Infamy.*

56. On the potential for ritualized pain to be communicative, see Glucklich, "Sacred Pain and the Phenomenal Self." For a suggestive approach to the study of religion outside the traditional analytic categories of the individual or the institutional, see Besecke, "Seeing Invisible Religion." Like Glucklich, Besecke considers the communicative aspects of religion. Focusing on the contemporary moment, she provides a framework for understanding religious behavior as a form of cultural communication. As she describes it, "Religion understood institutionally looks like a church, sect, or cult; religion looked at individually looks like psychological orientations and the occasional belief. Looked at culturally, religion looks like a *conversation*—a societal conversation about transcendent meanings" (190). This approach focuses analytic attention on how religious life fostered a dialogue about values and behavior and shares interesting parallels with Sabean's work on early modern German communities. "What is common in community," Sabean observes, "is not shared values or common understanding so much as the fact that members of a community are engaged in the same argument, the same *raisonnement*, the same *Rede*, the same discourse, in which alternative strategies, misunderstandings, conflicting goals and values are threshed out. . . . What makes community is the discourse." Sabean, *Power in the Blood*, 29–30. In the context of the Santas Escuelas and eighteenth-century Mexican Catholicism, the conversation often blurred the boundary between transcendent and mundane concerns.

57. For discussions of flagellant confraternities in early modern Italy, see Black, *Italian Confraternities in the Sixteenth Century;* Eisenbichler, ed., *Crossing the Boundaries;* Terpstra, *Lay Confraternities and Civic Religion in Renaissance Bologna;* Terpstra, ed., *The Politics of Ritual Kinship.* For early modern Spain, an important work is Flynn, *Sacred Charity.*

58. AGN, *Cofradías y Archicofradías*, vol. 10, exp. 8, fol. 245r, 1792. See also AGN, *Cultos Religiosos*, vol. 1, fol. 248v, August 27, 1799, report of the Santa Escuela of Santa Cruz y Soledad parish (Mexico City). *Celadores* also performed such functions in Mexico City's Good Death

Congregation. See Schroeder, "Jesuits, Nahuas, and the Good Death Society," 62. Similar practices could be found in other early modern confraternities, although the Holy Schools were much more attentive to collective monitoring than other sodalities in New Spain.

59. Baptist congregations in eighteenth-century rural Virginia employed similar methods of internal policing of moral failings as well as a public confession of sin. See Spangler, "Becoming Baptists."

60. AGN, *Cultos Religiosos*, vol. 1, fol. 207v, August 26, 1799, Juan Nicolás Abad, Santa Escuela of Espíritu Santo (Mexico City).

61. Almost all petitioners for new escuelas and officers of existing chapters were either ecclesiastics or laymen who carried the honorific Don, a rough marker of status in New Spain.

62. AGN, *Cultos Religiosos*, vol. 1, fol. 210r, August 26, 1799, Juan Nicolás Abad, Santa Escuela of Espíritu Santo (Mexico City).

63. Ibid., fols. 205r–v (Santa María la Redonda), fols. 249v–50r (Colegio de San Pedro), fol. 276r (Santa Veracruz). Seth Koven has examined a number of male religious brotherhoods in late nineteenth- and early twentieth-century London whose project of social uplift resonated with the goals of some proponents of the Holy School movement. See Koven, *Slumming*.

64. For a good example of such thinking applied to native peoples, see Francisco Antonio de Lorenzana (archbishop of Mexico 1766–72), Archivo Histórico Nacional, Madrid (AHNM), *Diversos*, 28, doc. 35, 1768, "Reglas para que los naturales de estos reynos sean felices en lo espiritual y temporal." A similar ethos of social and spiritual improvement through mimesis propelled the expansion of an association founded by Hernán Cortés in 1523 in Mexico City's Santa Veracruz church. The 1824 bylaws of the group, originally known as Archicofradía de Caballeros de la Santa Veracruz (renamed the Archicofradía de Ciudadanos after Mexican independence), recalled how "the exemplary conduct and Christian zeal of the dignified brothers aroused even the infamous plebe to piety, imitating the pursuits and Christian practices of the Archconfraternity." Following the model developed by the archicofradía, associations for the poor and persons of African descent were founded in "Tlamanalco, Córdova, Coyoacán, Puebla, Zacatecas and eventually in almost all of the cities and towns of America." Yet, in contrast to the escuelas, the exclusive archicofradía did not admit poor members to its ranks. *Constituciones de la muy ilustre Archicofradía de Ciudadanos de la Santa Veracruz, mandadas observar por acuerdo de su junta general celebrada en 29 de febrero de 1824* (Mexico City, 1824). I thank Bill Taylor for this reference.

65. AGN, *Cofradías y Archicofradías*, vol. 10, exp. 8, fols. 282r–v, May 8, 1798.

66. AGN, *Cultos Religiosos*, vol. 1, fol. 94v, August 3, 1796, Padre Luciano Joseph de Medina.

67. Ibid., fol. 210v, August 26, 1799, Juan Nicolás Abad, Padre Obediencia of the Santa Escuela of Espíritu Santo (Mexico City).

68. AGN, *Clero Regular y Secular*, vol. 120, exp. 3, fols. 54–103, "El Pbro. del Obispado de Michoacán, Bachiller Don José Miguel Lejarsa, sobre licencia para construir una escuela en la congregación de Irapuato," fols. 60r–61r.

69. AGN, *Cultos Religiosos*, vol. 1, fol. 251r (San Pedro); fols. 151r–53v (Jesús Nazareno).

70. For good examples, see *Constituciones de la congregación y Santa Escuela de Christo; Oraciones jaculatorias que practican los dicípulos de Christo Señor Nuestro en su Santa Escuela*; Juan Francisco Domínguez, *Catón christiano de la Santa Escuela de Christo Nuestro Señor* (Mexico City, 1805); Francisco Espinosa y Rosal, *Despertador de la vida espiritual; Poético devocionario: Con que en tierno metro se saludan las sagradas estaciones de la Vía Sacra para el ejercicio que practican todos los viernes del año los hermanos de la Santa Escuelas del Hospital de Nuestra Señora de la Concepción y Jesús Nazareno* (Mexico City, 1829); Luis de la Puente, *Místico relox: Que . . . señala las horas de la oración para todo el año, reguladas según el orden de las Dominicas y práctica de la Santa Escuela de Christo Señor Nuestro* (Mexico City, 1794).

71. For some examples, see AGN, *Indiferente Virreinal (Arzobispos y Obispos)*, caja 6164, exp. 2, 1804, "Petición del Prebendado de la Insigne y Real Colegiata de Santa María de Guadalupe, Doctor Don Antonio María Campos, de una licencia para el establecimiento de una santa escuela bajo las mismas reglas o constituciones . . ."; AGN, *Indiferente Virreinal (Cultos Religiosos)*, caja 4281, exp. 15, 1765 (Querétaro, Convent of San Francisco); AGN, *Clero Regular y Secular*, vol. 120, exp. 3, fols. 54–103, "El Pbro. del Obispado de Michoacán, Bachiller Don José Miguel Lejarsa, sobre licencia para construir una escuela en la congregación de Irapuato"; AGN, *Cofradías y Archicofradías*, vol. 10, exp. 8, 1792 (Querétaro).

72. See, for example, Haslip-Viera, *Crime and Punishment in Late Colonial Mexico City 1810*; Viqueira Albán, *¿Relajados o reprimidos?*; Sacristán, "El pensamiento ilustrado ante los grupos marginados"; Voekel, "Peeing on the Palace," 208; Scardaville, "(Hapsburg) Law and (Bourbon) Order."

73. For evidence of increasing fluidity in late colonial caste labels, see Chance and Taylor, "Estate and Class in a Colonial City"; Seed, "Social Dimensions of Race"; Valdés, "Decline of the Sociedad de Castas in Mexico City"; Castleman, "Social Climbers in a Colonial Mexican City."

74. AGN, *Indiferente Virreinal (Templos y Conventos)*, caja 4520, exp. 16, 1762–64, "Juicio ordinario seguido por el Juez Provisor y Vicario General del Arzobispado de México para que la Santa Escuela de Cristo en el convento de Sto. Domingo en la ciudad de México se apegue a sus constituciones."

75. See O'Hara, *A Flock Divided*, chapter 3. With the advent of Mexico's independence wars in 1810, which included the widespread participation of

Indians and *castas* (persons deemed to be of mixed race), the distinctions between Spaniard and non-Spaniard quickly became much starker. Although Spanish creoles formed much of the early leadership of the insurgency, many Spaniards, both Creole and peninsular, feared the racial implications of popular rebellion, a point discussed in chapter 6. One of the first major engagements between insurgents and royalists catalyzed such fears, when insurgents in the force led by the Creole priest Miguel Hidalgo slaughtered Spaniards barricaded inside the city of Guanajuato's granary. In the aftermath some Spaniards called aggressively for Creole and peninsular unity. In this context there is suggestive but limited evidence that the Holy Schools played a very conservative role during the insurgency and immediately following the eventual consummation of Mexican independence in 1821. Just weeks after Hidalgo launched his insurrection, for example, Mexico City's Santa Veracruz Escuela paid for the publication of an open letter by a cleric that railed against the insurrection, which had seduced "the simple Indians and ignorant laborers," and decried its indiscriminate attacks against all peninsulares. Nearly a decade later, while the independence struggle lingered on, the priest of Amecameca petitioned the viceroy for permission to establish a Santa Escuela in his parish. With the foundation he sought "to inspire loyalty in my flock, which has been stripped from most of them by the monstrous insurrection." For Santa Veracruz, see Pedro María Solano, *Carta familiar: Que para utilidad pública, y con anuencia de su obediencia perpetuo, el Exmo. e. Illmo. Señor Arzobispo, da a luz la venerable Santa Escuela de la Inmaculada Concepción de la parroquia de la Santa Veracruz* (Mexico City, 1810), 6. For Amecameca, see AGN, *Indiferente Virreinal (Colegios)*, caja 5674, exp. 36, 1819, "Cartas en que el Señor Cura de Amecameca le informa y piden permiso al Señor Virrey para construir una Santa Escuela la cuál estaría encargada de promover la fe de sus feligreses y alejarlos de los vicios."

76. AGN, *Cultos Religiosos*, vol. 1, fol. 210r, August 26, 1799, Juan Nicolás Abad, Padre Obediencia of the Santa Escuela of Espíritu Santo (Mexico City).

77. On this point, see Girard, "Innovation and Repetition."

Chapter Six. Promises

1. Hamill, *The Hidalgo Revolt*, 123, cited in Rodríguez O., *The Independence of Spanish America*, 161. In his discussion of these events, Rodríguez emphasizes Hidalgo's appeals to religious sentiment and a political culture that understood the king to be the source of justice and good government.

2. The latter phrase is borrowed from Auden, *The Age of Anxiety*. For the reference to Auden, see Bouwsma, "Anxiety and the Formation of Early

Modern Culture." Bouwsma discusses some of the theoretical and methodological difficulties of studying anxiety, given its close relationship to the human experience of time. On the "Age of Revolution" paradigm, see the original thesis and shorter periodization of Palmer, *The Age of Democratic Revolution*. For a more recent study focused on the Americas, see Langley, *The Americas in the Age of Revolution*.

3. For striking examples of the uncertainty that gripped New Spain during these years, see Van Young, *The Other Rebellion*, especially chapter 14, which examines the "oral culture of internal war" (312).

4. Joan Corominas with José A. Pascual, *Diccionario crítico etimológico Castellano e Hispánico* (Madrid: Editorial Gredos, 1980). On its usage in medicine, see, for example, the *Aforismos de Boerhave para conocer y curar las calenturas*, 234–39.

5. In his *Tesoro de la lengua castellana* (Madrid, 1611), Sebastián de Covarrubias described *ansia* as "the anguish and tightening of the heart."

6. Gortari Rabiela, "Julio-agosto de 1808," 185.

7. Herrejón Peredo, *Del sermón al discurso cívico*, 17. The other major work on sermons for this period is Connaughton, *Ideología y sociedad en Guadalajara*.

8. On these points, see Herrejón Peredo, *Del sermón al discurso cívico*, 18–19.

9. Rosenwein, *Emotional Communities in the Early Middle Ages*, 2.

10. Rosenwein, "Worrying About Emotions," 842.

11. Francisco Javier Lizana y Beaumont, *Sermón que en las solemnes rogativas que se hicieron en la Santa Iglesia Metropolitana de México implorando el auxîlio divino en las actuales ocurrencias de la monarquía española* (Mexico: María Fernández de Jáuregui, 1808).

12. For "Los asesinos del norte," see Manuel de la Bárcena, *Sermón: que en la jura del señor don Fernando VII (que Dios guarde) dixo en la catedral de Valladolid de Michoacán el Dr. Dn. Manuel de la Bárcena, Tesorero de la misma iglesia y rector del Colegio Seminario. El día 26 de Agosto de 1808* (Mexico City: Arizpe, 1808), 2. Preachers used a similar rhetoric of collective blame to explain the earthquake that wreaked havoc on Caracas in 1812. Rodríguez, "1812: El terremoto que interrumpió una revolución."

13. "Fac conclusionem: quoniam terra plena est judicio sanguinum, et Civitas plena iniquitate," Ezek. 7:23; Lizana y Beaumont, *Sermón que en las solemnes rogativas que se hicieron en la Santa Iglesia Metropolitana de México*, 1. Biblical references, especially to the Old Testament, remained a standard feature of late colonial sermons, even as a modern or neoclassical style emerged that privileged a more coherent and accessible preaching, in contrast to the dense allegories and erudite Latin references of baroque-era sermons. As Herrejón notes, however, biblical references served a different purpose in the neoclassical sermons, as they were primarily "to teach and guide one towards the practice of virtues." Herrejón Peredo, *Del sermón al discurso cívico*, 263–64, 288.

14. Ibid., 4–5.
15. Ibid., 24–25.
16. This was one of those rare historical moments when crisis made "groups" cohere into something worthy of the name, turning them into historical actors rather than just a convenient name for a number of people. On this issue, see Brubaker, *Ethnicity Without Groups.*
17. Reddy, "Against Constructionism," 331.
18. Ibid. and "Sentimentalism and Its Erasure," 152. The emotives framework both offers an epistemological justification for the study of emotions and places the subject on a surer methodological footing, allowing the researcher to examine how emotions might play a causal role in historical change. Reddy, "Historical Research on the Self and Emotions," 313.
19. Reddy, "Against Constructionism," 335.
20. Diego Miguel Bringas, *Sermón que en la solemne función que en acción de gracias por la insigne victoria conseguida contra los insurgentes, en la toma del fuerte de Tenango del Valle, el sábado seis de Junio de 1812, celebró en honor de María Santísima de Guadalupe la División mandada por el señor don Joaquín del Castillo y Bustamante* . . . (Mexico: Imprenta de María Fernández de Jáuregui, 1812), 4. Cited and discussed by Connaughton, "¿Politización de la religión o nueva sacralización de la política?" 172–73, and Herrejón Peredo, *Del sermón al discurso cívico*, 305–6.
21. On the role of fear in royalist propaganda, see Serrano Ortega, "El discurso de la unión," especially 173–74.
22. Bouwsma, "Anxiety and the Formation of Early Modern Culture," 222.
23. Vicente Ferrer, *Parte segunda del tratado posthumo de los impedimentos de la perseverancia en el bien* (Barcelona: Bernardo Pla, 1789).
24. Robert Westman's analysis of the great turmoil and warfare in sixteenth-century Europe and their relationship to the almanacs and prognostications resonates with that of Reddy's emotives. "The literature of annual prognostications," Westman writes, "—a literature of cities, towns, and regions—both exacerbated and lived off the anxiety, fear, and consolation that coincided with this development." "All the annual prognostications," he adds, "manipulated their readership along a spectrum between alarm and consolation," *Copernican Question*, 62, 64.
25. Heb. 4:15–16.
26. Francisco Javier Conde Pineda, *Oración moral deprecativa: a la milagrosa imagen de Jesús nazareno que se venera en la parroquia de señor San Josef de la ciudad de Puebla, implorando sus misericordias por las actuales necesidades de la monarquía, en la solemne función que celebró al efecto el Real Pontificio Seminario Palafoxiano el día 9 de julio de este año de 1809* (Mexico City: Arizpe, 1809), 2. Cited and discussed in Herrejón Peredo, *Del sermón al discurso cívico*, 305–6.
27. The emphasis that seventeenth-century Spanish and Spanish American political thinkers placed on moderating the passions is discussed in Cañeque, "The Emotions of Power."

28. Conde Pineda, *Oración moral deprecativa,* 5–6.

29. José Mariano Beristáin de Souza, *Discurso político-moral y cristiano: que en los solemnes cultos que rinde al santísimo sacramento en los días del carnaval la real congregación de eclesiásticos oblatos de México* (Mexico City: Oficina de María Fernández de Jáuregui, 1809), 17. For other examples, see Serrano Ortega, "El discurso de la unión."

30. Beristáin de Souza, *Discurso político-moral y cristiano,* 19.

31. Manuel de la Bárcena, *Exhortación que hizo al tiempo de jurarse la constitución política de la monarquía española* (Mexico City: Don Alejandro Valdés, 1820), cited in Eastman, "Forging Catholic National Identities," 5.

32. Coronado, *A World Not to Come,* notes how Spanish American political thought, even in the eighteenth and early nineteenth centuries, leaned heavily on ideas drawn from sixteenth-century Spanish thinkers such as Francisco Suárez, who linked sovereignty to the *corpus mysticum,* or social body, rather than the aggregation of the rights of individuals.

33. Vicente Navarro, *Sermón que a honra y gloria de la santísima Vírgen del Pilar de Zaragoza, y en honor de las triunfantes armas españolas* (Madrid: Viuda de Barco, 1808).

34. Ibid., 1.

35. Ibid., 7.

36. Scholars of British North America, and especially of Puritanism, have long recognized the importance of typological reading. More recent work on Spanish America also demonstrates the widespread use of typology as a way of interpreting the colonial experience. See Brading, *Mexican Phoenix,* and Cañizares-Esguerra, *Puritan Conquistadors;* Herrejón Peredo, *Del sermón al discurso cívico;* Connaughton, "¿Politización de la religión o nueva sacralización de la política?"

37. Frye, *The Great Code,* 79.

38. The process and metaphors are described in Carruthers, *Craft of Thought,* 14–21.

39. Brading, *Mexican Phoenix,* 20–24.

40. De la Bárcena, *Sermón: que en la jura,* 2. For another example, see Lizana y Beaumont, *Sermón que en las solemnes rogativas,* 3–4.

41. Bárcena, *Sermón que en la jura del señor don Fernando VII dixo en la catedral de Valladolid,* 2. For another example, see Lizana y Beaumont, *Sermón que en las solemnes rogativas que se hicieron en la Santa Iglesia Metropolitana de México,* 3–4.

42. Keith Thomas demonstrated a similar compatibility between anxiety and the acceptance of a providential future. See his *Religion and the Decline of Magic.*

43. Cited in Rodríguez O., *The Independence of Spanish America,* 54. The larger discussion draws on Rodríguez, 52–55; Guedea, "El pueblo de México y la política capitalina," and "The Process of Mexican Independence"; Herrejón Peredo, *Del sermón al discurso cívico,* 272.

44. Bárcena, *Sermón: que en la jura*, 23.
45. Ibid., 21.
46. Ibid.
47. Ibid., 22–23.
48. Beristáin de Souza, *Discurso político-moral y cristiano*, 30.
49. Ibid., 31.
50. This is the position of Scott Eastman, who suggests that "the common cultural idiom of religion and the language of national sovereignty provided a unifying symbolic repertoire for Spanish national identities during the transition from Old Regime to liberal ascendancy." Eastman, "Forging Catholic National Identities," 3. For other examples, see Herrejón Peredo, *Del sermón al discurso cívico*.
51. Beristáin even compiled a ten-page list of prominent Creole officials from the colonial era as a response to persistent claims of discrimination against Creoles. Hamill, "Early Psychological Warfare in the Hidalgo Revolt." On the use of kinship metaphors to describe the relationship between Spain and Spanish America, see Eastman, "Forging Catholic National Identities," 5, and Serrano Ortega, "El discurso de la unión," 160–67.
52. Pedro Josef de Mendizábal y Zubialdea, *Sermón que en el tercer día del solemne novenario de Nuestra Señora del Pueblito conducida en secreto* (Mexico City: Arizpe, 1810).
53. For a discussion of Nuestra Señora del Pueblito, including the frequent processions that featured her image in or near Querétaro, see Taylor, "Santuarios y milagros en la secuela de la Independencia mexicana."
54. Population data are drawn from Anna, *The Fall of Royal Government in Mexico City*, 6, cited in Van Young, *The Other Rebellion*, 46. For a case study of conflict (and fear) between Indian villagers and Spanish authorities near Querétaro in the years before 1810, see Jiménez, "El temor a la insurreción de los indios en Querétaro a principios del siglo XIX."
55. Matt. 22:21, RSV.
56. Mendizábal y Zubialdea, *Sermón que en el tercer día del solemne novenario de Nuestra Señora del Pueblito conducida en secreto*, 2.
57. José Antonio Ximenez de las Cuevas, *Plática moral y una de las treinta y tres [. . .] se han celebrado en la Iglesia del Espíritu Santo de la ciudad de la Puebla . . .* (Puebla: Imprenta de Pedro de la Rosa, 1810).
58. Manuel Alcayde y Gil, *Oración que en la solemne acción de gracias que anualmente celebra . . .* (Mexico City: María Fernández de Jaúregui, 1812), 27, cited and discussed in Herrejón, *Del sermón al discurso cívico*, 280–81.
59. Mijangos y González, *The Lawyer of the Church*, 8.
60. Herrejón Peredo, *Del sermón al discurso cívico*, 18–19.
61. Lomnitz, *Deep Mexico, Silent Mexico*, 84–86. Coronado discusses this point from the perspectives of both insurgents and royalists in *A World Not to Come*, 74 and passim.

62. Bárcena, *Sermón que en la jura del señor don Fernando VII dixo en la catedral de Valladolid*, 3.

63. On this point, see Bouwsma, "Anxiety and the Formation of Early Modern Culture," 218–19.

64. José María Alcalá, *Sermón que en la solemne función celebrada en la Santa Iglesia Metropolitana de México en honra y veneración de la Divina Providencia* (Mexico City: Mariano de Zúñiga y Ontiveros, 1810). Alcalá glossed passages from Luke 12:6 and Matt. 10:29. From Matthew, "Are not two sparrows sold for a penny? And not one of them will fall to the ground without your Father's will."

65. For intriguing examples from independence-era Texas, see Coronado, *A World Not to Come*, especially chapter 6.

66. Some of the most important recent work on the nineteenth-century Mexican church has shown the surprising blending of tradition with forward-looking ideas and pragmatic reforms. On this point, see García Ugarte, *Poder político y religioso*, passim and 21–29. See also Connaughton, *Ideología y sociedad*. On the crystallization of a more rigid conservatism around the time of the Mexican *Reforma*, see Mijangos y González, *The Lawyer of the Church*.

Chapter Seven. Epilogue, as Prologue

1. Lockhart, *The Nahuas After the Conquest*, 412.

2. Though these were often individuals without a great deal of formal training as scribes or notaries.

3. There is now a large literature on the *títulos primordiales* and related documents. In addition to the pioneering work of Lockhart, notable studies that discuss the titles include Wood, *Transcending Conquest*; Haskett, *Visions of Paradise*; Restall, *The Maya World*; Gruzinski, *The Conquest of Mexico*; Romero Frizzi and Oudijk, "Los títulos primordiales"; Tavárez, "Representations of Spanish Authority in Zapotec Calendrical and Historical Genres"; Florescano, "El canon memorioso forjado por los títulos primordiales"; Megged, *Social Memory in Ancient and Colonial Mesoamerica*. See also Nancy Farriss, "Remembering the Future, Anticipating the Past," where she provides vivid examples of how pre- and postconquest Maya texts combined linear and cyclical models of time.

4. See, for example, the discussions in Haskett, Wood, Tavárez, and Gruzinski.

5. Anderson, "Retrieving the Lost Worlds of the Past." Robert Orsi makes similar points when discussing the real presence of God / the Gods in the study of religion. "Once the gods return and once their presence is acknowledged, functionalism yields to a messier, less predictable, and perhaps less recognizable past, one that is not bound to a single account of

human life or to a single, short period of time or to a single ontology." *History and Presence*, 251.

6. Waldman, "Tradition as a Modality of Change." See also the suggestive arguments of Premo, "Custom Today."

7. Palti, "Time, Modernity and Time Irreversibility."

8. Lockhart, *Nahuas After the Conquest*, 412, 416.

9. "When change is made in or in the name of religion, it must usually be legitimized as nonchange." Waldman, "Tradition as a Modality of Change," 328.

10. Girard, "Innovation and Repetition."

Bibliography

Archival Sources

Archivo General de Indias, Seville, Spain (AGI) *México*
Archivo General de la Nación, Mexico City (AGN)
Arzobispos y Obispos
Bienes Nacionales
Clero Regular y Secular
Cofradías y Archicofradías
Colegios
Criminal
Cultos Religiosos
Indiferente Virreinal
Indios
Edictos de Inquisición
Inquisición
Templos y Conventos
Archivo Histórico del Arzobispado de México, Mexico City (AHAM)
Archivo Histórico Nacional, Madrid, Spain (AHNM) *Diversos*
Archivo Parroquial de la Santa Veracruz, Mexico City (APSV)
Bancroft Library, University of California, Berkeley
John Carter Brown Library, Providence, R.I.
Sutro Library, California State Historical Society, San Francisco

Printed Sources

Ackerman Smoller, Lauren. *History, Prophecy, and the Stars: The Christian Astrology of Pierre d'Ailly, 1350–1420*. Princeton: Princeton University Press, 1994.

Acosta, José de. *Natural and Moral History of the Indies*, ed. Jane E. Mangan. Durham: Duke University Press, 2002.

Adelman, Jeremy, ed. *Colonial Legacies: The Problem of Persistence in Latin American History*. New York: Routledge, 1999.

Aforismos de Boerhave para conocer y curar las calenturas. Madrid: Don Francisco de la Parte, 1817.

Aho, James. *Confession and Bookkeeping: The Religious, Moral, and Rhetorical Roots of Modern Accounting*. Albany: State University of New York Press, 2005.

Alberro, Solange. *Inquisición y sociedad en México, 1571–1700*. Mexico City: Fondo de Cultura Económica, 1988.

Alcalá, José María. *Sermón que en la solemne función celebrada en la Santa Iglesia Metropolitana de México en honra y veneración de la Divina Providencia*. Mexico City: Mariano de Zúñiga y Ontiveros, 1810.

Alcayde y Gil, Manuel. *Oración que en la solemne acción de gracias que anualmente celebra.* . . . Mexico City: María Fernández de Jaúregui, 1812.

Allen, Don Cameron. *The Star-Crossed Renaissance: The Quarrel About Astrology and Its Influence in England*. New York: Octagon Books, 1966.

Alva, Bartolomé de. *Confessionario mayor y menor en lengua mexicana*. Mexico: Imprenta de Francisco Salbago, 1634.

————. *A Guide to Confession Large and Small in the Mexican Language, 1634*. Translated and edited by Barry Sell, John F. Schwaller, and Lu Ann Homza. Norman: University of Oklahoma Press, 1999.

Amith, Jonathan. *The Möbius Strip: A Spatial History of Colonial Society in Guerrero, Mexico*. Stanford: Stanford University Press, 2005.

Anderson, Greg. "Retrieving the Lost Worlds of the Past: The Case for an Ontological Turn." *American Historical Review* 120, no. 3 (2015): 787–810.

Andrien, Kenneth J. "The Sale of *Juros* and the Politics of Reform in the Viceroyalty of Peru, 1608–1695." *Journal of Latin American Studies* 13, no. 1 (1981): 1–19.

Anna, Timothy. *The Fall of Royal Government in Mexico City*. Lincoln: University of Nebraska Press, 1978.

Anonymous. *Vocabulario castellano-zapoteco*. Mexico: Secretaría de Fomento/ Junta Colombina de México, 1893 (ca. 1793?).

Auden, W. H. *The Age of Anxiety: A Baroque Eclogue*. New York: Random House, 1947.

Augustine. *Confessions*. Translated by F. J. Sheed. Indianapolis: Hackett, 1992.

Ávila Blancas, Luis. "El venerable Padre Luis Felipe Neri de Alfaro." *Annales Oratorii* 3 (2003): 263–73.

Bakewell, Peter. *A History of Latin America*. Malden, Mass.: Blackwell, 1997.

Bárcena, Manuel de la. *Sermón: que en la jura del señor don Fernando VII (que Dios guarde) dixo en la catedral de Valladolid de Michoacán el Dr. Dn. Manuel de la Bárcena, Tesorero de la misma iglesia y rector del Colegio Seminario. El día 26 de Agosto de 1808*. Mexico City: Arizpe, 1808.

————. *Exhortación que hizo al tiempo de jurarse la constitución política de la monarquía española*. Mexico City: Don Alejandro Valdés, 1820.

Baskes, Jeremy. *Indians, Merchants, and Markets: A Reinterpretation of the* Repartimiento *and Spanish-Indian Economic Relations in Colonial Oaxaca, 1750–1821*. Stanford: Stanford University Press, 2000.

Bauer, Arnold J. "The Church in the Economy of Spanish America: Censos and Depósitos in the Eighteenth and Nineteenth Centuries." *Hispanic American Historical Review* 63, no. 4 (1983): 707–33.

Baumeister, Roy F., Kathleen D. Vohs, C. Nathan DeWall, and Liqing Zhang. "How emotion shapes behavior: Feedback, anticipation, and reflection, rather than direct causation." *Personality and Social Psychology Review* 11, no. 2 (2007): 167–203.

Bautista, Juan. *Advertencias para los confessores de los naturales*. Mexico: M. Ocharte, 1600.

Bazarte Martínez, Alicia. *Las cofradías de españoles en la ciudad de México (1526–1860)*. Mexico City: Universidad Autónoma Metropolitana-Azcapotzalco, 1989.

Bazarte Martínez, Alicia, and José Antonio Cruz Rangel. "Las Santas Escuelas de Cristo en la segunda mitad siglo XVIII: Ciudad de México." In *Corporaciones religiosas y evangelización en Iberoamérica: Siglos XVI–XVIII*, ed. Diego Lévano Medina and Kelly Montoya Estrada, 89–110. Lima: Universidad Nacional Mayor de San Marcos, 2010.

Beeler, Madison S. *The Ventureño Confesionario of José Señán, O.F.M.* Berkeley: University of California Press, 1967.

Belanger, Brian C. "Secularization and the Laity in Colonial Mexico: Querétaro, 1598–1821." Ph.D. diss., Tulane University, 1990.

Beristáin de Souza, José Mariano. *Discurso político-moral y cristiano: que en los solemnes cultos que rinde al santísimo sacramento en los días del carnaval la real congregación de eclesiásticos oblatos de México*. Mexico City: Oficina de María Fernández de Jáuregui, 1809.

Berthe, Jean Pierre. "Contribución a la historia del crédito en la Nueva España (siglos XVI, XVII, XVIII)." In *Prestar y pedir prestado: Relaciones sociales y crédito en México del siglo XVI al XX*, ed. Marie-Nöelle Chamoux, et al., 25–52. Mexico City: Centro de Investigaciones y Estudios Superiores en Antropología Social, 1993.

Besecke, Kelly. "Seeing Invisible Religion: Religion as a Societal Conversation about Transcendent Meaning." *Sociological Theory* 23, no. 2 (2005): 179–96.

Bhambra, Gurminder K. "Historical Sociology, Modernity, and the Postcolonial Critique." *American Historical Review* 116, no. 3 (2011): 653–62.

Biernacki, Richard. *The Fabrication of Labor: Germany and Britain, 1640–1914*. Berkeley: University of California Press, 1995.

Black, Christopher F. *Italian Confraternities in the Sixteenth Century*. New York: Cambridge University Press, 1989.

Bonfil Batalla, Guillermo. *México profundo.* Mexico City: SEP, 1987.

Borja Ochoa de la Rea, Francisco. *Septenario y exercicio a mayor culto de la milagrosa imagen del Santo Christo que se venera en la parroquia de la Sta Veracruz, de esta ciudad de México, con el título del Señor de los Siete Velos.* Mexico, 1788.

Borobio, Dionisio. "The Tridentine Model of Confession in Its Historical Context." In *The Fate of Confession,* ed. Mary Collins and David Power, 21–37. Edinburgh: T. and T. Clark, 1987.

Bouwsma, William B. "Anxiety and the Formation of Early Modern Culture." In *After the Reformation: Essays in Honor of J. H. Hexter,* ed. Barbara C. Malament. Manchester: Manchester University Press, 1980.

Brading, David A. "Tridentine Catholicism and Enlightened Despotism in Bourbon Mexico." *Journal of Latin American Studies* 15, no. 1 (1983): 1–22.

———. *The First America: The Spanish Monarchy, Creole Patriots, and the Liberal State, 1492–1867.* New York: Cambridge University Press, 1991.

———. *Church and State in Bourbon Mexico: The Diocese of Michoacán, 1749–1810.* Cambridge: Cambridge University Press, 1994.

———. *Mexican Phoenix: Our Lady of Guadalupe, Image and Tradition Across Five Centuries.* Cambridge: Cambridge University Press, 2001.

Braudel, Fernand. *The Wheels of Commerce.* London: Collins, 1982.

Bricker, Victoria Reifler. *The Indian Christ, the Indian King: The Historical Substrate of Maya Myth and Ritual.* Austin: University of Texas Press, 1981.

Breen, Benjamin, and Jorge Cañizares-Esguerra. "Hybrid Atlantics: Future Directions for the History of the Atlantic World." *History Compass* 11, no. 8 (2013): 597–609.

Bringas, Diego Miguel. *Sermón que en la solemne función que en acción de gracias por la insigne victoria conseguida contra los insurgentes, en la toma del fuerte de Tenango del Valle, el sábado seis de Junio de 1812, celebró en honor de María Santísima de Guadalupe la División mandada por el señor don Joaquín del Castillo y Bustamante. . . .* Mexico: Imprenta de María Fernández de Jáuregui, 1812.

Brubaker, Rogers. *Ethnicity Without Groups.* Cambridge: Harvard University Press, 2004.

Brubaker, Rogers, and Frederick Cooper. "Beyond 'Identity.'" *Theory and Society* 29, no. 1 (2000): 1–47.

Buc, Philippe. "Ritual and Interpretation: The Early Medieval Case." *Early Medieval Europe* 9, no. 2 (2000): 183–210.

———. *The Dangers of Ritual: Between Early Medieval Texts and Social Scientific Theory.* Princeton: Princeton University Press, 2001.

Burkhart, Louise M. *The Slippery Earth: Nahua–Christian Moral Dialogue in Sixteenth-Century Mexico.* Tucson: University of Arizona Press, 1989.

Burns, Kathryn. *Colonial Habits: Convents and the Spiritual Economy of Cuzco, Peru.* Durham: Duke University Press, 1999.

Butler, Jon. "Magic, Astrology, and the Early American Religious Heritage, 1600–1760." *American Historical Review* 84, no. 2 (1979): 317–46.

Cañeque, Alejandro. "The Emotions of Power: Love, Anger, Fear, or How to Rule the Spanish Empire." In *Emotions and Daily Life in Colonial Mexico*, ed. Javier Villa-Flores and Sonya Lipsett-Rivera, 89–121. Albuquerque: University of New Mexico Press, 2014.

Cañizares-Esguerra, Jorge. "New World, New Stars: Patriotic Astrology and the Invention of Indian and Creole Bodies in Colonial Spanish America, 1600–1650." *American Historical Review* 104, no. 1 (1999): 36–68.

———. *How to Write the History of the New World: Histories, Epistemologies, and Identities in the Eighteenth-Century Atlantic World*. Stanford: Stanford University Press, 2001.

———. *Puritan Conquistadors: Iberianizing the Atlantic, 1550–1700*. Stanford: Stanford University Press, 2006.

———. *Nature, Empire, and Nation: Explorations of the History of Science in the Iberian World*. Stanford: Stanford University Press, 2006.

Carmagnani, Marcello. *The Other West: Latin America from Invasion to Globalization*. Berkeley: University of California Press, 2011.

Carruthers, Mary. *The Craft of Thought: Meditation, Rhetoric, and the Making of Images, 400–1200*. New York: Cambridge University Press, 1998.

Cartilla breve de los rudimentos mas necesarios que debe observar el discípulo de Christo, Nuestro Señor y maestro. Mexico City, 1797.

Castanien, Donald G. "The Mexican Inquisition Censors a Private Library, 1655." *Hispanic American Historical Review* 34, no. 3 (1954): 374–92.

Castleman, Bruce A. "Social Climbers in a Colonial Mexican City: Individual Mobility Within the *Sistema de Castas* in Orizaba, 1777–1791." *Colonial Latin American Review* 10, no. 2 (2001): 229–49.

Cervantes, Fernando. *The Devil in the New World: The Impact of Diabolism in New Spain*. New Haven: Yale University Press, 1994.

Chakrabarty, Dipesh. "The Muddle of Modernity." *American Historical Review* 116, no. 3 (2011): 663–75.

Chance, John K., and William B. Taylor. "Estate and Class in a Colonial City: Oaxaca in 1792." *Comparative Studies in Society and History* 19, no. 4 (1977): 454–87.

———. "Cofradías and Cargos: An Historical Perspective on the Mesoamerican Civil-Religious Hierarchy." *American Ethnologist* 12, no. 1 (1985): 1–26.

Chowning, Margaret. *Wealth and Power in Provincial Mexico: Michoacán from the Late Colony to the Revolution*. Stanford: Stanford University Press, 1999.

———. "Convent Reform, Catholic Reform, and Bourbon Reform in Eighteenth-Century New Spain: The View from the Nunnery." *Hispanic American Historical Review* 85, no. 1 (2005): 1–37.

———. *Rebellious Nuns: The Troubled History of a Mexican Convent, 1752–1863*. New York: Oxford University Press, 2006.

Christensen, Mark Z. *Nahua and Maya Catholicisms: Texts and Religion in Colonial Central Mexico and Yucatan.* Stanford: Stanford University Press; Berkeley: Academy of American Franciscan History, 2013.

Conde Pineda, Francisco Javier. *Oración moral deprecativa: a la milagrosa imagen de Jesús nazareno que se venera en la parroquia de señor San Josef de la ciudad de Puebla, implorando sus misericordias por las actuales necesidades de la monarquía, en la solemne función que celebró al efecto el Real Pontificio Seminario Palafoxiano el día 9 de julio de este año de 1809.* Mexico City: Arizpe, 1809.

Connaughton, Brian. *Ideología y sociedad en Guadalajara (1788–1853).* Mexico City: Universidad Nacional Autónoma de México and Consejo Nacional para la Cultura y las Artes, 1992.

———. "¿Politización de la religión o nueva sacralización de la política? El sermón en las mutaciones públicas de 1808–24." In *Religión, política e identidad en la Independencia de México,* ed. Brian Connaughton, 160–200. Mexico City: Universidad Autónoma Metropolitana and Benemérita Universidad Autónoma de Puebla, 2010.

Constituciones de la Congregación, y Escuela de Christo, fundada debajo del patrocinio de la SS. Virgen María, Nra. Sra. y del glorioso S. Phelippe Neri. Mexico City, 1735.

Constituciones de la Congregación del Oratorio de Roma: Fundada por el glorioso patriarca San Felipe Neri, con la bula de su confirmación, por las que se goviernan todas las congregaciones del Oratorio. Mexico City, 1780.

Constituciones de la congregación y Santa Escuela de Christo: Fundada baxo del patrocinio de la Santísima Virgen María Nra. Sra. y del glorioso San Felipe Neri. Mexico City, 1789.

Constituciones de la muy ilustre Archicofradía de Ciudadanos de la Santa Veracruz, mandadas observar por acuerdo de su junta general celebrada en 29 de febrero de 1824. Mexico City, 1824.

Constituciones de la Santa Escuela de Christo Señor Nuestro: Fundada bajo la protección de la Virgen María, Nuestra Señora y de los gloriosos S. Juan Nepomuceno y S. Felipe Neri en el Hospital de Nuestra Señora de la Concepción y Jesus Nazareno de esta ciudad. Mexico City, 1774.

Cooper, Frederick. *Colonialism in Question: Theory, Knowledge, History.* Berkeley: University of California Press, 2005.

Cope, Douglas R. *The Limits of Racial Domination: Plebeian Society in Colonial Mexico City, 1660–1720.* Madison: University of Wisconsin Press, 1994.

Corcuera de Mancera, Sonia. *Del amor al temor: Borrachez, catequesis y control en la Nueva España (1555–1771).* Mexico City: Fondo de Cultura Económica, 1994.

Corominas, Joan, with José A. Pascual. *Diccionario crítico etimológico Castellano e Hispánico.* Madrid: Editorial Gredos, 1980.

Corona, Carmen. *Lunarios: Calendarios novohispanos del siglo XVII.* Mexico City: Día en libros, 1991.

Coronado, Raúl. *A World Not to Come: A History of Latino Writing and Print Culture.* Cambridge: Harvard University Press, 2013.

Covarrubias, Sebastián de. *Tesoro de la lengua castellana.* Madrid, 1611.

Crewe, Ryan. "Brave New Spain: An Irishman's Plot in Seventeenth-Century Mexico." *Past and Present* 207 (2010): 53–87.

Cruz, Juan de la. *Doctrina christiana en la lengua Guasteca co[n] la lengua castellana.* Mexico City: Casa de Pedro Ocharte, 1571.

Cummins, Victoria Hennessy. "The Church and Business Practices in Late Sixteenth Century Mexico." *The Americas* 44, no. 4 (1988): 421–40.

Curry, Patrick. *Prophecy and Power: Astrology in Early Modern England.* Malden, Mass.: Polity Press, 1989.

———, ed. *Astrology, Science and Society: Historical Essays.* Suffolk: Boydell Press, 1987.

Dehouve, Danièle. "El pueblo de indios y el mercado: Tlapa en el siglo XVIII." In *Empresarios, indios y estado: perfil de la economía mexicana (siglo XVIII)*, ed. Arij Ouweneel and Cristina Torales Pacheco, 86–102. Amsterdam: Centro de Estudios y Documentación Latinoamericanos, 1988.

———. "El sistema de crédito al día en los pueblos indígenas durante el siglo XVIII." In *Prestar y pedir prestado: relaciones sociales y crédito en México del siglo XVI al XX*, ed. Marie-Nöelle Chamoux et al., 93–109. Mexico City: Centro de Investigaciones y Estudios Superiores en Antropología Social, 1993.

———. "El crédito de repartimiento por los alcaldes mayores: Entre la teoría y la práctica." In *El crédito en la Nueva España*, ed. María del Pilar Martínez López-Cano and Guillermina del Valle Pavón, 151–75. Mexico City: Instituto Mora, El Colegio de Michoacán, and Instituto de Investigaciones Históricas–UNAM, 1998.

Díaz de Gamarra y Dávolos, Juan Benito. *El sacerdote fiel, y según el corazón de Dios.* Mexico City, 1776.

Domínguez, Juan Francisco. *Catón christiano de la Santa Escuela de Christo Nuestro Señor.* Mexico City, 1805.

Ducey, Michael T. *A Nation of Villages: Riot and Rebellion in the Mexican Huasteca, 1750–1850.* Tucson: University of Arizona Press, 2004.

Earle, Rebecca. *The Body of the Conquistador: Food, Race, and the Colonial Experience in Spanish America.* New York: Cambridge University Press, 2012.

Eastman, Scott. "Forging Catholic National Identities in the Transatlantic Spanish Monarchy, 1808–1814." Working Paper. Berkeley: U.C. Berkeley, Institute of European Studies, 2008.

Eire, Carlos M. N. *From Madrid to Purgatory: The Art and Craft of Dying in Sixteenth-Century Spain.* New York: Cambridge University Press, 1995.

Eisenbichler, Konrad, ed. *Crossing the Boundaries: Christian Piety and the Arts in Italian Medieval and Renaissance Confraternities.* Kalamazoo: Medieval Institute Publications, Western Michigan University, 1991.

Elliot, J. H. *Spain and Its World: 1500–1700*. New Haven: Yale University Press, 1989.

Enrigue, Álvaro. "Sor Juana, contadora." *Letras Libres*. May 9, 2013.

Escobar Ohmstede, Antonio. "La población en el siglo XVIII y principios del siglo XIX, ¿Conformación de una sociedad multiétnica en las Huastecas?" In *Población y estructura urbana en México, siglos XVIII y XIX*, ed. Carmen Blázquez, Carlos Contreras, and Sonia Pérez, 277–99. Xalapa: Universidad Veracruzana/Instituto Mora/UAM-Ixtapalapa, 1996.

———. *De la costa a la sierra: Las huastecas, 1750–1900*. Mexico City: Centro de Investigaciones Superiores en Antropología Social, 1998.

———. "El comercio en las Huastecas: Los indígenas y su participación, siglo XVIII." In *Mercados indígenas en México, Chile y Argentina, siglos XVIII–XIX*, ed. Jorge Silva Riquer and Antonio Escobar Ohmstede, 87–115. Mexico City: Instituto de Investigaciones Dr. José María Luis Mora, Centro de Investigaciones Superiores en Antropología Social, 2000.

Escobar Ohmstede, Antonio, and Ricardo A. Fagoaga Hernández. "Indígenas y comercio en las Huastecas." *Historia Mexicana* 55, no. 2 (2005): 333–417.

Espinosa y Rosal, Francisco. *Despertador de la vida espiritual; Poético devocionario: Con que en tierno metro se saludan las sagradas estaciones de la Vía Sacra para el ejercicio que practican todos los viernes del año los hermanos de la Santa Escuelas del Hospital de Nuestra Señora de la Concepción y Jesús Nazareno*. Mexico City, 1829.

Estabilidad y firmeza de la Santa Escuela de Christo Sr. Nro: Fundada con autoridad apostólica y ordinaria en el Convento de N.S.P. Sr. San Francisco de México. Mexico City, 1756?

Fara, Patricia. "Marginalized Practices." In *The Cambridge History of Science*, vol. 4, ed. Roy Porter, 485–510. New York: Cambridge University Press, 2003.

Farriss, Nancy. "Remembering the Future, Anticipating the Past: History, Time, and Cosmology Among the Maya of Yucatan." *Comparative Studies in Society and History* 29, no. 3 (1987): 566–93.

Ferguson, Niall. *The Ascent of Money: A Global History of Finance*. New York: Penguin, 2009.

Ferrer, Vicente. *Parte segunda del tratado posthumo de los impedimentos de la perseverancia en el bien*. Barcelona: Bernardo Pla, 1789.

Fisher, Andrew B. "Worlds in Flux, Identities in Motion: A History of the Tierra Caliente of Guerrero, Mexico, 1521–1821." Ph.D. diss., University of California, San Diego, 2002.

Flint, Valerie. "The Transmission of Astrology in the Early Middle Ages." *Viator* 21 (1990): 1–27.

Florescano, Enrique. *Memory, Myth, and Time in Mexico: From the Aztecs to Independence*. Austin: University of Texas Press, 1994.

———. "El canon memorioso forjado por los títulos primordiales." *Colonial Latin American Review* 11, no. 2 (2002): 183–230.

Flynn, Dennis. "A New Perspective of the Spanish Price Revolution: The Monetary Approach to the Balance of Payments." *Explorations in Economic History* 15 (1978): 388–406.

Flynn, Maureen. *Sacred Charity: Confraternities and Social Welfare in Spain, 1400–1700.* Ithaca: Cornell University Press, 1989.

———. "The Spiritual Uses of Pain in Spanish Mysticism." *Journal of the American Academy of Religion* 64, no. 2 (1996): 257–78.

Foster, George M. *Hippocrates' Latin American Legacy: Humoral Medicine in the New World.* Amsterdam: Gordon and Breach, 1994.

Foucault, Michel. *The History of Sexuality.* Volume 1: *An Introduction.* Translated by Robert Hurly. New York: Random House, 1990.

Frank, Andre Gunder. *ReOrient: Global Economy in the Asian Age.* Berkeley: University of California Press, 1998.

Freyre, Gilberto. *Casa-grande & Senzala.* (1933). Reprint, Recife: Imprensa Official, 1966.

Frye, Northrop. *The Great Code: The Bible and Literature.* New York: Harcourt Brace Jovanovich, 1982.

Fukuyama, Francis, ed. *Falling Behind: Explaining the Development Gap Between Latin America and the United States.* New York: Oxford University Press, 2008.

García Ayluardo, Clara. "Confraternity, Cult, and Crown in Colonial Mexico City, 1700–1810." Ph.D. diss., Cambridge University, 1989.

García, Bartholome. *Manual para administrar los santos sacramentos de penitencia, eucharistia, extrema-unción y matrimonio.* Mexico: Herederos de Doña María de Rivera, 1760.

García Ugarte, Marta Eugenia. *Poder político y religioso: México siglo XIX.* 2 vols. Mexico: Universidad Autónoma de México/Miguel Ángel Porrua, 2010.

Geneva, Ann. *Astrology and the Seventeenth-Century Mind: William Lilly and the Language of the Stars.* New York: St. Martin's Press, 1995.

Gerhard, Peter. *A Guide to the Historical Geography of New Spain.* Norman: University of Oklahoma Press, 1993.

Gill, Katherine. "*Scandala:* Controversies Concerning *Clausura* and Women's Religious Communities in Late Medieval Italy." In *Christendom and Its Discontents: Exclusion, Persecution, and Rebellion, 1000–1500,* ed. Scott L. Waugh and Peter D. Diehl, 177–203. New York: Cambridge University Press, 1996.

Girard, René. "Innovation and Repetition." *Substance* 19, no. 2/3 (1990): 7–20.

Glucklich, Ariel. "Sacred Pain and the Phenomenal Self." *Harvard Theological Review* 91, no. 4 (1998): 389–412.

Gómez Camacho, Francisco. "Crédito y usura en el pensamiento de los doctores escolásticos (siglos XVI–XVII)." In *Iglesia, estado y economía, siglos XVI al XIX,* ed. María del Pilar Martínez López-Cano, 63–79. Mexico City: Universidad Nacional Autónoma de México, Instituto de Investigaciones Dr. José María Luis Mora, 1995.

González Obregón, Luís. *D. Guillén de Lampart, la Inquisición, y la independencia en el siglo XVII.* Mexico City: Viuda de C. Bouret, 1908.

Gortari Rabiela, Hira de. "Julio–agosto de 1808: 'La lealtad mexicana.'" *Historia Mexicana* 39, no. 1 (1989): 181–203.

Graeber, David. *Debt: The First 5,000 Years.* Brooklyn: Melville House, 2012.

Grafton, Anthony. *Cardano's Cosmos: The Worlds and Works of a Renaissance Astrologer.* Cambridge: Harvard University Press, 1999.

Grafton, Anthony, and William R. Newman, eds. *Secrets of Nature: Astrology and Alchemy in Early Modern Europe.* Cambridge: MIT Press, 2001.

Greenleaf, Richard E. "The Inquisition and the Indians of New Spain: A Study in Jurisdictional Confusion." *The Americas* 22, no. 2 (1965): 138–66.

Grice-Hutchinson, Marjorie. *The School of Salamanca: Readings in Spanish Monetary Theory, 1544–1605.* Oxford: Clarendon Press, 1952.

Gruzinski, Serge. "La 'conquista de los cuerpos.'" In *Familia y sexualidad en la Nueva España,* ed. Solange Alberro, 177–206. Mexico City: Fondo de Cultura Económica, 1982.

———. "La 'segunda aculturación': El estado ilustrado y la religiosidad indígena en Nueva España (1775–1800)." *Estudios de historia novohispana* 8 (1985): 175–201.

———. "Confesión, alianza, y sexualidad entre los indios de la Nueva España." In *El Placer de pecar y el afán de normar,* 169–215. Mexico City: Fondo de Cultura Económica, 1987.

———. "Individualization and Acculturation: Confession Among the Nahuas of Mexico from the Sixteenth to the Eighteenth Century." In *Sexuality and Marriage in Colonial Latin America,* ed. Asunción Lavrin, 96–115. Lincoln: University of Nebraska Press, 1992.

———. *The Conquest of Mexico: The Incorporation of Indian Societies into the Western World, 16th–18th Centuries.* Cambridge, Mass.: Polity Press, 1993.

———. *What Time Is It There?: America and Islam at the Dawn of Modern Times.* Malden, Mass.: Polity Press, 2010.

Guedea, Virginia. "El pueblo de México y la política capitalina, 1808 y 1812." *Mexican Studies / Estudios Mexicanos* 10, no. 1 (1994): 27–61.

———. "The Process of Mexican Independence." *American Historical Review* 105, no. 1 (2000): 116–30.

Gunnarsdóttir, Ellen. *Mexican Karismata: The Baroque Vocation of Francisca de los Ángeles, 1674–1744.* Lincoln: University of Nebraska Press, 2004.

Haber, Stephen, ed. *How Latin America Fell Behind: Essays on the Economic Histories of Brazil and Mexico, 1800–1914.* Stanford: Stanford University Press, 1997.

Haliczer, Stephen. *Between Exaltation and Infamy: Female Mystics in the Golden Age of Spain.* New York: Oxford University Press, 2002.

Hamill, Hugh M. "Early Psychological Warfare in the Hidalgo Revolt." *Hispanic American Historical Review* 41, no. 2 (1961): 206–35.

———. *The Hidalgo Revolt: Prelude to Mexican Independence.* Gainesville: University of Florida Press, 1966.

Harrison, Regina. *Sin and Confession in Colonial Peru: Spanish–Quechua Penitential Texts, 1565–1650.* Austin: University of Texas Press, 2014.

Haskett, Robert S. *Visions of Paradise: Primordial Titles and Mesoamerican History in Cuernavaca.* Norman: University of Oklahoma Press, 2005.

Haslip-Viera, Gabriel. *Crime and Punishment in Late Colonial Mexico City.* Albuquerque: University of New Mexico Press, 1999.

Hernández, Jorge F. *La soledad del silencio: Microhistoria del santuario de Atotonilco.* Mexico City: Fondo de Cultura Económica, 1991.

Herr, Richard. *The Eighteenth-Century Revolution in Spain.* Princeton: Princeton University Press, 1958.

Herrejón Peredo, Carlos. *Del sermón al discurso cívico: México, 1760–1834.* Zamora: El Colegio de Michoacán; Mexico City: Colegio de México, 2003.

Hoberman, Louisa Schell. "Enrico Martínez: Printer and Engineer." In *Struggle and Survival in Colonial America,* ed. David G. Sweet and Gary B. Nash, 331–46. Berkeley: University of California Press, 1981.

———. *Mexico's Merchant Elite, 1590–1660: Silver, State, and Society.* Durham: Duke University Press, 1991.

———. "El crédito colonial y el sector minero en el siglo XVII: Aportación del mercader de plata a la economía colonial." In *El crédito en la Nueva España,* ed. María del Pilar Martínez López-Cano and Guillermina del Valle Pavón, 61–82. Mexico City: Instituto Mora, Colegio de Michoacán, and Instituto de Investigaciones Históricas–UNAM, 1998.

Jaffary, Nora E. *False Mystics: Deviant Orthodoxy in Colonial Mexico.* Lincoln: University of Nebraska Press, 2004.

Jiménez, Juan Ricardo. "El temor a la insurrección de los indios en Querétaro a principios del siglo XIX." In *Una historia de los usos del miedo,* ed. Pilar Gonzalbo Aizpuru, Anne Staples, and Valentina Torres Septién, 55–75. Mexico City: Colegio de México and Universidad Iberoamericana, 2009.

Jiménez Rueda, Julio. *Herejías y supersticiones en la Nueva España (los heterodoxos en México).* Mexico City: Universidad Nacional Autónoma de México, 1946.

Juana Inés de la Cruz, Sister. *Sor Juana Inés de la Cruz: Poems.* Edited and translated by Margaret Sayers Peden. Binghamton, N.Y.: Bilingual Press/ Editorial Bilingüe, 1985.

Juana Inés de la Cruz, Sor. *Sor Juana Inés de la Cruz: Selected Works,* ed. Anna More. Translated by Edith Grossman. New York: W. W. Norton, 2016.

Kagan, Richard L. *Urban Images of the Hispanic World, 1493–1780.* New Haven: Yale University Press, 2000.

Kamen, Henry. *Empire: How Spain Became a World Power, 1492–1763.* New York: HarperCollins, 2003.

Kerridge, Eric. *Usury, Interest, and the Reformation.* Burlington, Vt.: Ashgate, 2002.

Klein, Herbert S., and Ben Vinson. *African Slavery in Latin America and the Caribbean.* New York: Oxford University Press, 2007.

Klor de Alva, J. Jorge. "Sin and Confession Among the Colonial Nahuas: The Confessional as a Tool for Domination." In *La ciudad y el campo en la historia de México,* ed. Eric Van Young and Gisela von Wobeser, 1:91–101. Mexico City: Universidad Autónoma de México, 1992.

Koselleck, Reinhart. *Futures Past: On the Semantics of Historical Time.* Cambridge: MIT Press, 1985.

———. *The Practice of Conceptual History.* Stanford: Stanford University Press, 2002.

Kourí, Emilio. *A Pueblo Divided: Business, Property, and Community in Papantla, Mexico.* Stanford: Stanford University Press, 2004.

Koven, Seth. *Slumming: Sexual and Social Politics in Victorian London.* Princeton: Princeton University Press, 2004.

Kuhn, Thomas. *The Structure of Scientific Revolutions.* Chicago: University of Chicago Press, 1962.

Kuri Camacho, Ramón. *El barroco jesuita novohispano: La forja de un México posible.* Xalapa: Universidad Veracruzana, 2008.

Labarga García, Fermín. "Mons. García Lahiguera y la revitalización de la Santa Escuela de Cristo." In *El caminar histórico de la santidad cristiana: De los inicios de la época contemporánea hasta el Concilio Vaticano II,* ed. Josep-Ignasi Saranyana, Santiago Casas, María Rosario Bustillo, Juan Antonio Gil-Tamayo, and Eduardo Flandes, 455–66. Pamplona: Universidad de Navarra, 2004.

Langley, Lester D. *The Americas in the Age of Revolution, 1750–1850.* New Haven: Yale University Press, 1996.

Larkin, Brian. "The Splendor of Worship: Baroque Catholicism, Religious Reform, and Last Wills and Testaments in Eighteenth-Century Mexico City." *Colonial Latin American Historical Review* 8, no. 4 (1999): 404–42.

———. "Liturgy, Devotion, and Religious Reform in Eighteenth-Century Mexico City." *The Americas* 60, no. 4 (2004): 493–518.

———. "Confraternities and Community: The Decline of the Communal Quest for Salvation in Eighteenth-Century Mexico City." In *Local Religion in Colonial Mexico,* ed. Martin Austin Nesvig, 189–213. Albuquerque: University of New Mexico Press, 2006.

———. *The Very Nature of God: Baroque Catholicism and Religious Reform in Bourbon Mexico City.* Albuquerque: University of New Mexico Press, 2010.

Lavrin, Asunción. "La congregación de San Pedro: Una cofradía urbana del México colonial, 1604–1730." *Historia Mexicana* 29, no. 4 (1980): 562–601.

———. "Mundos en contraste: Cofradías rurales y urbanas en México a fines del siglo XVIII." In *La iglesia en la economía de América latina, siglos XVI a*

XVIII, ed. Arnold J. Bauer, 235–76. Mexico City: Instituto Nacional de Antropología e Historia, 1986.

——. "Cofradías novohispanas: Economía material y espiritual." In *Cofradías, capellanías y obras pías en la América Colonial*, ed. Pilar Martínez López-Cano, Gisela von Wobeser, and Juan Guillermo Muñoz Correa, 49–64. Mexico: Universidad Nacional Autónoma de México, 1998.

Le Goff, Jacques. *Your Money or Your Life: Economy and Religion in the Middle Ages*. New York: Zone Books, 1990.

Leonard, Irving. *Baroque Times in Old Mexico: Seventeenth-Century Persons, Places, and Practices*. Ann Arbor: University of Michigan Press, 1966.

Lewis, Laura A. *Hall of Mirrors: Power, Witchcraft, and Caste in Colonial Mexico*. Durham: Duke University Press, 2003.

Lizana y Beaumont, Francisco Javier. *Sermón que en las solemnes rogativas que se hicieron en la Santa Iglesia Metropolitana de México: implorando el auxílio divino en las actuales ocurrencias de la monarquía española*. Mexico: María Fernández de Jáuregui, 1808.

Llombart, Vicent. *Campomanes, economista y político de Carlos III*. Madrid: Alianza, 1992.

Lockhart, James. *The Nahuas After the Conquest: A Social and Cultural History of the Indians of Central Mexico, Sixteenth Through Eighteenth Centuries*. Stanford: Stanford University Press, 1992.

Lomnitz, Claudio. *Deep Mexico, Silent Mexico: An Anthropology of Nationalism*. Minneapolis: University of Minnesota Press, 2001.

——. "Time of Crisis: Historicity, Sacrifice, and the Spectacle of Debacle in Mexico City." *Public Culture* 15, no. 1 (2003): 127–47.

——. *Death and the Idea of Mexico*. New York: Zone Books, 2005.

Lucas, Scott. *Astrology and Numerology in Medieval and Early Modern Catalonia*. Leiden: Brill, 2003.

Luque Alcaide, Elisa. "Debates doctrinales en el IV Concilio Provincial Mexicano (1771)." *Historia Mexicana* 55, no. 1 (2005): 5–66.

Lynch, John. *Spain, 1516–1598: From Nation State to World Empire*. Cambridge, Mass.: Basil Blackwell, 1992.

MacLachlan, Colin M., and Jaime E. Rodríguez O. *The Forging of the Cosmic Race: A Reinterpretation of Colonial Mexico*. Berkeley: University of California Press, 1990.

Mann, Charles C. *1493: Uncovering the New World Columbus Created*. New York: Alfred A. Knopf, 2011.

Marcus, Hannah. "Banned Books: Medicine, Readers, and Censors in Early Modern Italy, 1559–1664." Ph.D. diss., Stanford University, 2016.

Mariátegui, José Carlos. *Siete ensayos de interpretación de la realidad peruana*. 1928; Reprint, Caracas: Biblioteca Ayacucho, 1979.

Marichal, Carlos. "The Spanish American Silver Peso: Export Commodity and Global Money of the Ancien Regime, 1550–1800." In *From Silver to Cocaine: Latin American Commodity Chains and the Building of the World*

Economy, 1500–2000, ed. Steven Topik, Carlos Marichal, and Zephyr Frank, 25–52. Durham: Duke University Press, 2006.

Marshall, Patricia A. "When Money Talks: Material Culture and the Creation of Meaning in Quevedo." *South Atlantic Review* 72, no. 1 (2007): 172–90.

Martínez López-Cano, María del Pilar. "Aproximación al crédito eclesiástico en el siglo XVI en la Ciudad de México." In *Iglesia, estado y economía, siglos XVI al XIX*, ed. María del Pilar Martínez López-Cano, 101–17. Mexico City: Universidad Nacional Autónoma de México, Instituto de Investigaciones Históricas, Instituto de Investigaciones Dr. José María Luis Mora, 1995.

———. *El crédito a largo plazo en el siglo XVI: Ciudad de México, 1550–1620*. Mexico City: Universidad Nacional Autónoma de México, 1995.

———. "La usura a la luz de los Concilios Provinciales Mexicanos e instrumentos de pastoral." In *Los concilios provinciales en Nueva España: Reflexiones e influencias*, ed. María del Pilar Martínez López-Cano and Francisco Javier Cervantes Bello, 284–314. Mexico City: Universidad Nacional Autónoma de México and Benemérita Universidad Autónoma de Puebla, 2005.

Martínez López-Cano, Mariá del Pilar, Gisela von Wobeser, and Juan Guillermo Muñoz Correa, eds. *Cofradías, capellanías y obras pías en la América colonial*. Mexico City: Universidad Nacional Autónoma de México, 1998.

Mazín Gómez, Oscar. *Entre dos majestades: El obispo y la iglesia del Gran Michoacán ante las reformas borbónicas, 1758–1772*. Zamora: Colegio de Michoacán, 1987.

McSweeney, Brendan. "Looking Forward to the Past." *Accounting, Organizations, and Society* 25 (2000): 767–86.

Medina, Joseph Mariano de. *Heliotropio crítico racional prognóstico computado a el meridiano de la Puebla de los Ángeles para el año 1752*. Puebla: Viuda de Miguel de Ortega. In *Historia de la ciencia en México: Estudios y textos, Siglo XVII*, vol. 2, ed. Elías Trabulse. Mexico City: Conacyt/Fondo de Cultura Económica, 1984.

Megged, Amos. *Social Memory in Ancient and Colonial Mesoamerica*. New York: Cambridge University Press, 2010.

Melvin, Karen. *Building Colonial Cities of God: Mendicant Orders and Urban Culture in New Spain*. Stanford: Stanford University Press, 2012.

Mendizábal y Zubialdea, Pedro Josef de. *Sermón que en el tercer día del solemne novenario de Nuestra Señora del Pueblito conducida en secreto*. Mexico City: Arizpe, 1810.

Mercado, Tomás de. *Tratos y contratos de mercaderes* (Salamanca, 1569). In Marjorie Grice-Hutchinson, *The School of Salamanca: Readings in Spanish Monetary Theory, 1544–1605*. Oxford: Clarendon Press, 1952.

Meza González, Javier. *El laberinto de la mentira: Guillén de Lamporte y la Inquisición*. Mexico City: Universidad Autónoma Metropolitana (Xochimilco), 1997.

Mijangos y González, Pablo. *The Lawyer of the Church: Bishop Clemente de Jesús Munguía and the Clerical Response to the Mexican Liberal Reforma*. Lincoln: University of Nebraska Press, 2015.

Mills, Kenneth. *Idolatry and Its Enemies: Colonial Andean Religion and Extirpation, 1640–1750*. Princeton: Princeton University Press, 1997.

Molina, Alonso de. *Confessionario mayor en lengua mexicana y castellana*. Mexico, 1569.

Molina, J. Michelle. "Spirituality and Colonial Governmentality: The Jesuit Spiritual Exercises in Europe and Abroad." In *Postcolonial Moves: Medieval Through Modern*, ed. Patricia Ingham and Michelle Warren, 133–52. New York: Palgrave Macmillan, 2003.

———. *To Overcome Oneself: The Jesuit Ethic and Spirit of Global Expansion, 1520–1767*. Berkeley: University of California Press, 2013.

———. "Father of My Soul: Reason and Affect in a Shipboard Conversion Narrative." *Journal of Jesuit Studies* 2, no. 4 (2015): 641–58.

More, Anna. *Baroque Sovereignty: Carlos de Sigüenza y Góngora and the Creole Archive of Colonial Mexico*. Philadelphia: University of Pennsylvania Press, 2013.

Morin, Claude. *Michoacán en la Nueva España del siglo XVIII: Crecimiento y desigualdad en una economía colonial*. Mexico City: Fondo de Cultura Económica, 1979.

Muriel, Josefina. *Las indias caciques de Corpus Christi*. 1963. Reprint, Mexico City: Universidad Autónoma de México, 2001.

Myers, David. *"Poor, Sinning Folk": Confession and Conscience in Counter-Reformation Germany*. Ithaca: Cornell University Press, 1996.

Navarro, Vicente. *Sermón que a honra y gloria de la santísima Vírgen del Pilar de Zaragoza, y en honor de las triunfantes armas españolas*. Madrid: Viuda de Barco, 1808.

Nesvig, Martin. "'Heretical Plagues' and Censorship Cordons: Colonial Mexico and the Transatlantic Book Trade." *Church History* 75, no. 1 (2006): 1–37.

———. *Ideology and Inquisition: The World of the Censors in Early Mexico*. New Haven: Yale University Press, 2009.

Noonan, John T. *The Scholastic Analysis of Usury*. Cambridge: Harvard University Press, 1957.

O'Banion, Patrick J. *The Sacrament of Penance and Religious Life in Golden Age Spain*. University Park: Pennsylvania State University Press, 2012.

O'Gorman, Edmundo. *México, el trauma de su historia*. Mexico City: Universidad Nacional Autónoma de México, 1977.

O'Hara, Matthew D. "The Orthodox Underworld of Colonial Mexico." *Colonial Latin American Review* 17, no. 2 (2008): 233–50.

———. *A Flock Divided: Race, Religion, and Politics in Mexico, 1749–1857*. Durham: Duke University Press, 2010.

Oraciones jaculatorias que practican los dicípulos de Christo Señor Nuestro en su Santa Escuela: Fundada con autoridad ordinaria y arreglada a las constituciones pontificias en una de las iglesias de N.S.P. Sr. S. Francisco de la ciudad de Querétaro. Mexico City, 1789.

Orsi, Robert A. *History and Presence.* Cambridge: Harvard University Press, 2016.

Ortner, Sherry B. *Anthropology and Social Theory: Culture, Power, and the Acting Subject.* Durham: Duke University Press, 2006.

Palmer, R. R. *The Age of Democratic Revolution: A Political History of Europe and America, 1760–1800.* 2 vols. Princeton: Princeton University Press, 1959–64.

Palti, Elías José. "Time, Modernity and Time Irreversibility." *Philosophy and Social Criticism* 23, no. 5 (1997): 27–62.

Pardo, Osvaldo F. *The Origins of Mexican Catholicism: Nahua Rituals and Christian Sacraments in Sixteenth-Century Mexico.* Ann Arbor: University of Michigan Press, 2004.

Paz, Octavio. *El laberinto de la soledad.* 1950. Reprint, Mexico City: Fondo de Cultura Económica, 1981.

Peña, Margarita. "Quiromancia y adivinación en la Nueva España." In *Literatura y cultura populares de la Nueva España*, ed. Mariana Masera, 59–90. Barcelona: Azul Editorial; Mexico City: Universidad Nacional Autónoma de México, 2004.

———. "De varios infortunios en un tratado de quiromancia novohispano." *Revista de la Universidad de México* 31 (2006): 21–26.

Peraza-Rugeley, Aurora Margarita. "Los almanaques de Carlos de Sigüenza y Góngora: Aspectos literarios y herramienta para analizar Infortunios de Alonso Ramírez y Parayso Occidental." Ph.D. diss., University of Oklahoma, 2011.

Pérez, Manuel. *Farol indiano y guía de curas de indios.* Mexico City: Francisco de Rivera Calderón, 1713.

Pescador, Juan Javier. *De bautizados a fieles difuntos: Familia y mentalidades en una parroquia urbana, Santa Catarina de México, 1568–1820.* Mexico City: Colegio de México, 1992.

Peterson, Heather R. "Heavenly Influences: The Cosmic and Social Order of New Spain at the Turn of the Seventeenth-Century." Ph.D. diss., University of Texas, Austin, 2009.

Pomeranz, Kenneth. *The Great Divergence: Europe, China, and the Making of the Modern World Economy.* Princeton: Princeton University Press, 2000.

Premo, Bianca. "Custom Today: Temporality, Customary Law, and Indigenous Enlightenment." *Hispanic American Historical Review* 94, no. 3 (2014): 355–79.

Puente, Luis de la. *Místico relox: Que en las breves meditaciones del V.P. Luis de la Puente señala las horas de la oración para todo el año, reguladas según el orden de las Dominicas y práctica de la Santa Escuela de Christo Señor Nuestro.* Mexico City, 1794.

Quintana, Augustín de. *Confessonario en lengua mixe.* Puebla: Viuda de Miguel de Ortega, 1733.

Quintana, José Miguel. *La astrología en la Nueva España en el siglo XVII.* Mexico City: Ediciones Oasis, 1969.

Rafael, Vicente L. *Contracting Colonialism: Translation and Christian Conversion in Tagalog Society Under Early Spanish Rule.* Durham: Duke University Press, 1993.

Ramírez, Paul F. "Mendacious Texts: The Art of Confessional Dissimulation." In *Imagining Histories of Colonial Latin America: Synoptic Methods and Practices,* ed. Karen Melvin and Sylvia Sellers-García, 217–24. Albuquerque: University of New Mexico Press, 2017.

Ramos, Gabriela. *Death and Conversion in the Andes: Lima and Cuzco, 1532–1670.* South Bend: University of Notre Dame Press, 2010.

Reddy, William M. "Against Constructionism: The Historical Anthropology of Emotions." *Current Anthropology* 38, no. 3 (1997): 327–51.

———. "Sentimentalism and Its Erasure: The Role of Emotions in the Era of the French Revolution." *Journal of Modern History* 72, no. 1 (2000): 109–52.

———. "Historical Research on the Self and Emotions." *Emotion Review* 1, no. 4 (2009): 302–15.

Reith, Gerda. "Uncertain Times: The Notion of 'Risk' and the Development of Modernity." *Time and Society* 13, no. 2/3 (2004): 383–402.

Rivadeneira, Antonio de. *Disertación primera, sobre los depósitos irregulares* (1774). In *El Cardenal Lorenzana y el IV Concilio Provincial Mexicano,* ed. Luisa Zahino Peñafort. Mexico City: Universidad Nacional Autónoma de Mexico, 1999.

Restall, Matthew. *The Maya World: Yucatec Culture and Society, 1550–1850.* Stanford: Stanford University Press, 1997.

Rodríguez, Pablo. "1812: El terremoto que interrumpió una revolución." In *Una historia de los usos del miedo,* ed. Pilar Gonzalbo Aizpuru, Anne Staples, and Valentina Torres Septién, 247–71. Mexico City: Colegio de México and Universidad Iberoamericana, 2009.

Rodríguez O., Jaime E. *The Independence of Spanish America.* New York: Cambridge University Press, 1998.

Romero Frizzi, María de los Ángeles, and Michael R. Oudijk. "Los títulos primordiales: Un género de tradición mesoamericana: Del mundo prehispánico al siglo XXI." *Relaciones* 24, no. 95 (2003): 19–48.

Ronan, Charles E. *Francisco Javier Clavigero, S.J. (1731–1787): Figura de la ilustración mexicana, su vida y obras.* Guadalajara: Universidad de Guadalajara, 1993.

Ronan, Gerard. *The Irish Zorro: The Extraordinary Adventures of William Lamport (1610–1659).* Dingle, Ireland: Brandon Books, 2004.

Rosenwein, Barbara H. *Emotional Communities in the Early Middle Ages.* Ithaca: Cornell University Press, 2002.

———. "Worrying About Emotions." *American Historical Review* 107, no. 3 (2002): 821–45.

Saavedra, Marcos de. *Confessonario breve, activo y passivo, en lengua mexicana.* Mexico: Doña María de Rivera, 1746.

Sabean, David Warren. *Power in the Blood: Popular Culture and Village Discourse in Early Modern Germany.* New York: Cambridge University Press, 1984.

Sacristán, María Cristina. "El pensamiento ilustrado ante los grupos marginados de la ciudad de México, 1767–1824." In *La ciudad de México en la primera mitad del Siglo XIX.* Volume 1: *Economía y estructura urbana,* ed. Regina Hernández Franyuti, 187–249. Mexico City: Instituto Mora, 1994.

Sánchez Castañer, Francisco. "José María Blanco White y Alberto Lista en las Escuelas de Cristo Hispalenses." *Archivo Hispalense: Revista histórica, literaria y artística* 42, no. 130 (1965): 229–48.

Santiago Silva, José de. *Atotonilco: Alfaro y Pocasangre.* Guanajuato: Ediciones la Rana, 2004.

Scardaville, Michael C. "(Hapsburg) Law and (Bourbon) Order: State Authority, Popular Unrest, and the Criminal Justice System in Bourbon Mexico City." *The Americas* 50, no. 4 (1994): 501–25.

Schneider, Robert A. "Mortification on Parade: Penitential Processions in Sixteenth- and Seventeenth-Century France." *Renaissance and Reformation* 22, no. 1 (1986): 123–46.

———. *Public Life in Toulouse, 1463–1789: From Municipal Republic to Cosmopolitan City.* Ithaca: Cornell University Press, 1989.

Schroeder, Susan. "Jesuits, Nahuas, and the Good Death Society in Mexico City, 1710–1767." *Hispanic American Historical Review* 80, no. 1 (2000): 43–76.

Schwaller, John F. *Church and Clergy in Sixteenth-Century Mexico.* Albuquerque: University of New Mexico Press, 1987.

———. "La iglesia y el crédito comercial en la Nueva España en el siglo XVI." In *Iglesia, estado y economía, siglos XVI al XIX,* ed. María del Pilar Martínez López-Cano, 81–93. Mexico City: Universidad Nacional Autónoma de México, Instituto de Investigaciones Dr. José María Luis Mora, 1995.

Schwaller, Robert C. "The Importance of Mestizos and Mulatos as Bilingual Intermediaries in Sixteenth-Century New Spain." *Ethnohistory* 59, no. 4 (2012): 713–38.

Schwartz, Stuart. *All Can Be Saved: Religious Tolerance and Salvation in the Iberian Atlantic World.* New Haven: Yale University Press, 2008.

Scott, Heidi. "A Geography of Mineral Wealth: Herman Moll's Map of South America." John Carter Brown Library, *Cartographic Conversation,* accessed February 18, 2016, www.brown.edu/Facilities/John_Carter_Brown_Library/cartographic/pages/scott.html.

Seed, Patricia. "Social Dimensions of Race: Mexico City, 1753." *Hispanic American Historical Review* 62, no. 4 (1982): 569–606.

Seligman, Martin E. P., Peter Railton, Roy F. Baumeister, and Chandra Sripada. *Homo Prospectus.* New York: Oxford University Press, 2016.

Serra, Ángel. *Manual de administrar los santos sacramentos a los españoles, y naturales de esta provincia.* Mexico: Joseph Bernardo de Hogal, 1697.

Serrano Ortega, José Antonio. "El discurso de la unión: El patriotismo novohispano en la propaganda realista durante el movimiento insurgente de Hidalgo." *Estudios de Historia Novohispana* 14 (1994): 157–77.

Sewell, William H. "A Theory of Structure: Duality, Agency, and Transformation." *American Journal of Sociology* 98, no. 1 (1992): 1–29.

Sigüenza y Góngora, Carlos de. *Pronóstico para 1678.* In José Miguel Quintana, *La astrología en la Nueva España en el siglo XVII.* Mexico City: Ediciones Oasis, 1969.

Silverblatt, Irene. *Modern Inquisitions: Peru and the Colonial Origins of the Civilized World.* Durham: Duke University Press, 2004.

Sokol, Alina. "Unequal Words: Sor Juana and the Poetics of Money in New Spain." *Early American Literature* 41, no. 3 (2006): 455–71.

Solano, Pedro María. *Carta familiar: Que para utilidad pública, y con anuencia de su obediencia perpetuo, el Exmo. e. Illmo. Señor Arzobispo, da a luz la venerable Santa Escuela de la Inmaculada Concepción de la parroquia de la Santa Veracruz.* Mexico City, 1810.

Spangler, Jewel L. "Becoming Baptists: Conversion in Colonial and Early National Virginia." *Journal of Southern History* 67, no. 2 (2001): 243–86.

Stein, Stanley J., and Barbara H. Stein. *Silver, Trade, and War: Spain and America in the Making of Early Modern Europe.* Baltimore: Johns Hopkins University Press, 2000.

Swidler, Ann. "Culture in Action: Symbols and Strategies." *American Sociological Review* 51, no. 2 (1986): 273–86.

Tavárez, David. "Legally Indian: Inquisitorial Readings of Indigenous Identity in New Spain." In *Imperial Subjects: Race and Identity in Colonial Latin America,* ed. Andrew B. Fisher and Matthew D. O'Hara, 81–100. Durham: Duke University Press, 2009.

———. "Representations of Spanish Authority in Zapotec Calendrical and Historical Genres." In *The Conquest All Over Again: Nahuas and Zapotecs Thinking, Writing, and Painting Spanish Colonialism,* ed. Susan Schroeder, 206–25. Portland, Ore.: Sussex Academic Press, 2010.

———. *The Invisible War: Indigenous Devotions, Discipline, and Dissent in Colonial Mexico.* Stanford: Stanford University Press, 2011.

Taylor, William B. *Magistrates of the Sacred: Priests and Parishioners in Eighteenth-Century Mexico.* Stanford: Stanford University Press, 1996.

———. "Santuarios y milagros en la secuela de la Independencia mexicana." In *Religión, política e identidad en la Independencia de México,* ed. Brian Connaughton, 515–89. Mexico City: Universidad Autónoma Metropolitana, 2010.

Tena Villeda, Rosalba. "Gabriel López Bonilla, un astrónomo-astrólogo en el siglo XVII mexicano." In *Del estamento ocupacional a la comunidad científica: Astrónomos-astrólogos e ingenieros, siglos XVII al XIX,* ed. María Luisa

Rodríguez-Sala and Rosalba Tena Villeda, 33–55. Mexico City: Universidad Nacional Autónoma de México, Instituto de Investigaciones Sociales, 2004.

Tenorio-Trillo, Mauricio. *Historia y celebración*. Mexico City: Tusquets Editores, 2009.

Tentler, Thomas. *Sin and Confession on the Eve of the Reformation*. Princeton: Princeton University Press, 1977.

Terpstra, Nicholas. *Lay Confraternities and Civic Religion in Renaissance Bologna*. New York: Cambridge University Press, 1995.

———, ed. *The Politics of Ritual Kinship: Confraternities and Social Order in Early Modern Italy*. New York: Cambridge University Press, 2000.

Tester, S. J. *A History of Western Astrology*. Suffolk: Boydell Press, 1987.

Thomas, Keith. *Religion and the Decline of Magic: Studies in Popular Beliefs in Sixteenth and Seventeenth Century England*. London: Weidenfeld and Nicolson, 1971.

Trabulse, Elías. *El círculo roto: Estudios históricos sobre la ciencia en México*. Mexico City: Fondo de Cultura Económica, 1982.

———, ed. *Historia de la ciencia en México: Estudios y textos, Siglo XVII*, vol. 2. Mexico City: Conacyt/Fondo de Cultura Económica, 1984.

———. *La ciencia perdida: Fray Diego Rodríguez, un sabio del siglo XVII*. Mexico City: Fondo de Cultura Económica, 1985.

———. *Los orígenes de la ciencia moderna en México (1630–1680)*. Mexico City: Fondo de Cultura Económica, 1994.

Trexler, Richard C. *Reliving Golgotha: The Passion Play of Iztapalapa*. Cambridge: Harvard University Press, 2003.

Tutino, John. *Making a New World: Founding Capitalism in the Bajío and Spanish North America*. Durham: Duke University Press, 2011.

Vaggi, Gianni, and Peter Groenewegen. *A Concise History of Economic Thought: From Mercantilism to Monetarism*. New York: Palgrave Macmillan, 2003.

Valdés, Dennis Nodin. "Decline of the Sociedad de Castas in Mexico City." Ph.D. diss., University of Michigan, 1978.

Valdés-Ugalde, Francisco. "Janus and the Northern Colossus: Perceptions of the United States in the Building of the Mexican Nation." *Journal of American History* 86, no. 2 (1999): 568–600.

Van Young, Eric. "Conflict and Solidarity in Indian Village Life: The Guadalajara Region in the Late Colonial Period." *Hispanic American Historical Review* 64, no. 1 (1984): 55–79.

———. *The Other Rebellion: Popular Violence, Ideology, and the Mexican Struggle for Independence, 1810–1821*. Stanford: Stanford University Press, 2001.

Velázquez de Cárdenas, Carlos Celedonio. *Breve práctica y régimen del confessonario de indio, en mexicano y castellano; para instrucción del confessor principiante, habilitación y examen del penitente*. Mexico City: Imprenta de la Bibliotecha Mexicana, 1761.

Viguri Arribas, M. *Trescientos veinticinco años de historia: Santa Escuela de Cristo y la Semana Santa en la ciudad de Orduña*. Bilbao: Ediciones Mensajero, 2001.

Vilches, Elvira. *New World Gold: Cultural Anxiety and Monetary Disorder in Early Modern Spain*. Chicago: University of Chicago Press, 2010.

Villa Flores, Javier. "Talking Through the Chest: Divination and Ventriloquism Among African Slave Women in Seventeenth-Century Mexico." *Colonial Latin American Review* 14, no. 2 (2005): 299–321.

Viqueira Albán, Juan Pedro. *¿Relajados o reprimidos? Diversiones públicas y vida social en la Ciudad de México durante el siglo de las luces*. Mexico City: Fondo de Cultural Económica, 1987.

Vitoria, Francisco de. *Confesionario util y provechoso*. Zaragoza, 1564.

Voekel, Pamela. "Peeing on the Palace: Bodily Resistance to Bourbon Reforms in Mexico City." *Journal of Historical Sociology* 5, no. 2 (1992): 183–208.

——. *Alone Before God: The Religious Origins of Modernity in Mexico*. Durham: Duke University Press, 2002.

von Wobeser, Gisela. "Mecanismos crediticios en la Nueva España: El uso del censo consignativo." *Mexican Studies / Estudios Mexicanos* 5, no. 1 (1989): 1–23.

——. "La postura de la Iglesia católica frente a la usura." *Memorias de la Academia Mexicana* 36 (1993): 121–45.

——. *El crédito eclesiástico en la Nueva España (siglo XVIII)*. Mexico City: Universidad Autónoma de México, 1994.

——. "Los créditos de las instituciones eclesiásticas de la ciudad de México en el siglo XVIII." In *El crédito en la Nueva España*, ed. María del Pilar Martínez López-Cano and Guillermina del Valle Pavón, 176–202. Mexico City: Instituto Mora, Colegio de Michoacán, and Instituto de Investigaciones Históricas–UNAM, 1998.

——. "Certezas, incertidumbres y expectativas en torno a la salvación del alma: Creencias escatológicas en Nueva España, siglos XVI–XVIII." *Historia Mexicana* 61, no. 4 (2012): 1311–48.

Waldman, Marilyn. "Tradition as a Modality of Change: Islamic Examples." *History of Religions* 25, no. 4 (1986): 318–40.

Walker, Charles F. *Shaky Colonialism: The 1746 Earthquake-Tsunami in Lima, Peru, and Its Long Aftermath*. Durham: Duke University Press, 2008.

Westman, Robert S. *The Copernican Question: Prognostication, Skepticism, and Celestial Order*. Berkeley: University of California Press, 2011.

Wittrock, Björn. "Modernity, One, None, or Many?: European Origins and Modernity as a Global Condition." *Daedalus* 129, no. 1 (2000): 31–60.

Wood, Stephanie. *Transcending Conquest: Nahua Views of Spanish Colonial Mexico*. Norman: University of Oklahoma Press, 2003.

Wright-Ríos, Edward. *Searching for Madre Matiana: Prophecy and Popular Culture in Modern Mexico*. Albuquerque: University of New Mexico Press, 2014.

Ximenez de las Cuevas, José Antonio. *Plática moral y una de las treinta y tres, que por mañana, tarde y noche se tuvieron en el solemnísimo Novenario y quatro días posteriores, que con suma edificación de los fieles se han celebrado en la Iglesia del Espíritu Santo de la ciudad de la Puebla.* . . . Puebla: Imprenta de Pedro de la Rosa, 1810.

Zahino Peñafort, Luisa, ed., *El Cardenal Lorenzana y el IV Concilio Provincial Mexicano.* Mexico City: Universidad Nacional Autónoma de México, 1999.

Zammito, John. "Koselleck's Philosophy of Historical Time(s) and the Practice of History." *History and Theory* 43, no. 1 (2004): 124–35.

Index

Note: Page numbers in italic type refer to illustrations

Bacon, Francis, 49–50
banquillo ritual, 135–36, 140
Bárcena, Manuel de la, 164–65, 167, 171
Baskes, Jeremy, 115
Beristáin de Souza, José Mariano, 162–63, 167
Bernabé, Leonardo, 45, 72–73, 74
Beteta, Juan, 67
binary models of culture, 8–9, 23–24, 43
body and embodiment, 134–35, 139–40
Bonaparte, Joseph (King José I), 151, 162
Bonaparte, Napoleon, 151
Bourbon Reforms, 125–27, 146, 152
Bouwsma, William, 160
Brahe, Tycho, 64
Bringas, Diego Miguel, 159
Brotherhood of the Little Oratory, 131
Buc, Philippe, 122–23, 131
Burkhart, Louise, 24–25
Butler, Jon, 70

caciques (local leaders), 113
Calderón de la Barca, Pedro, 69
Calvin, John, 21
Calvinism, 70
Cañas, Salvador de, 102
Carrera de Indias, 84–85
Carruthers, Mary, 35, 188n41
Casimiro de Montenegro, Antonio, 69
Catholicism and Catholic Church: and astrology, 43–46, 53–75; common political identity grounded in, 162–63, 167; as conceptual foundation for futuremaking in New Spain, 15, 40; and confession, 26–40; and credit system, 100, 101, 105–9, 115–16; and futuremaking, 163; human nature in theology of, 20–21; insurgents' appeal to, 170–71; reformist, 119–21, 126–28, 131–35, 146; scholarship on, 9–11; and sin, 20–25; social control exercised by, 25, 37, 186n16; and

usury, 94–98, 105, 111–12, 115–16. *See also* Inquisition
causality, 23
celadores, 140
censo (contract of sale), 97–102, 105–6, 202nn73–74
Chakrabarty, Dipesh, 184n14
chaos, Nahua concept of, 23–24
Charles IV, King of Spain, 151, 162
Charles V, Holy Roman Emperor, 85, 88
China, 86–87
chiromancy. *See* palm reading
Chowning, Margaret, 203n103
Christ crucified, *124*
collective religious behavior, 16, 40, 118–21, 126–29, 131, 134, 136–37, 140, 147–48, 209n38
colonial Mexico. *See* New Spain
colonial preachers, 155–73
comets, 62–63
Conde Pineda, Francisco Javier, 160–61, 172
confession: agency in, 37–38; in calendar, 28; defined, 19; description of ritual of, 27–30; historical sources on, 25–26; Holy Schools' public practice of, 135–36; institutional role of, 27–28; instructional role of, 28; manuals associated with, 29–33, *30*, *33*, 39, *39*, 41; memory and, 35–37, *36*; in mission work, 27–28, 32; precursors of, 26–27; priest-penitent relations in, 37–38; private and public aspects of, 27; questions concerning conduct of, 37–38; risks of, 32–34, 188n34; role of sins in, 31–32; subjectivity and, 27, 31, 34–41; temporality of, 20, 34–37; as underlying cultural concept, 19–20. *See also* sin and fallibility
contracts, justness of, 114
Cope, Douglas, 102
Cortés, Hernán, 174, 176